American
Home Front in
World War II
Primary Sources

American Home Front in World War II Primary Sources

Sharon M. Hanes

**Allison McNeill,
Project Editor**

U·X·L

An imprint of Thomson Gale, a part of The Thomson Corporation

THOMSON

GALE

Detroit • New York • San Francisco • San Diego • New Haven, Conn. • Waterville, Maine • London • Munich

American Home Front in World War II: Primary Sources

Sharon M. Hanes

Project Editor
Allison McNeill

Permissions
Emma Hull

Imaging and Multimedia
Robyn Young, Lezlie Light, Dan Newell

Product Design
Michelle Dimercurio, Pamela Galbreath

Composition
Evi Seoud

Manufacturing
Rita Wimberley

For permission to use material from this product, submit your request via Web at http://www.gale-edit.com/permissions, or you may download our Permissions Request form and submit your request by fax or mail to:

Permissions Department
Thomson Gale
27500 Drake Rd.
Farmington Hills, MI 48331-3535
Permissions Hotline:
248-699-8006 or 800-877-4253, ext. 8006
Fax: 248-699-8074 or 800-762-4058

Cover photographs reproduced courtesy of the Library of Congress.

While every effort has been made to ensure the reliability of the information presented in this publication, Thomson Gale does not guarantee the accuracy of the data contained herein. Thomson Gale accepts no payment for listing; and inclusion in the publication of any organization, agency, institution, publication, service, or individual does not imply endorsement by the editors or publisher. Errors brought to the attention of the publisher and verified to the satisfaction of the publisher will be corrected in future editions.

LIBRARY OF CONGRESS CATALOGING-IN-PUBLICATION DATA

American home front in World War II. Primary sources / [edited by] Sharon M. Hanes ; Allison McNeill, project editor.
p. cm. – (American home front in World War II reference library)
Includes bibliographical references and index.
ISBN 0-7876-7653-5
1. World War, 1939-1945–United States–Juvenile literature. 2. World War, 1939-1945–United States–Sources–Juvenile literature. 3. United States–History–1933-1945–Juvenile literature. 4. United States–History–1933-1945–Sources–Juvenile literature. I. Title: Primary sources. II. Hanes, Sharon M. III. McNeill, Allison. IV. Series.
D769.1.A655 2004 973.917–dc22
2004009394

This title is also available as an e-book.
ISBN 0-7876-9385-5 (Set)
Contact your Thomson Gale sales representative for ordering information.

Printed in the United States of America
10 9 8 7 6 5 4 3 2 1

Contents

Introduction

Many people who lived on the American home front during World War II (1939–45; U.S. involvement 1941–45) proclaimed the period as "the best of times and worst of times." In the 1930s the United States and much of the rest of the world had been in the throes of the Great Depression. The Depression was marked by dramatically slowed business activity, high unemployment, and, for a significant portion of the population, much hunger. In the United States, society seemed, at times, to be falling apart as violent labor conflicts, food riots, and race riots punctuated the 1930s. Change came in 1940 as the United States began gearing up for a war that was already raging in Europe. As industries began receiving sizable government contracts to produce war materials, good-paying jobs once again became available for anyone who wanted to work. On December 7, 1941, the Japanese surprised and shocked the United States with a deadly attack on U.S. military bases at Pearl Harbor, Hawaii. Immediately an overwhelming spirit of patriotic fervor consumed America. A common cause and a common enemy became well-defined.

The war years were the "best of times" because the war effort united Americans as never before. The factories were humming, men and women were working and earning livable wages, even rationing of food and gasoline was viewed as necessary for the push to victory. At the same time, the "worst" aspect of the early 1940s involved separation from loved ones as millions joined the military and went overseas to fight for their country. Americans held their collective breath until their sons, husbands, brothers, and even daughters returned to the home front.

The United States was clearly a different nation in 1942 than the previous decade. Just about everything aspect of society was affected. Changes came in employment, living locations, and in driving and eating habits. Millions of new jobs caused personal income to rise dramatically and an improved standard of living. Taking advantage of new employment, individuals and whole families migrated to the war industry centers on each coast and the Great Lakes region. Millions of American men joined the military service and left for far off places. Change also came as everyone on the home front pitched in to do their part for the war effort. They volunteered for civil defense duties, complied with food and gasoline rationing, planted "victory gardens," and collected scrap metal and rubber tires that contained materials needed in producing war materials. Cities staged practice air raid drills with blackouts, as volunteer air raid wardens patrolled the streets and neighborhoods. Citizens, fearing spies and saboteurs, kept a vigilant watch, viewing anyone with an accent with suspicion. Housewives shopped with ration coupons and adapted recipes to find substitutes for sugar and meat, which were rationed items. Families readjusted transportation priorities to make do on four gallons of gasoline a week. Citizens on the home front also helped feed the nation and free up a portion of commercially grown fruits and vegetables for shipment overseas. Over twenty million home gardens, known as victory gardens, were planted. They provided one-third of all vegetables eaten in America. Youth joined the effort by rounding up scrap materials in the form of discarded pots and pans, bedsprings, tin cans, and rubber tires for use in manufacturing war materials.

The entertainment industry participated in the war effort as well. Hollywood directors produced war documentaries aimed at bolstering the wave of patriotism. New movie releases showed Japanese and German characters as villainous, while promoting traditional American cultural values and creating American heroes. Celebrities contributed to war bond drives, leading to the sales of millions of dollars of bonds. Others volunteered at canteens where servicemen could stop for food and entertainment before departing for overseas assignments. Still others enlisted in the regular armed services or volunteered in civilian defense roles.

Through the major government and private industry mobilization efforts and the patriotic fervor of the population, the American home front became the leading industrial and agricultural producer in the world. Existing factories were converted from production of civilian consumer goods, such as cars, toasters, alarm clocks, and refrigerators, to wartime materials such as warplanes, tanks, guns, ammunition, and military trucks. Major new factories were built, as well as massive new shipyards where thousands of freight transports, known as "Liberty" ships, were produced. U.S. industry produced almost three hundred thousand warplanes, over eighty-six thousand tanks, and almost twelve thousand ships between 1941 and 1945. Long workweeks became commonplace for war industry workers.

Corporations and farmers saw their investments grow. Corporate assets almost doubled as the government guaranteed profits on war production. Farmers also saw their prosperity rise to new heights by growing food for the armies of the Allied forces. Big business and military services formed a long lasting powerful alliance known as the military-industrial complex. The alliance would influence U.S. foreign policy and industrial production for decades following the war.

Despite the vastly improved economic outlook, for some Americans not all was rosy. Racial discrimination increased. With war quickly expanding in Europe in 1940, Congress passed the Smith Act requiring four million aliens, those not yet U.S. citizens, but living in America, to register with U.S. authorities. Following the bombing of Pearl Harbor, President Franklin D. Roosevelt signed an order labeling German, Italian, and Japanese immigrants as enemy aliens. Though restrictions on Germans and Italians would soon ease, Japanese aliens experienced harsh discrimination. In the spring of 1942 the U.S. government hastily rounded up some 112,000 Japanese aliens, as well as

Japanese Americans with full U.S. citizenship, from their homes and businesses. They were transported to remote detention camps where they were held for the remainder of the war. Meanwhile their constitutionally protected rights were trampled.

Black Americans experienced much needed gains in the newly expanded job markets, but only after non-minorities were fully employed and labor shortages had become critical. Some new opportunities in the military services also opened for blacks. However the armed services remained racially segregated, as was civilian life in much of the home front. Triggered by job discrimination and severe housing shortages in the war industry centers, violent race riots broke out on the home front in 1943. The worst racial rioting occurred in Detroit, Michigan, where thirty-four were killed and seven hundred injured.

As with minorities, women found new opportunities in jobs never available before, such as factory assembly-line jobs. "Rosie the Riveter" became a mythical caricature symbolic of all women who took jobs in war industries. Millions of women entered the workforce during the war years. By late 1944 women made up some 40 percent of the workforce in aircraft factories and 12 percent in shipyards. Much of the wartime home front gains proved short-lived. Women were expected to leave their jobs at the war's end so that returning veterans could find work to support their families.

Though the home front worker had money to spend, fewer goods were available to purchase because factory production and raw materials were directed to military use. No new automobiles, radios, or appliances were produced during the war. The government introduced a rationing system to ensure fair distribution of limited goods. Rationed items and materials included sugar, coffee, meat, canned goods, leather shoes, and dairy products. Gasoline for automobiles was rationed in a complex system based on demonstrated need.

The most difficult home front shortage to overcome was the shortage of housing. Twenty million Americans relocated to industrial centers or military bases only to find little available housing. Because of war needs for war materials, few new houses were built.

With little to spend money on, savings grew and personal debt declined. The government encouraged citizens to invest their extra funds in war bonds to help finance the very expensive war effort. The war bond drives served to keep home front Americans involved in actively supporting the war. Congress also passed and instituted the modern federal income tax system. Forty million Americans were paying income tax by 1945, up from just five million in 1939.

By 1943 the war became a test of will and endurance. Most affected by war on the home front were those with loved ones in the military service, particularly those serving overseas. American casualties mounted as the war continued, with the most deaths occurring in the last twelve months. Ultimately fifteen million Americans served in the wartime military. Of those, three hundred thousand were killed and seven hundred thousand injured. As a reward to those who served in the military, the government introduced sweeping programs of financial assistance amounting to $100 billion in benefits for millions of war veterans and their families. The funds provided a significant boost to the U.S. postwar economy as veterans used the funds to buy homes and fund their education.

Early 1945 brought a rapid sequence of events. Germany surrendered on May 7. The following day became known as V-E Day for Victory in Europe. The Japanese surrendered on August 14, and the following day became known as V-J Day for Victory Over Japan. The war's end in mid-1945 brought wild jubilation on the American home front. As time passed and new generations grew up, the prominent place of World War II became fixed in U.S. history. Despite vast destruction of parts of Europe and Asia, the United States home front, with the exception of Pearl Harbor, was spared any physical harm. Many Americans later looked nostalgically back at World War II as a simpler time of patriotic unity and adventure.

Richard C. and Sharon M. Hanes

Reader's Guide

American Home Front in World War II: Primary Sources tells the story of the American home front during World War II in the words of the people who lived and shaped it. Approximately thirty excerpted documents provide a wide range of perspectives on this period of history. Included are excerpts from presidential addresses and proclamations; government pamphlets; magazine articles; and reflections by individuals who lived through the tumultuous times.

Format

The excerpts in *American Home Front in World War II: Primary Sources* are divided into eight chapters. Each of the chapters focuses on a specific theme: Mobilizing America, Civil Defense, Working Women on the Home Front, Home Front Communities, Black American and Japanese American Experiences on the Home Front, Through a Youngster's Eyes, Praise and Practical Advice, and Newlyweds and Families. Every chapter opens with an historical overview, followed by reprinted documents.

Each excerpt (or section of excerpts) includes the following additional features:

- **Introductory material** places the document and its author in an historical context.

- **Things to remember while reading** offers important background information about the featured text.

- **Excerpt** presents the document in its original spelling and format.

- **What happened next . . .** discusses the impact of the document and/or relevant historical events following the date of the document.

- **Did you know . . .** provides interesting fact about the document and its author.

- **Consider the following . . .** poses questions about the material for the reader to consider.

- **For More Information** offers resources for further study of the document and its author as well as sources used by the authors in writing the material.

Other features of *American Home Front in World War II: Primary Sources* include numerous sidebar boxes highlighting interesting, related information. More than sixty-five black-and-white photos illustrate the text. In addition, each excerpt is accompanied by a glossary running in the margin alongside the reprinted document that defines terms, people, and ideas. The volume begins with a timeline of events and a "Words to Know" section, and concludes with a general bibliography and subject index of people, places, and events discussed throughout *American Home Front in World War II: Primary Sources*.

American Home Front in World War II Reference Library

American Home Front in World War II: Primary Sources is only one component of the three-part U•X•L American Home Front in World War II Reference Library. The other two titles in this set are:

- *American Home Front in World War II: Almanac* (one volume) presents a comprehensive overview of events and everyday life that occurred within the United States while the nation was at war from 1941 to 1945. The volume concentrates on the actual events related to the World War II effort rather than simply relating all general happenings of the time period. Each of the thirteen chapters focuses on a particular topic, such as mobilization of American industry and agriculture, the miracles of war production and economic growth, the experience of women and minorities on the home front, growth of civil defense and other organizations to assist the war effort, the changes to various home front communities, the effects of war on everyday life, and the preparations for a changed postwar world.

- *American Home Front in World War II: Biographies* (one volume) presents the life stories of twenty-six individuals who played key roles on the American home front while the nation was at war from 1941 to 1945. Individuals from all walks of life are included. Some held prominent national roles in guiding America through the war, others were among the millions who eagerly did their share in contributing to the war effort. Profiled are well-known figures such as President Franklin D. Roosevelt, First Lady Eleanor Roosevelt, Secretary of War Henry Stimson, painter Norman Rockwell, social activist A. Philip Randolph, industrialists Donald Douglas and Henry Kaiser, entertainers Betty Grable and Dorothy Lamour, movie director Frank Capra, and journalist Elmer Davis, as well as lesser-known individuals such as industrial worker Peggy Terry, artist and author Mine Okubo, physicist Elda Anderson, and labor leader Luisa Moreno.

A cumulative index of all three titles in the U•X•L American Home Front in World War II Reference Library is also available.

Dedication

The *American Home Front in World War II* volumes are dedicated to our new grandson Luke Clay Hanes. May he and his generation be spared the trauma and ravages of war.

Special Thanks

Kelly Rudd contributed importantly to the *Biographies* volume. Catherine Filip typed much of the manuscript for the

Primary Sources volume. Constance Carter, head of the Library of Congress science research department, assisted in searching out primary source materials.

Comments and Suggestions

We welcome your comments on *American Home Front in World War II: Primary Sources* and suggestions for other topics to consider. Please write: Editors, *American Home Front in World War II: Primary Sources,* U•X•L, 27500 Drake Rd. Farmington Hills, Michigan 48331-3535; call toll free: 1-800-877-4253; fax to (248) 699-8097; or send e-mail via http://www.gale.com.

Timeline of Events

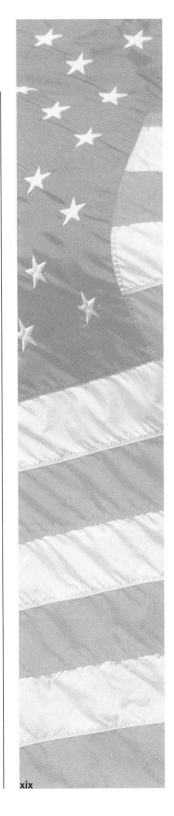

October 1929   The Great Depression arrives, leading to high unemployment rates and social unrest; over the next few years the Depression spreads worldwide, hitting Germany particularly hard.

September 18, 1931   Japan invades and occupies Manchuria to gain access to its natural resources, beginning Japan's military expansion in the Far East through the next decade.

January 30, 1933   Adolf Hitler becomes Germany's head of government.

March 4, 1933   Franklin D. Roosevelt is inaugurated as the thirty-second president.

1935   Germany introduces a military draft and begins mobilizing its industries to produce military materials, including tanks and war planes.

October 3, 1935   Italy invades Ethiopia and gains control by May 1936.

July 7, 1937   Japan invades China, capturing many of its major cities including its capital, Peking (Beijing).

March 12, 1938   Germany announces a union with Austria.

October 15, 1938   Germany gains control of part of Czechoslovakia, beginning its military expansion in Europe.

1939   Pocket Book Company introduces the paperback book, which will become highly popular through the war, selling 40 million in 1943 alone.

September 1, 1939   Germany invades Poland, thereby starting World War II. Several nations, including Britain and France, declare war on Germany two days later; President Roosevelt declares U.S. neutrality in the following days.

September 5, 1939   Congress revises the Neutrality Acts, ending the ban of sales of military supplies to foreign nations; the United States establishes a cash and carry program to sell war materials to Great Britain.

September 8, 1939   President Roosevelt issues a limited national emergency declaration and creates the War Resources Board (WRB) to begin planning for war.

1940   Roosevelt creates the Office of Emergency Management (OEM), located in the White House, to oversee war preparations.

March 16, 1940   Roosevelt, in a speech, asks for construction of 50,000 warplanes in preparation for war and sale to Britain.

April 9, 1940   Germany begins a military assault on Western Europe, first invading Denmark and Norway, eventually leading to the fall of France on June 22.

June 1940   Dr. Vannevar Bush meets with President Roosevelt, leading to the creation of the National Defense Research Committee (NRDC) to coordinate technological research benefiting advanced military equipment.

June 28, 1940   Congress passes the Alien Registration Act, more commonly known as the Smith Act, one week after the fall of France, making it illegal to advocate the overthrow of the U.S. government.

July 10, 1940   The German bombing of Britain begins; it lasts for eight months. Italy declares war on France and Great Britain.

September 15, 1940 Congress passes the first peacetime military draft in U.S. history.

September 27, 1940 Germany, Italy, and Japan form a military alliance.

November 5, 1940 With the public fearful of looming war, President Roosevelt is elected to an unprecedented third term in office.

December 29, 1940 In a Fireside Chat, Roosevelt delivers his "Arsenal of Democracy" speech calling for greater efforts in supporting the war against Germany.

January 1941 Roosevelt creates the Office of Production Management (OPM) to spur industrial war mobilization.

February 4, 1941 United Service Organizations (USO) is created to provide entertainment to American troops; it establishes Camp Shows, Inc., through which entertainers volunteer to perform for military servicemen, amounting to over 428,000 shows by 1947.

March 1941 The National Defense Mediation Board is formed to resolve labor disputes in industry and to ease the process of war mobilization.

March 6, 1941 The first houses in the Linda Vista housing development in San Diego, California, are completed for war industry workers; 16,000 residents are housed here by April 1943.

March 11, 1941 Congress passes the Lend-Lease Act, authorizing the United States to lend Britain and other nations fighting Germany money to purchase or lease military equipment and supplies from U.S. industry; the United States would spend $50 billion through the war, essentially ending the Great Depression.

April 11, 1941 Roosevelt creates the Office of Price Administration and Civilian Supply (OPACS) to control the prices of goods and corporate profits.

May 1941 Congress creates the Office of Scientific Research and Development (OSRD) to coordinate technological research.

May 20, 1941 Roosevelt creates the Office of Civilian Defense (OCD) to help communities prepare for war.

May 27, 1941 Roosevelt issues an unlimited national emergency declaration in response to continued Japanese expansion in Southeast Asia; the U.S. begins economic restrictions against Japan.

June 22, 1941 Germany invades the Soviet Union, drawing the Soviets into World War II; Roosevelt extends the Lend-Lease program to the Soviets.

June 25, 1941 Under pressure from A. Philip Randolph and other black American leaders, Roosevelt signs an executive order calling for an end to racial discrimination in hiring practices by war industries.

August 14, 1941 Roosevelt and British leader Winston Churchill sign the Atlantic Charter, spelling out their goals in the war.

August 28, 1941 Roosevelt creates the Supplies Priorities and Allocations Board (SPAB) to guide OPM in war mobilization.

December 1, 1941 The Civil Air Patrol is established to patrol the nation's borders and coastal areas by air.

December 7, 1941 Japan launches a surprise air attack on U.S. military installations at Pearl Harbor, Hawaii, drawing the United States into World War II; the United States declares war on Japan; the following day Germany and Italy declare war on the United States.

1942 Congress establishes the Emergency Farm Labor Program.

1942 The War Labor Board (WLB) is created to control wages.

January 1942 German submarines become more prevalent off the U.S. East Coast.

January 2, 1942 Japanese forces capture the capital city of the Philippines as American forces begin a retreat to the Bataan Peninsula.

January 16, 1942 Roosevelt creates the War Production Board (WPB), headed by Donald Nelson, to oversee mobilization and determine which consumer goods should be discontinued or limited in production and to set war production goals.

January 30, 1942 Congress passes the Emergency Price Control Act creating the Office of Price Administration (OPA), which has greater authority to control prices.

February 1942 A Japanese submarine briefly shells a coastal oil field near Santa Barbara, California; President Roosevelt establishes the Volunteer Port Security Force to protect ports and waterfront facilities.

February 7, 1942 The Pittsburgh *Courier,* a prominent black American newspaper, introduces the Double V campaign representing victory over the enemies abroad and victory over racial prejudice on the home front.

February 10, 1942 The WPB bans production of civilian automobiles, paving the way for conversion of the Michigan auto industry to production of warplanes, tanks, military trucks, and other military equipment.

February 19, 1942 Roosevelt signs Executive Order 9066 authorizing removal of Japanese aliens and Japanese Americans to detention centers.

March 21, 1942 The evacuation of Japanese Americans and Japanese aliens to internment camps begins.

April 1942 Roosevelt creates the War Manpower Commission (WMC) to direct workers to more critical industries and areas of workforce shortages.

April 6, 1942 By this date some six million citizens had planted victory gardens, leading to a major contribution to the nation's food supply.

April 28, 1942 OPA issues the General Maximum Price Regulation, known as General Max, setting price controls.

May 1942 Food rationing begins; War Ration Book One is issued, with sugar being the first table food rationed.

May 1942 The United States and Mexico reach agreement on the *bracero* program, which allows some one hundred thousand Mexican citizens to enter the United States to help solve the farm labor shortage.

May 8, 1942 In an early key military victory in the Pacific, the U.S. defeats a Japanese fleet in the Battle of the Coral Sea.

May 14, 1942 Congress creates the Women's Army Auxiliary Corp (WAAC); some 150,000 would serve.

June 7, 1942 In another major U.S. victory in the Pacific, the U.S. Navy defeats the Japanese fleet in the Battle of Midway.

June 13, 1942 Roosevelt creates the Office of War Information (OWI), with Elmer Davis as its head, to coordinate release of war information to the public.

July 16, 1942 The National War Labor Board (NWLB) establishes the "Little Steel Formula" to control wage increases.

July 30, 1942 Roosevelt signs a bill authorizing women to be accepted into the U.S. Navy, Coast Guard, and U.S. Marines, including the navy's Women Accepted for Volunteer Emergency Service (WAVES) in which 90,000 would serve.

August 7, 1942 U.S. forces begin the offensive in the Pacific with the invasion of Guadalcanal in the Solomon Islands.

September 1942 The first Hollywood World War II combat movie is released titled *Wake Island.*

September 9, 1942 A lone Japanese float plane, launched from a submarine, drops incendiary bombs in a remote forest area of southwest Oregon causing little damage.

September 10, 1942 The U.S. Army creates the Women's Auxiliary Ferry Squadron (WAFS) to fly planes to needed destinations.

October 3, 1942 Congress passes the Economic Stabilization Act creating the Office of Economic Stabilization (OES), headed by James F. Byrnes, to control the economy and guide the complex rationing program.

October 21, 1942 Congress passes the Revenue Act, restructuring the U.S. income tax system to help finance the war.

November 8, 1942 Allied forces launch a major military offensive in North Africa against German forces.

November 23, 1942 The Coast Guard creates their women's reserves, known as SPAR.

November 29, 1942 Coffee is rationed.

December 1, 1942 A complex system of gasoline rationing begins.

1943 Over 3.5 million American Red Cross volunteers repair military clothing, wrap bandages, and put together care packages for servicemen overseas.

January 12, 1943 Roosevelt declares this date Farm Mobilization Day, claiming food was also a weapon in the war.

January 15, 1943 The Pentagon building is dedicated in the Washington, D.C., area to house the War Department; construction had started in September 1941.

January 31, 1943 Russian troops defeat German forces at Stalingrad marking the first major defeat of Germany and a turning point in the war.

February 1943 Congress establishes a national farm policy for solving farm labor shortages with such programs as the Women's Land Army (WLA) and the Victory Farm Volunteers (VFV).

February 1943 Roosevelt signs an order expanding normal workweeks from 40 to 48 hours.

February 1943 War Ration Book Two is issued as canned goods, dried beans, and peas come under rationing; shoe rationing also begins to conserve the use of leather.

February 13, 1943 U.S. Marine Corps adds the Women's Reserve; 23,000 women joined.

March 29, 1943 The rationing of meat begins.

April 1943 Florence Hall is named head of the newly formed Women's Land Army (WLA).

May 28, 1943 Roosevelt creates the Office of War Mobilization (OWM) to resolve disputes over workforce and raw material shortages.

June 1943 Congress passes the Bolton Act establishing the Cadet Nurse Corps program to recruit and train nurses for wartime duty; 59,000 would serve in the Army Nurse Corps and 11,000 in the Navy Nurse Corps.

June 1943 A series of violent racial conflicts erupts in the United States, including one in Detroit, Michigan, and the "Zoot Suit Riot" in Los Angeles, California.

June 1943 Congress passes the Smith-Connolly War Labor Disputes Act that gives the government power to seize and operate plants where workers are on strike.

July 1943 War mobilization is complete, as industry is able to meet ongoing military needs through the remainder of the war.

July 3, 1943 The WAAC becomes the Women's Army Corp (WAC) to become a regular part of the army.

July 10, 1943 Following victory in North Africa, Allied forces invade Sicily, a large island south of Italy, and then Italy itself on September 3.

July 25, 1943 The Women's Aircraft Service Program (WASP) is formed from the WAFS and other organizations; it is ended December 20, 1944.

September 8, 1943 Italy surrenders to Allied forces.

November 28, 1943 Roosevelt, Churchill, and Joseph Stalin, premier of the Soviet Union, convene a three day meeting at Tehran, Iran, to discuss war strategies against Germany and Italy.

January 10, 1944 Congress passes the Servicemen's Readjustment Act, known as the GI Bill, that provides generous benefits in housing, education, and business loans to U.S. war veterans.

March 7, 1944 The United States reports that women constitute 42 percent of the workers in West Coast aircraft plants.

June 6, 1944 Allied forces launch the largest sea invasion in history, called Operation Overlord, on the shores of Normandy, France.

August-October 1944 An international conference held at Dumbarton Oaks in Washington, D.C., creates the beginning of the United Nations.

August 25, 1944 Paris, France, is liberated from German occupation by Allied forces.

September 13, 1944 Allied ground forces enter Germany.

October 26, 1944 In the largest naval battle in history, known as the Battle of Leyte Gulf, the U.S. Navy largely destroys the Japanese fleet.

November 1944   The WAVES and SPAR are opened to black American women; the WAC has been open to blacks since its beginning.

November 1944   Japanese begin launching balloon bombs, designed to float across the Pacific Ocean and explode in North America, from Japan; nine thousand are launched over the next several months.

November 7, 1944   Roosevelt wins reelection to a fourth term as U.S. president.

December 1944   Roosevelt revamps OWM to the Office of War Mobilization and Reconversion (OWMR) to coordinate change of war industries back to peacetime production.

December 16, 1944   German forces launch a major counterattack against advancing Allied forces, known as the Battle of the Bulge.

February 1, 1945   Soviet forces advance through Poland and into Germany to within one hundred miles of the German capital of Berlin.

February 4, 1945   The Yalta Conference, held in the Crimean region of the Soviet Union, begins and runs for seven days. The three key allied leaders, U.S. President Franklin D. Roosevelt, British Prime Minister Winston Churchill, and Soviet Premier Joseph Stalin, discuss German surrender terms, a Soviet attack against Japanese forces, and the future of Eastern Europe.

April 12, 1945   Roosevelt dies suddenly from a brain hemorrhage; he is replaced by Harry Truman.

April 18, 1945   Noted war correspondent Ernie Pyle is killed by enemy fire near Okinawa, Japan.

April 25, 1945   Fifty nations begin meeting in San Francisco, California, to write the United Nations (UN) charter.

April 28, 1945   Italian dictator Benito Mussolini is captured and executed by Italian resistance fighters.

April 30, 1945   German dictator Adolf Hitler commits suicide in a fortified bunker beneath Berlin.

May 1945   Six people are killed in southern Oregon by a Japanese balloon bomb.

May 7, 1945 Germany surrenders to allied forces leaving Germany and its capital of Berlin divided into four military occupation zones with American, British, French, and Soviet forces; Americans celebrate the following day, known as V-E Day (Victory in Europe Day).

June 21, 1945 Japanese forces are essentially defeated in major fighting for over two months on the island of Okinawa.

June 26, 1945 Fifty nations meeting in San Francisco, California, sign the United Nations charter.

July 16, 1945 First successful U.S. atomic bomb test occurs at Alamogardo, New Mexico.

July 26, 1945 U.S. president Harry S. Truman, Stalin, and Churchill meet at Potsdam to discuss postwar conditions of Germany.

August 6, 1945 The United States drops an atomic bomb on Hiroshima, Japan, followed by a second bomb on August 9 on Nagasaki.

August 14, 1945 Japan surrenders, ending World War II. Americans celebrate the following day, known as V-J Day (Victory over Japan Day).

September 2, 1945 Formal surrender papers are signed by Japan aboard a U.S. warship in Tokyo Bay.

June 12, 1948 Congress makes the Women's Army Corp (WAC) a permanent part of the U.S. Army.

1988 The U.S. government issues a formal apology to Japanese Americans for their treatment during World War II on the home front.

1997 The Franklin D. Roosevelt Memorial is dedicated in Washington, D.C., commemorating his leadership through the Great Depression and World War II.

June 29, 2001 A national monument is dedicated in Washington, D.C., in the memory of Japanese Americans in World War II.

May 2004 The World War II Memorial is dedicated in Washington, D.C. The memorial honors not only those who fought in the war, but commemorates the great efforts and sacrifices made by those on the American home front as well.

Words to Know

A

aliens: Immigrants who hold citizenship in a foreign country.

Allies: Over thirty nations, including the United States, Great Britain, and Soviet Union, who united in the fight against Germany, Italy, and Japan during World War II.

appeasement: Giving in to the demands of another nation in order to maintain peace.

atomic bomb: A bomb whose massive explosive force comes from the nuclear fission of uranium or plutonium.

Authoritarian: A political system in which authority is centered in a ruling party that demands complete obedience of its citizens and is not legally accountable to the people.

auxiliary: Volunteers who provide additional or supplementary assistance, or an organization that is supplemental to a larger one, such as the auxiliary police or firemen.

Axis powers: Nations who fought against the Allies in World War II including Germany, Italy, and Japan.

B

baby boomers: The population of 76 million children born after World War II, between 1946 and 1964.

barrage balloons: A network of balloons, steel cables, and nets placed over a town or city to protect against attacking enemy aircraft.

bereavement: Grieving over the death of a loved one.

black market: Illegally selling goods in violation of government regulations, such as selling rationed items at very high prices.

blackouts: Completely concealing or turning off all lights from outside view to guard against air raids.

Braceros: Mexican workers recruited by the United States to fill wartime labor shortages, particularly in the area of farm labor.

C

canteen: A place where food, rest, and entertainment are available, usually operated by volunteers.

capital: Money and property.

capitalism: An economic system in which private business and markets, largely free of government intervention, determine the prices, distribution, and production of goods.

cash and carry: The program established in late 1939 by the United States to sell war materials to Great Britain, but Britain had to transport them in their own ships.

civil defense: Non-military programs designed to protect U.S. citizens from enemy attack or disasters on the home front.

civil liberties: Protection of certain basic rights from government interference, such as freedom of speech and religion.

coalition: A temporary alliance of different groups.

Cold War: A prolonged conflict for world dominance from 1945 to 1991 between the two superpowers, the democratic, capitalist United States and the communist Soviet Union. The weapons of conflict were commonly words of propaganda and threats, not military conflicts.

commodity: An economic good produced by industry.

communism: A political and economic system where a single party controls all aspects of citizens' lives and private ownership of property is banned.

conservatism: Opposition to a large federal government and extensive social programs.

D

deficit spending: A government spending more money than the revenue coming in.

democracy: A system of government, such as that of the United States, that allows multiple political parties. Their members are elected to various government offices by popular vote of the people.

dictatorship: A form of government in which one person wields absolute power and control over the people.

dimouts: To turn out some lights, such as along a coastal shore area, particularly those lights pointed toward or easily seen from the ocean to guard against attacks from the sea.

draft: A legal requirement that young men serve in the military for their country for certain periods of time; also more formally known as selective service system.

E

espionage: Using spies to acquire information about the activities of a foreign nation.

F

fascism: A political system in which a strong central government, usually run by a dictator, controls the nation, gaining support through promotion of strong nationalism and often racism; promotes the good of the state above individual rights.

furlough: A brief leave of absence from duty granted to a soldier.

G

G.I.: Nickname for military servicemen derived from the term "government issue."

G.I. Bill: Formally known as the Servicemen's Readjustment Act of 1944; provided extensive economic benefits to World War II veterans, including school expenses and low interest loans for buying homes and starting businesses and farms.

Great Depression: A major economic crisis lasting from 1929 to 1941 leading to massive unemployment and widespread hunger in the U.S. and abroad.

Gross National Product (GNP): The total value of goods and services produced in a country for a particular period of time, such as annually.

I

incendiary bombs: Two- to ten-pound bombs designed to start fires.

incentives: Providing a reward to cause people to take specific actions, such as industries promised certain levels of profits to switch from production of consumer goods to war materials.

induction: A civilian enrolling into the military.

internment camps: A series of ten guarded camps mostly in the western United States where a total of 112,000 Japanese Americans and Japanese aliens were detained during the war for fear of sabotage or espionage. Also known as relocation camps.

isolationism: Opposition to foreign commitments or involvement in foreign disputes.

Issei: Japanese immigrants to the United States.

J

Jim Crow: Jim Crow laws enforced legal segregation, keeping races separated in every aspect of life from schools to restrooms and water fountains; particularly common in the South.

L

Lend-Lease: A U.S. program to supply war materials to foreign countries with payment to be delayed until after the war.

liberal: Those who look to social improvement through government action, such as providing financial security and healthcare not traditionally provided by the national government.

M

market: The world of commerce operating relatively free of government interventions, where demand and availability of goods and materials determines prices, distribution, and production levels.

mass production: To produce in large quantities in an assembly line fashion with the process broken down into many small steps.

mechanization: To replace human or animal labor with machines, such as tanks and trucks.

merchant marines: Officers and crews of U.S. vessels that engage in commerce.

migrant: A person who travels from place to place, often searching for work.

military-industrial complex: A politically powerful alliance of the military services and industry that provides materials to the military.

mobilization: To transform the national economy·from peacetime production of goods and foods to wartime production.

munitions: Various types of ammunition such as guns, grenades, and bombs.

N

nationalism: Holding a strong loyalty to one's country and seeking or maintaining independence from other nations.

Nazi: A political party in Germany, more formally known as the National Socialist German Worker's Party, led by Adolf Hitler from 1920 to 1945.

New Deal: The 1930s programs designed by President Franklin D. Roosevelt to promote economic recovery from the Great Depression.

O

organized labor: A collective effort by workers and labor organizations to seek better working conditions.

P

patriotism: Love or devotion to one's country.

prefabricated: To build the parts in separate locations and assemble them at another site, such as a ship or a house.

propaganda: Information aimed at shaping opinions of people, usually by a government.

R

racism: To be prejudiced against people of another race.

rationing: A government system to limit the amount of certain foods and other items in short supply that could be sold to citizens to conserve materials.

riveter: One who fastens metal pieces together, such as airplane or ship parts, with flattened metal bolts.

Rosie the Riveter: A fictional female character appearing on posters and in advertisements recruiting women to work in the war industries.

S

sabotage: To destroy military or industrial facilities.

scrap drives: A public program of gathering discarded or unused items made of materials needed by the defense industry, such as rubber tires, metal pots and pans, and nylon hose.

segregation: To keep races separate, such as in public places and the U.S. military during World War II.

Social Security: A federal program that provides economic assistance for citizens including the aged, retired, unemployed, and disabled.

socialism: An economic and political system in which the government controls all means of production.

strike: A work stoppage to force an employer to meet worker demands.

subversive: People working secretly to overthrow a government.

T

theater of war: Specific regions of the world where World War II was fought, such as the European theater or the Pacific theater.

totalitarian states: Countries where every aspect of life is tightly controlled by a dictator and all citizens must conform.

V

V-E Day: The day victory in Europe was celebrated, May 8, 1945.

victory gardens: Small fruit and vegetable gardens grown by individuals or families, planted in their own yards and public places, such as parks, to supplement the commercial production of food.

V-J Day: The day victory over Japan was celebrated, August 15, 1945.

V-mail: Personal letters written to servicemen overseas on special forms that were photographed onto microfilm, transported to their destination, then printed on paper and delivered to the addressee; designed to conserve cargo space.

W

war bonds: Government certificates sold to individuals and corporations to raise money to finance the war, with the purchaser receiving their money back plus interest at a future time.

wildcat strikes: Worker strikes that do not have the support of organized labor unions.

Text Credits

The following is a list of the copyright holders who have granted us permission to reproduce excerpts from primary source documents in *American Home Front in World War II: Primary Sources*. Every effort has been made to trace copyright; if omissions have been made, please contact us.

Copyrighted excerpts were reproduced from the following periodicals:

House & Garden, v. 81, February, 1942 for "Houses for Defense," by Anonymous. Copyright © 1942, renewed 1969 by The Conde Nast Publications, Inc. Reproduced by permission.

House & Garden, January, 1944 for "Still Keep 'Em Growing," by H. W. Hochbaum. Copyright © 1943, renewed 1971 by The Conde Nast Publications, Inc. Reproduced by permission.

Ladies Home Journal, v. LX, August, 1943; September 19, 1943; October, 1943; November, 1943. Copyright © 1943 by The Curtis Publishing Company. Renewed 1971 by Downe Publishing, Inc. All reproduced by permission.

Terkel, Studs. From *The Good War: An Oral History of World War Two*. Ballantine Books, 1984. Copyright © 1984 by Studs Terkel. All rights reserved. Reproduced by permission of Donadio & Olson, Inc.

Copyrighted excerpts were reproduced from the following sources:

Hanes, Hazel. From "Hazel Hanes Recalls Transferring Across the Country, in personal interview, 2003. Reproduced by permission of Sharon M. Hanes.

American
Home Front in
World War II
Primary Sources

Mobilizing America

In 1939, the year that World War II (1939–45) began in Europe, America was just beginning to emerge from the Great Depression (1929–41). The Great Depression was the longest and worst economic crisis in U.S. history. During the early 1930s, twelve million American workers, approximately 25 percent of the workforce, were jobless. Among people who were employed, incomes dropped an average of 40 percent between 1929 and 1932. In 1939 between eight million and ten million willing workers, roughly 17 percent of the workforce, were still unemployed. The Great Depression did not end until 1941, when the United States stepped up its mobilization efforts for World War II. Mobilization involved a major shift in U.S. industry; manufacturers had to switch from the production of civilian goods to the production of massive quantities of war materials, including tanks, planes, ships, mortars (a cannon for shooting shells at high angles), bombs, and small ammunition.

In the late 1930s President Franklin D. Roosevelt (1882–1945; served 1933–45) had asked American industry to voluntarily retool for the production of armaments so that the

United States could provide weapons for the Allied forces. The Allies included all the countries that were battling the so-called Axis powers of Germany, Italy, and Japan. During the 1930s and early 1940s, German dictator Adolf Hitler (1889–1945), Italian dictator Benito Mussolini (1883–1945), and Japanese military leaders ordered their respective armies to invade and subdue neighboring countries. Like most Americans at that time, President Roosevelt did not want to be directly involved in the war, but he believed the United States should support the Allies in resisting the aggression of the Axis powers. Providing American-made weapons was one way to fulfill this sense of obligation.

In response to Roosevelt's call for mobilization, U.S. industry began a slow and gradual shift toward the production of war materials. Most U.S. industrial leaders were hesitant to make this change, because they were just beginning to enjoy a strong consumer goods market. As the Depression lifted, Americans were eager to buy consumer goods, and profits were rising. Business leaders wanted to continue supplying those goods. They were not sure that war materials would bring them enough profit, and they did not want to build massive war production plants that would become useless after the war.

President Roosevelt faced a considerable challenge in rallying Americans to mobilization. Businessmen and Congress opposed the president's early mobilization efforts, calling them an intrusion of government into private business. The following three excerpts, all from speeches by President Roosevelt, illustrate Roosevelt's increasing belief that the United States needed to mobilize for its own national security. All three excerpts can be found in *The Public Papers and Addresses of Franklin D. Roosevelt.*

The first excerpt, **"There Can Be No Appeasement with Ruthlessness ... We Must Be the Great Arsenal of Democracy"**, was part of a "fireside chat" that President Roosevelt delivered on the evening of December 29, 1940. (Most Americans did not have televisions in their homes at this time, so Roosevelt, in 1933, instituted radio broadcasts, which he called fireside chats, to keep the American public informed of events and issues of the time.) Having been reelected to a third term as president in November 1940, Roosevelt felt confident in making a bold call for a rapid increase in mobilization. He wanted the United States to provide armaments to Great Britain and the other countries that were fighting against Germany, Italy, and Japan. Roosevelt stressed his belief that this action was vital to America's national security. He explained that the United States might be able to avoid direct involvement in the war by providing help—namely, weapons—to the Allies in Europe. This fireside chat quickly became known as the "Arsenal of Democracy" speech.

Approximately five months later, in May 1941, President Roosevelt acknowledged that the situation in Europe had steadily worsened. Yugoslavia and Greece had both fallen under Axis control. At this time Roosevelt determined he must declare an "unlimited national emergency." He announced this decision on May 27, 1941, speaking in the East Room of the White House before a group of Latin American diplomats. The second excerpt, **"The President Proclaims That an Unlimited National Emergency Confronts the Country, Proclamation No. 2487,"** comes from this speech. After the speech, Roosevelt delivered another evening fireside chat via radio, explaining to the American public why mobilization needed to proceed as quickly as possible and what dangers the home front could face if the Axis powers were not stopped.

The third excerpt in this chapter is titled **"We Are Going to Win the War and We Are Going to Win the Peace That Follows."** It comes from another fireside chat, delivered by President Roosevelt on December 9, 1941, two days after Japan's attack on a U.S. military base at Pearl Harbor, Hawaii. In his radio broadcast the president described precisely what the world situation was. He then outlined specific mobilization plans and reassured Americans that with total cooperation from all of its citizens the United States would indeed prevail. Full mobilization, which Roosevelt had been asking for since his "Arsenal of Democracy" speech, would at last become the nation's first priority.

Franklin D. Roosevelt

Excerpt from "There Can Be No Appeasement with Ruthlessness . . . We Must Be the Great Arsenal of Democracy," *a radio address delivered on December 29, 1940*

Reprinted from *The Public Papers and Addresses of Franklin D. Roosevelt, 1940 Volume.* Published in 1941.

"We must be the great arsenal of democracy. . . . We must apply ourselves to our task with the same resolution, the same sense of urgency, the same spirit of patriotism and sacrifice as we would show were we at war."

President Roosevelt's calls for mobilization in 1940 were well-founded. By late spring of 1940 German dictator Adolf Hitler had successfully directed his Nazi army in conquests over Denmark, Luxembourg, the Netherlands, and Belgium. In May the relentless Nazis entered northern France, and by June 14 they were in the streets of Paris. The French government was forced to sign an armistice (truce) on June 22. With the fall of France, Hitler turned his attention across the English Channel to Great Britain. The German air force, the *Luftwaffe,* attempted to destroy Britain's Royal Air Force and commenced bombing London in September. Italy had also declared war on Britain and France. Meanwhile in Asia, Japan had invaded various provinces in China, and Japanese military leaders were eyeing the Southeast Asian countries of Vietnam, Laos, and Cambodia.

On September 27, 1940, representatives from Germany, Italy, and Japan (collectively known as the Axis powers) met in Berlin, the capital of Germany. With the ultimate goal of world domination, the three countries boldly signed an agreement that threatened united aggression against the United States if it tried to halt their expansion objectives.

By late fall of 1940 it was clear to Roosevelt that the only way to stop the Axis powers and to keep them off American soil was to supply Britain with war materials. The United States had already been slowly moving toward mobilization in the previous twelve months. When France fell to the Nazis, President Roosevelt had asked Congress to appropriate money to manufacture more military aircraft, and Congress authorized $1 billion for fifty thousand new warplanes. However, these measures would not be enough to stop the Axis powers. Therefore, in late December 1940, Roosevelt asked the nation to become "the arsenal of democracy," that is, to produce and stockpile weapons for the nations that were defending democracy against the dictatorial Axis regimes. The tone of Roosevelt's speech was urgent and determined. Roosevelt spoke to convince Americans that they were indeed vulnerable to attack if the Axis powers were not defeated. America's best defense, Roosevelt said, was to rearm its own military and to supply Britain with everything needed to defeat the German assault.

Things to remember while reading the excerpt from "Arsenal of Democracy" . . .

- The United States remained detached from international events throughout the 1930s. As the war expanded in Europe and Asia, however, Americans experienced great uncertainty about the nation's future foreign policy.

- Although they hoped British forces would be victorious over Germany and Italy, many Americans opposed giving aid to Britain and other nations involved in the European war. Separated from Europe by the vast expanse of the Atlantic Ocean and from Japan by the Pacific Ocean, Americans generally felt secure against foreign attack, and they did not believe it would serve U.S. interests to get involved in the war. Americans who did not want the United States to become involved in the war in Europe were known as isolationists (people who wanted to remain uninvolved from what they viewed as Europe's problems) or pacifists (people who oppose using military force for any reason).

- President Roosevelt, with his broad overall world vision, believed that the United States needed to provide weapons to Britain immediately; otherwise, he feared, U.S. forces would ultimately be drawn into the war. Roosevelt was deeply concerned about America's lack of military preparedness and wanted to build up all the U.S. armed services as rapidly as possible. Americans who agreed with Roosevelt and supported U.S. intervention into the war in Europe were known as interventionists.

Excerpt from "Arsenal of Democracy"

*My friends: This is not a fireside chat on war. It is a talk on national security; because the **nub** of the whole purpose of your President is to keep you now, and your children later, and your grandchildren much later, out of a last-ditch war for the preservation of American independence and all of the things that American independence means to you and to me and to ours.*

Nub: Main point.

Tonight, in the presence of a world crisis, my mind goes back eight years to a night in the midst of a **domestic crisis**. It was a time when the wheels of American industry were grinding to a full stop, when the whole banking system of our country had ceased to function.

I well remember that while I sat in my study in the White House, preparing to talk with the people of the United States, I had before my eyes the picture of all those Americans with whom I was talking. I saw the workmen in the mills, the mines, the factories; the girl behind the counter; the small shopkeeper; the farmer doing his Spring plowing; the widows and the old men wondering about their life's savings. I tried to convey to the great mass of American people what the banking crisis meant to them in their daily lives.

Tonight I want to do the same thing, with the same people, in this new crisis which faces America.

We met **the issue of 1933** with courage and realism. We face this new crisis—this new threat to the security of our nation—with the same courage and realism. Never before since Jamestown and Plymouth Rock has our American civilization been in such danger as now.

For on September 27, 1940—this year—by an agreement signed in Berlin, three powerful nations, two in Europe and one in Asia, joined themselves together in the threat that if the United States of America interfered with or blocked the expansion program of these three nations—a program aimed at world control— they would unite in ultimate action against the United States.

The **Nazi masters** of Germany have made it clear that they intend not only to dominate all life and thought in their own country, but also to enslave the whole of Europe, and then to use the resources of Europe to dominate the rest of the world. It was only three weeks ago that their leader stated this: "There are two worlds that stand opposed to each other." And then in defiant reply to his opponents he said this: "Others are correct when they say: 'With this world we cannot ever **reconcile ourselves**' . . . I can beat any other power in the world." So said the leader of the Nazis.

In other words, the **Axis** not merely admits but the Axis proclaims that there can be no ultimate peace between **their philosophy**—their philosophy of government—and **our philosophy** of government . . . .

Some of our people like to believe that wars in Europe and in Asia are of no concern to us. But it is a matter of most vital concern

Domestic crisis: The economic decline of the 1930s known as the Great Depression.

The issue of 1933: Widespread bank failures in early 1933 that threatened survival of the nation at the height of the Great Depression.

Nazi masters: German dictator Adolf Hitler and his close staff.

Reconcile ourselves: Settle differences and live in peace.

Axis: The nations who fought against the Allies in World War II including Germany, Italy, and Japan.

Their philosophy: Dictatorship.

Our philosophy: Democracy.

to us that European and Asiatic war-makers should not gain control of the oceans which lead to this hemisphere. . . .

Some of us like to believe that even if Britain falls, we are still safe, because of the broad expanse of the Atlantic and of the Pacific.

But the width of those oceans is not what it was in the days of clipper ships. At one point between Africa and Brazil the distance is less than it is from Washington [D.C.] to Denver, Colorado, five hours for the latest type of bomber. And at the north end of the Pacific Ocean, America and Asia almost touch each other. Why, even today we have planes that could fly from the British Isles to New England and back again without refueling. And remember that the range of the modern bomber is ever being increased. . . .

Frankly and definitely there is danger ahead—danger against which we must prepare. But we well know that we cannot escape danger, or the fear of danger, by crawling into bed and pulling the covers over our heads. . . .

There are those who say that the Axis powers would never have any desire to attack the Western Hemisphere. That is the same dangerous form of wishful thinking which has destroyed the powers of resistance of so many conquered peoples. The plain facts are that the Nazis have proclaimed, time and again, that all other races are their inferiors and therefore subject to their orders. And most important of all, the vast resources and wealth of this American hemisphere constitute the most tempting loot in all of the round world. . . .

The experience of the past two years has proven beyond doubt that no nation can appease the Nazis. No man can tame a tiger into a kitten by stroking it. There can be no **appeasement** with ruthlessness. There can be no reasoning with an **incendiary bomb**. We know now that a nation can have peace with the Nazis only at the price of total surrender. . . .

Thinking in terms of today and tomorrow, I make the direct statement to the American people that there is far less chance of the United States getting into war if we do all we can now to support the nations defending themselves against attack by the Axis than if we **acquiesce in** their defeat, submit tamely to an Axis victory, and wait our turn to be the object of attack in another war later on.

If we are to be completely honest with ourselves, we must admit that there is risk in any course we may take. But I deeply believe that the great majority of our people agree that the course that I **advocate**

Appeasement: Giving in to the demands of another nation in order to maintain peace.

Incendiary bomb: A bomb designed to start fires, usually dropped on civilian targets.

Acquiesce in: Passively accept.

Advocate: To argue for or support.

Emphatically: Strongly or forcefully pursue.

involves the least risk now and the greatest hope for world peace in the future.

The people of Europe who are defending themselves do not ask us to do their fighting. They ask us for the implements of war, the planes, the tanks, the guns, the freighters which will enable them to fight for their liberty and for our security.

Emphatically *we must get these weapons to them, get them to them in sufficient volume and quickly enough so that we and*

A factory worker at a Philadelphia, Pennsylvania, arsenal. War supplies manufactured in the United States were shipped to Great Britain beginning in early 1941 to help in the fight against Germany. *AP/Wide World Photos. Reproduced by permission.*

our children will be saved the agony and suffering of war which others have had to endure. . . .

*In a military sense Great Britain and the British Empire are today the **spearhead** of resistance to world conquest. And they are putting up a fight which will live forever in the story of human **gallantry**. . . .*

Our national policy is not directed toward war. Its sole purpose is to keep war away from our country and away from our people.

Democracy's fight against world conquest is being greatly aided, and must be more greatly aided, by the rearmament of the United States and by sending every ounce and every ton of munitions and supplies that we can possibly spare to help the defenders who are in the front lines. . . .

This nation is making a great effort to produce everything that is necessary in this emergency—and with all possible speed. And this great effort requires great sacrifice. . . .

*If our capacity to produce is limited by machines, it must ever be remembered that these machines are operated by the skill and the **stamina** of the workers. As the government is determined to protect the rights of the workers, so the nation has a right to expect that the men who man the machines will **discharge their full responsibilities to the urgent needs of defense**. . . .*

*The nation expects our defense industries to continue operation without interruption by **strikes or lockouts**. It expects and insists that management and workers will reconcile their differences by voluntary or legal means, to continue to produce the supplies that are so sorely needed. . . .*

*Nine days ago I announced the setting up of **a more effective organization** to direct our gigantic efforts to increase the production of munitions. The appropriation of vast sums of money and a well-coordinated executive direction of our defense efforts are not in themselves enough. Guns, planes, ships and many other things have to be built in the factories and the arsenals of America. They have to be produced by workers and managers and engineers with the aid of machines which in turn have to be built by hundreds of thousands of workers throughout the land.*

In this great work there has been splendid cooperation between the government and industry and labor. And I am very thankful.

Spearhead: Leading the attack.

Gallantry: Heroic bravery.

Stamina: Energy and endurance.

Discharge their full responsibilities to the urgent needs of defense: Workers in war industries will be dedicated and work diligently to achieve war production goals.

Strikes or lockouts: Various forms of work stoppages.

A more effective organization: Roosevelt is referring to the Office of Production Management (OPM), which actually began operation the following month.

*American industrial genius, unmatched throughout all the world in the solution of production problems, has been called upon to bring its resources and its talents into action. Manufacturers of watches, of farm implements, of **Linotypes** and cash registers and automobiles, and sewing machines and lawn mowers and locomotives, are now making **fuses** and bomb packing crates and telescope mounts and shells and pistols and tanks.*

But all of our present efforts are not enough. We must have more ships, more guns, more planes—more of everything. . . .

I want to make it clear that it is the purpose of the nation to build now with all possible speed every machine, every arsenal, every factory that we need to manufacture our defense material. We have the men—the skill—the wealth—and above all, the will.

I am confident that if and when production of consumer or luxury goods in certain industries requires the use of machines and raw materials that are essential for defense purposes, then such production must yield, and will gladly yield, to our primary and compelling purpose.

*So I appeal to the owners of plants—to the managers—to the workers—to our own government employees—to put every ounce of effort into producing these munitions swiftly and without **stint**. With this appeal I give you the pledge that all of us who are officers of your government will devote ourselves to the same wholehearted extent to the great task that lies ahead. . . .*

We must be the great arsenal of democracy. For us this is an emergency as serious as war itself. We must apply ourselves to our task with the same resolution, the same sense of urgency, the same spirit of patriotism and sacrifice as we would show were we at war. . . .

I have the profound conviction that the American people are now determined to put forth a mightier effort than they have ever yet made to increase our production of all the implements of defense, to meet the threat to our democratic faith.

As President of the United States, I call for that national effort. I call for it in the name of this nation which we love and honor and which we are privileged and proud to serve. I call upon our people with absolute confidence that our common cause will greatly succeed.

Linotypes: Typesetting machines used in printing and publishing.

Fuses: A combustible cord used to ignite explosives.

Stint: An old term for pausing or stopping.

The "Four Freedoms" Speech

Franklin D. Roosevelt was reelected to an unprecedented third term as U.S. president in November 1940. In late December of that year he delivered his "Arsenal of Democracy" fireside chat to the American people. He asked American industries to speed up their production of war materials, for U.S. military stockpiles and for shipment to Great Britain, whose armed forces were fighting against German aggression.

Roosevelt addressed Congress and the nation in his State of the Union address on January 6, 1941, a week after his "Arsenal" speech. In the address he repeated his call for accelerated mobilization, saying "I am not satisfied with the progress thus far."

Toward the end of the speech Roosevelt explained that mobilization was necessary to rid the world of dictatorships and military rule, the types of power wielded by Adolf Hitler in Germany, Benito Mussolini in Italy, and Japanese leaders in Southeast Asia. The president then eloquently described "four essential human freedoms" that the United States hoped to secure for the world community: freedom of speech and expression, religious freedom, freedom from want, and freedom from fear. Posters illustrating the four freedoms were widely distributed across America. Hanging in homes and stores, these posters reminded Americans what the nation was fighting for in World

What happened next . . .

In January 1941 President Roosevelt established the Office of Production Management (OPM), put industrial leaders in charge, and directed it to get production of war materials going immediately. Mobilization began in earnest. For example, ground was broken in March to build the gigantic Willow Run plant in Michigan for the production of B-24 bombers. Meanwhile a major problem emerged. As the United States tooled up for massive war production, Britain ran out of money to pay for the U.S. war supplies. In response Congress established the Lend-Lease program in March 1941 to loan Britain money for its purchases. The shipments of American armaments indeed helped Britain to hang on. In May 1941 Germany ended its attempt to defeat Britain from the air. The Lend-Lease program also helped the Soviet Union when Germany invaded Soviet borders in June 1941.

War II. Here are President Roosevelt's famous words about the four freedoms:

In the future days which we seek to make secure, we look forward to a world founded upon four essential human freedoms.

The first is freedom of speech and expression—everywhere in the world.

The second is freedom of every person to worship God in his own way—everywhere in the world.

The third is freedom from want, which, translated into world terms, means economic understandings which will secure to every nation a healthy peacetime life for its inhabitants—everywhere in the world.

The fourth is freedom from fear, which, translated into world terms, means a worldwide reduction of armaments to such a point and in such a thorough fashion that no nation will be in a position to commit an act of physical aggression against any neighbor—anywhere in the world. That is no vision of a distant millennium. It is a definite basis for a kind of world attainable in our own time and generation. That kind of world is the very antithesis [the opposite] of the so-called "new order" of tyranny which the dictators seek to create with the crash of a bomb.

—Reprinted from *The Public Papers and Addresses of Franklin D. Roosevelt, 1940 Volume.* Published in 1941.

Did you know . . .

- Franklin D. Roosevelt was the first and only U.S. president reelected to a third term. This unprecedented event occurred in November 1940, a month before the "Arsenal of Democracy" speech.

- Although mobilization had occurred only on a limited basis in 1940, war-related jobs created new work opportunities for many Americans who had been unemployed during the Great Depression. With more people receiving steady paychecks, demand for consumer goods began to rise. Anticipating better economic times and increasing consumer demand, American industries were eager to make civilian goods such as automobiles and kitchen appliances. Therefore, they did not want to switch to war production and resisted President Roosevelt's call to mobilization.

- In 1940, under heavy German air attack, Britain depended for its survival on American-made war supplies including food. The United States shipped these supplies over the Atlantic Ocean on freighters. The freighter traffic led to the so-called Battle of the Atlantic. German U-boats (short for *Unterseeboot,* which means submarine) patrolled the waters just off the eastern U.S. coastline and sank thousands of tons of supplies before the United States and Britain figured out how to better protect the ships. Soon, the U.S. was making ships, the Liberty ships, faster than Germany could sink them.

Consider the following . . .

- How did the increasing mobilization in 1941 affect unemployment rates?

- In "Arsenal of Democracy" President Roosevelt addresses Americans who have an isolationist viewpoint. What does he say to contradict their beliefs?

- Note that the United States was not yet at war when President Roosevelt delivered this speech. According to Roosevelt's words, why was the United States mobilizing to build massive amounts of war materials?

For More Information

Books

Adams, Henry H. *Years of Deadly Peril: The Coming of the War, 1939–1941.* New York: David McKay Co., 1969.

Goodwin, Doris Kearns. *No Ordinary Time: Franklin and Eleanor Roosevelt, the Home Front in World War II.* New York: Simon & Schuster, 1994.

Harris, Mark J., Franklin D. Mitchell, and Steven J. Schechter, eds. *The Homefront: America during World War II.* New York: Putnam, 1984.

Roosevelt, Franklin D. *The Public Papers and Addresses of Franklin D. Roosevelt, 1940 Volume.* New York: Macmillan, 1941.

Franklin D. Roosevelt

Excerpt from "The President Proclaims That an Unlimited National Emergency Confronts the Country, Proclamation No. 2487," *delivered on May 27, 1941*

Reprinted from *The Public Papers and Addresses of Franklin D. Roosevelt, 1941 Volume.* Published in 1950.

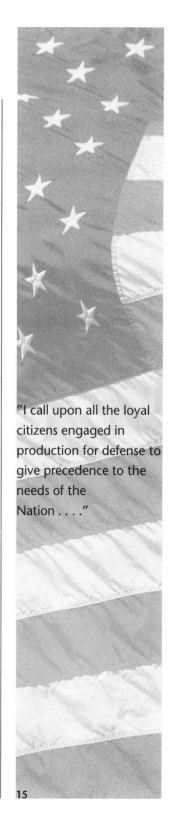

"I call upon all the loyal citizens engaged in production for defense to give precedence to the needs of the Nation . . . ."

In the spring of 1941 German dictator Adolf Hitler continued his aggression in Europe. By mid-April Yugoslavia had fallen under German occupation. By the end of April German and Italian forces had subdued Greece. Meanwhile Japanese military forces threatened to expand into the Southeast Asian nations of Vietnam, Laos, and Cambodia and appeared to cast an eye upon the U.S. territories of Guam and the Philippines. The United States became concerned about its economic interests in those regions.

President Roosevelt's "Arsenal of Democracy" speech in December 1940, in which he called for voluntary mobilization to manufacture more war materials, had produced considerably less action than he had hoped. Although leaders from industry, labor, and agriculture had made progress, much more needed to be done—and at a much faster pace. Roosevelt and his advisers believed that if U.S. business leaders continued their sluggish, foot-dragging approach to mobilization, America's own shores might soon come under Axis attack. In May 1941, as Axis expansion continued,

In 1941, this Chrysler automotive factory switched from manufacturing cars to assembling tanks to contribute to the war mobilization efforts on the home front.
© Bettman/Corbis. Reproduced by permission.

President Roosevelt felt it necessary to proclaim an "unlimited national emergency." His proclamation was brief, firm, and to the point. Roosevelt stated that Axis powers were bent on dominating the world, and he demanded the authorization to strengthen the U.S. military for defense against foreign attack. Military and civil defenses (civilian programs designed to protect U.S. citizens from enemy attack on the home front) were put on notice to be ready to turn back any aggression in the Western Hemisphere. President Roosevelt then called upon private businesses to put production of much needed war materials ahead of all domestic production wants or needs. He called upon workers and employers to put aside their differences for the sake of uninterrupted production. Finally Roosevelt directed all state and local government officials to work with civil defense agencies to protect the home front of the United States.

Things to remember while reading the excerpt from "Proclamation No. 2487" . . .

- President Roosevelt first called for U.S. mobilization to build up America's defense capabilities in September 1939, when Nazi Germany invaded Poland. His call had largely been ignored; most Americans saw no reason to be involved in another European war. In late December 1940, in his "Arsenal of Democracy" speech, Roosevelt again urged U.S. industry to mobilize and convert to war armament production.

- In Proclamation No. 2487 Roosevelt specifically addressed workers and employers, because their utmost cooperation with each other was vital to the war production effort. In the late 1930s membership in labor unions increased as worker dissatisfaction with wages and work conditions increased. The union supported many strikes (work stoppages) to press their demands for improved conditions. In some cases the confrontations led to violent clashes between union members and management's security guards.

- Many industry leaders had continued to balk at switching from production of civilian consumer goods to war armaments. They wanted assurances from the government and the military that the production of war materials would be profitable. Manufacturers were also reluctant to build war production plants, fearing that these would become useless when the war ended.

Excerpt from "Proclamation No. 2487"

WHEREAS on September 8, 1939, because of the outbreak of war in Europe a proclamation was issued declaring a limited national emergency and directing measures "for the purpose of strengthening our national defense within the limits of peacetime ***authorizations.****"*

WHEREAS a succession of events makes plain that the objectives of the ***Axis belligerents*** *in such war are not confined to* ***those avowed at its commencement,*** *but include overthrow throughout the world of existing democratic order, and a worldwide domination*

Authorizations: Annual funding levels for government.

Axis belligerents: Germany, Italy, and Japan.

Those avowed at its commencement: Agreements made between Germany, Britain, and France just prior to the war to turn over certain territories to Germany; in return, Germany had promised to make no more territorial demands.

of peoples and economies through the destruction of all resistance on land and sea and in the air, AND

WHEREAS **indifference** on the part of the United States to the increasing menace would be **perilous**, and common **prudence** requires that for the security of this Nation and of this hemisphere we should pass from peacetime authorizations of military strength to such a basis as will enable us to cope instantly and decisively with any attempt at **hostile encirclement of this hemisphere**, or the establishment of any base for aggression against it, as well as to repel the threat of **predatory incursion** by foreign agents into our territory and society,

NOW, THEREFORE, I, Franklin D. Roosevelt, President of the United States of America, do proclaim that an unlimited national emergency confronts this country, which requires that its military, naval, air, and civilian defenses be put on the basis of readiness to repel any and all acts or threats of aggression directed toward any part of the Western Hemisphere.

I call upon all the loyal citizens engaged in production for defense to give **precedence** to the needs of the Nation. . . .

I call upon all our loyal workmen as well as employers to merge their **lesser differences** in the larger effort to insure the survival of the only kind of government which recognizes the rights of labor or of **capital**.

I call upon loyal State and local leaders and officials to cooperate with the civilian defense agencies of the United States to assure our internal security against foreign directed **subversion**. . . .

I call upon all loyal citizens to place the Nation's needs first in mind and in action to the end that we may mobilize and have ready for instant defensive use all of the physical powers, all of the moral strength, and all of the material resources of this Nation.

What happened next . . .

After delivering "Proclamation No. 2487" to a group of foreign diplomats, President Roosevelt addressed the nation that same evening in a radio broadcast titled "We Choose

Indifference: Lack of interest.

Perilous: Dangerous.

Prudence: Practical wisdom.

Hostile encirclement of this hemisphere: Axis control over areas surrounding the United States.

Predatory incursion: Invasion.

Precedence: Top priority.

Lesser differences: Differences between labor union members and management, such as disputes over working conditions. Roosevelt calls them "lesser" because these are less important than the survival of American society in general.

Capital: Money and property.

Subversion: Attempt to overthrow the government.

A World War II poster encouraging union workers and union management to work together for the greater good of producing massive amounts of war materials. *The Library of Congress.*

Human Freedom." In this address, published in *The Public Papers and Addresses of Franklin D. Roosevelt, 1941 Volume,* he explained in detail the world situation. According to Roosevelt, German dictator Adolf Hitler planned "to strangle the United States of America and the Dominion of Canada." Roosevelt described what American life might be like in a world dominated by Hitler, stating that "American labor would have to compete with slave labor in the rest of the world . . . wages and hours would be fixed by Hitler . . . the American farmer would get for his products exactly what Hitler wanted to give . . . the whole fabric of working life as we know it—business and manufacturing, mining and agriculture—all would be mangled and crippled under such a system."

Roosevelt's call for mobilization inspired a modest increase in defense spending and a slow but steady conversion of industry to the production of war materials. These changes created many new jobs for Americans. More and more people began to migrate to urban industrial centers, where war production jobs were plentiful. Nevertheless, a full and massive mobilization effort did not occur until late 1941, when Japan attacked Pearl Harbor, a U.S. naval installation in Hawaii. Approximately twenty-seven hundred U.S. soldiers and sailors were killed in the attack. After the Pearl Harbor attack, Americans changed their attitude toward mobilization; they were outraged by the incident and ready to defend their nation against further harm. Industry leaders and everyday workers realized they would have to move into high gear to reach the level of mobilization that President Roosevelt had been asking for since his "Arsenal of Democracy" speech a year earlier.

Did you know . . .

- Proclamation No. 2487 was broadcast over radio in the United States. It was also translated into fourteen languages and transmitted worldwide by shortwave radio.

- President Roosevelt broadcast his address from the historic East Room in the White House. Representatives from twenty Latin American countries and Canada were present for the speech. They were attending a meeting on Western Hemisphere security; the subject of the proclamation.

- A few months after Roosevelt's proclamation of an unlimited national emergency, a Gallup Poll showed that 85 percent of Americans thought the United States would be drawn into the war in Europe. By late fall of 1941, in another Gallup Poll, 68 percent of Americans said it was more important to defeat Germany than for the United States to stay out of the war.

Consider the following . . .

- Review the text surrounding the first excerpt (the "Arsenal of Democracy" speech) and the commentary on this excerpt to find reasons why U.S. industry was slow to heed President Roosevelt's requests for mobilization.

- In fall of 1941, even though most Americans had come to believe that the United States would be drawn into the war, the general population was not particularly serious about preparing for war. Think about human nature as you understand it and offer reasons for this lack of concern. Also remember that Americans were just emerging from the economic hard times of the Great Depression (1929–41).

For More Information

Books

Lingeman, Richard R. *Don't You Know There's a War On? The American Home Front, 1941–1945*. New York: Putnam, 1970.

Roosevelt, Franklin D. *The Public Papers and Addresses of Franklin D. Roosevelt, 1941 Volume*. New York: Harper & Brothers, 1950.

Wiltz, John E. *From Isolation to War, 1931–1941*. New York: Thomas Y. Crowell Co., 1968.

Franklin D. Roosevelt

Excerpt from "We Are Going to Win the War and We Are Going to Win the Peace That Follows," *a speech delivered on December 9, 1941*

Reprinted from *The Public Papers and Addresses of Franklin D. Roosevelt, 1941 Volume.* Published in 1950.

"Together with other free peoples, we are now fighting to maintain our right to live among our world neighbors in freedom and in common decency, without fear of assault . . . ."

On December 8, 1941, President Roosevelt made a now famous speech, later published in 1950 in the *The Public Papers and Addresses of Franklin D. Roosevelt, 1941 Volume*, to Congress about the Japanese surprise attack on Pearl Harbor. The president asked Congress to declare a state of war between the United States and Japan. He began with these words: "Yesterday, December 7, 1941—a date which will live in infamy—the United States of America was suddenly and deliberately attacked by naval and air forces of the Empire of Japan." He went on to explain that Japan had "undertaken a surprise offensive extending throughout the Pacific area." Thirty-three minutes after Roosevelt concluded his "Day of Infamy" speech, Congress completed and passed a joint resolution declaring that "war existed between the United States and Japan."

On the evening of December 9, 1941, President Roosevelt spoke directly to the American public via radio broadcast, calmly explaining how U.S. participation in the war would affect the home front. Roosevelt had used the "fireside chat" format, radio broadcasts that addressed everyday

citizens in an informal, comforting manner, since he first took office in 1933. The first fireside chat occurred on March 12, 1933, in which Roosevelt explained to the nation the measures he was taking to solve the banking crisis that was gripping the nation at the height of the Great Depression. On December 9, as on many other occasions, the president's clear reassuring voice infused Americans with confidence as they listened. Roosevelt first recapped the world situation and then summarized that portion of his speech by saying, "We are all in it—all the way." Next Roosevelt explained that the U.S. government would be checking all news reports from the war zones for accuracy, and he asked American journalists to keep rumors and hearsay out of their reports. The president also stated that news stories would be screened before publication so that any information that might be valuable to the enemy could be removed.

In the next part of his speech, Roosevelt called for all-out production in the war industry and announced an

President Franklin D. Roosevelt speaking to the U.S. Congress on December 8, 1941, one day after the Pearl Harbor attack. During this speech Roosevelt requests a declaration of war against Japan; thirty-three minutes after concluding the speech, Congress passed the resolution declaring war between the United States and Japan. © *Corbis. Reproduced by permission.*

extended workweek for all existing production facilities. He also announced that taxes would go up to help pay for the war. The president advised the public that they might also experience shortages of consumer goods. Lastly Roosevelt described the lesson that the Pearl Harbor attack had taught the nation. His words on this point would be brought to mind almost sixty years later, after terrorists attacked the U.S. mainland on September 11, 2001 (see sidebar on page 30).

Things to remember while reading the excerpt from "We Are Going to Win the War and We Are Going to Win the Peace That Follows" . . .

- Before Pearl Harbor was attacked, most Americans had not taken war preparation to heart. After the attack, Roosevelt knew that the public's attitude had changed through telegrams and letters to the White House and through media reports on the public mood.

- After the attack on Pearl Harbor, the voices of isolationism (the belief in remaining uninvolved in another country's problems) and pacifism (opposition to the use of military force for any reason) quieted immediately.

- The Pearl Harbor attack shattered Americans' hope that vast ocean distances would protect the United States from involvement in World War II.

Excerpt from "We Are Going to Win the War and We Are Going to Win the Peace That Follows"

*The sudden **criminal attacks** perpetrated by the Japanese in the Pacific provide the climax of a **decade of international immorality**.*

*Powerful and **resourceful gangsters** have banded together to make war upon the whole human race. Their challenge has now been flung at the United States of America. The Japanese have*

Criminal attacks: The attack on Pearl Harbor, December 7, 1941.

Decade of international immorality: The Axis powers invaded country after country in Europe, North Africa, and Asia from 1931 to 1941.

Resourceful gangsters: The leaders of the Axis powers—Germany, Italy, and Japan.

treacherously violated the long-standing peace between us. Many American soldiers and sailors have been killed by enemy action. American ships have been sunk; American airplanes have been destroyed.

The Congress and the people of the United States have accepted that challenge.

Together with other free peoples, we are now fighting to maintain our right to live among our world neighbors in freedom and in common decency, without fear of assault. . . .

I can say with utmost confidence that no Americans, today or a thousand years hence, need feel anything but pride in our patience and in our efforts through all the years toward achieving a peace in the Pacific which would be fair and honorable to every Nation, large or small. And no honest person, today or a thousand years hence, will be able to suppress a sense of **indignation** and horror at the treachery committed by the military dictators of Japan. . . .

President Franklin D. Roosevelt signing the declaration of war against Japan, December 8, 1941. *National Archives.*

The course that Japan has followed for the past ten years in Asia has paralleled the course of Hitler and Mussolini in Europe and in Africa. Today, it has become far more than a parallel. It is actual **collaboration** so well calculated that all the continents of the world, and all the oceans, are now considered by the **Axis strategists** as one gigantic battlefield.

In 1931, ten years ago, Japan invaded Manchukuo—without warning.

In 1935, Italy invaded Ethiopia—without warning.

In 1938, Hitler occupied Austria—without warning.

In 1939, Hitler invaded Czechoslovakia—without warning.

Later in 1939, Hitler invaded Poland—without warning.

In 1940, Hitler invaded Norway, Denmark, the Netherlands, Belgium, and Luxembourg—without warning.

Indignation: Anger at an injustice.

Collaboration: Cooperation.

Axis strategists: Military planning experts of Germany, Italy, and Japan.

In 1941, also, Hitler invaded Russia—without warning.

And now Japan has attacked Malaya and Thailand—and the United States—without warning.

It is all of one pattern.

We are now in this war. We are all in it—all the way. Every single man, woman, and child is a partner in the most tremendous undertaking of our American history. We must share together the bad news and the good news, the defeats and the victories—the changing fortunes of war. . . .

*This Government will put its trust in the **stamina** of the American people, and will give the **facts** to the public just as soon as two conditions have been fulfilled: first, that the information has been definitely and officially confirmed; and, second, that the release of the information at the time it is received will not prove valuable to the enemy directly or indirectly. . . .*

It must be remembered by each and every one of us that our free and rapid communication these days must be greatly restricted in wartime. It is not possible to receive full, speedy, accurate reports from distant areas of combat. This is particularly true where naval operations are concerned. For in these days of the marvels of radio it is often impossible for the commanders of various units to report their activities by radio at all, for the very simple reason that this information would become available to the enemy, and would disclose their position and their plan of defense or attack.

Of necessity there will be delays in officially confirming or denying reports of operations but we will not hide facts from the country if we know the facts and if the enemy will not be aided by their disclosure.

To all newspapers and radio stations—all those who reach the eyes and ears of the American people—I say this: You have a most grave responsibility to the Nation now and for the duration of this war.

*If you feel that your Government is not disclosing enough of the truth, you have every right to say so. But—in the absence of all the facts, as revealed by official sources—you have no right in the **ethics of patriotism** to deal out unconfirmed reports in such a way as to make people believe that they are gospel truth.*

Every citizen, in every walk of life, shares this same responsibility. The lives of our soldiers and sailors—the whole future of this

Stamina: Endurance, strength.

Facts: News of happenings in the war.

Ethics of patriotism: The manner in which to be supportive of one's country.

Nation—depend upon the manner in which each and every one of us fulfills his obligation to our country.

Now a word about the recent past—and the future. A year and a half has elapsed since the fall of France, when the whole world first realized the **mechanized might** which the Axis Nations had been building for so many years. America has used that year and a half to great advantage. Knowing that the attack might reach us in all too short a time, we immediately began greatly to increase our industrial strength and our capacity to meet the demands of modern warfare.

Precious months were gained by sending vast quantities of our war material to the Nations of the world still able to resist Axis aggression. Our policy rested on the fundamental truth that the defense of any country resisting Hitler or Japan was in the long run the defense of our own country. That policy has been justified. It has given us time, invaluable time, to build our American assembly lines of production.

Assembly lines are now in operation. Others are being rushed to completion. A steady stream of tanks and planes, of guns and ships, and shells and equipment—that is what these eighteen months have given us.

But it is all only a beginning of what still has to be done. We must be set to face a long war against crafty and powerful bandits. The attack at Pearl Harbor can be repeated at any one of many points, points in both oceans and along both our coast lines and against all the rest of the hemisphere.

It will not only be a long war, it will be a hard war. That is the basis on which we now lay all our plans. That is the yardstick by which we measure what we shall need and demand; money, materials, doubled and quadrupled production—ever-increasing. The production must be not only for our own Army and Navy and Air Forces. It must reinforce the other armies and navies and air forces fighting the Nazis and the **war lords** of Japan throughout the Americas and throughout the world.

I have been working today on the subject of production. Your Government has decided on two broad policies.

The first is to speed up all existing production by working on a seven-day-week basis in every war industry, including the production of essential raw materials.

Mechanized might: Superior war materials such as tanks, aircraft, and submarines.

War lords: Aggressive military leaders exercising power over the civilian society.

A World War II poster featuring the powerful image of the American eagle, calling all Americans to do what they can to defend the United States against its enemies.
The Library of Congress.

AMERICA CALLING

Take your place in Civilian Defense

Obstacles and difficulties, divisions and disputes: Referring to labor disputes with management and tough management stances trying to break the unions.

Callousness: Insensitivity.

An organization in Washington: The federal government, including all the private industry leaders hired to advise government.

The second policy, now being put into form, is to rush additions to the capacity of production by building more new plants, by adding to old plants, and by using the many smaller plants for war needs.

Over the hard road of the past months, we have at times met **obstacles and difficulties, divisions and disputes,** *indifference and* **callousness.** *That is now all past—and, I am sure, forgotten.*

The fact is that the country now has **an organization in Washington** *[D.C.] built around men and women who are* *recognized experts in their own fields.—I think the country knows that the people who are actually responsible in each and every one of these many fields are pulling together with a teamwork that has never before been excelled.*

On the road ahead there lies hard work—grueling work—day and night, every hour and every minute.

I was about to add that ahead there lies sacrifice for all of us.

But it is not correct to use that word. The United States does not consider it a sacrifice to do all one can, to give one's best to our Nation, when the Nation is fighting for its existence and its future life.

It is not a sacrifice for any man, old or young, to be in the Army or the Navy of the United States. Rather is it a privilege.

*It is not a sacrifice for the industrialist or the wage earner, the farmer or the shopkeeper, the trainman or the doctor, to pay more taxes, to buy more **bonds**, to **forego** extra profits, to work longer or harder at the task for which he is best fitted. Rather is it a privilege.*

It is not a sacrifice to do without many things to which we are accustomed if the national defense calls for doing without.

A review this morning leads me to the conclusion that at present we shall not have to curtail the normal use of articles of food. There is enough food today for all of us and enough left over to send to those who are fighting on the same side with us.

But there will be a clear and definite shortage of metals of many kinds for civilian use, for the very good reason that in our increased program we shall need for war purposes more than half of that portion of the principal metals which during the past year have gone into articles for civilian use. Yes, we shall have to give up many things entirely.

*And I am sure that the people in every part of the Nation are prepared in their **individual living** to win this war. I am sure that they will cheerfully help to pay a large part of its financial cost while it goes on. I am sure they will cheerfully give up those material things that they are asked to give up.*

*And I am sure that they will retain all those **great spiritual things** without which we cannot win through.*

Bonds: Reference to war bonds that was a form of governmental borrowing by selling certificates to the public to help finance the war; purchasers were guaranteed their money back plus interest; it was a form of investment for the purchasers.

Forego: Do without.

Individual living: For citizens to live with fewer new consumer goods while industry converted to war production; to make personal sacrifices in terms of normal comfort.

Great spiritual things: Roosevelt is referring to the ideals of human freedom and dignity.

Chilling Words Applied Sixty Years Later

In his fireside chat on December 9, 1941, President Franklin D. Roosevelt delivered the following words:

It is our obligation to our dead—it is our sacred obligation to their children and to our children—that we must never forget what we have learned.

And what we all have learned is this:

There is no such thing as security for any Nation—or any individual—in a world ruled by the principles of gangsterism.

There is no such thing as impregnable defense against powerful aggressors who sneak up in the dark and strike without warning.

We have learned that our ocean-girt hemisphere is not immune from severe attack—that we cannot measure our safety in terms of miles on any map any more.

We may acknowledge that our enemies have performed a brilliant feat of deception, *perfectly timed and executed with great skill. It was a thoroughly dishonorable deed . . . We don't like it—we didn't want to get in it—but we are in it and we're going to fight it with everything we've got.*

I do not think any American has any doubt of our ability to administer proper punishment to the perpetrators of these crimes.

These chilling words applied to the Japanese attack on the U.S. Naval installation at Pearl Harbor in Hawaii on December 7, 1941. They also apply with an amazing degree of appropriateness to the terrorist attack on the World Trade Center towers in New York City on September 11, 2001. Discuss the similarities and differences between America's response to the Pearl Harbor attack and America's reaction to the September 11, 2001, terrorist attacks on the U.S. mainland.

*I repeat that the United States can accept no result **save** victory, final and complete. Not only must the shame of Japanese **treachery** be wiped out, but the sources of international brutality, wherever they exist, must be absolutely and finally broken.*

In my message to the Congress yesterday I said that we "will make it very certain that this form of treachery shall never again endanger us." In order to achieve that certainty, we must begin the great task that is before us by abandoning once and for all the illusion that we can ever again isolate ourselves from the rest of humanity.

In these past few years—and, most violently, in the past three days—we have learned a terrible lesson.

Save: Except for.

Treachery: Act of betrayal or deception.

It is our obligation to our dead—it is our sacred obligation to their children and to our children—that we must never forget what we have learned.

And what we all have learned is this:

There is no such thing as security for any Nation—or any individual—in a world ruled by the principles of gangsterism.

*There is no such thing as **impregnable** defense against powerful aggressors who sneak up in the dark and strike without warning.*

*We have learned that our **ocean-girt** hemisphere is not immune from severe attack—that we cannot measure our safety in terms of miles on any map any more.*

We may acknowledge that our enemies have performed a brilliant feat of deception, perfectly timed and executed with great skill. It was a thoroughly dishonorable deed, but we must face the fact that modern warfare as conducted in the Nazi manner is a dirty business. We don't like it—we didn't want to get in it—but we are in it and we're going to fight it with everything we've got.

I do not think any American has any doubt of our ability to administer proper punishment to the perpetrators of these crimes. . . .

We are going to win the war and we are going to win the peace that follows. . . .

What happened next . . .

Germany and Italy officially declared war on the United States on December 11, 1941. The U.S. government immediately infused American industry with massive amounts of money to convert to a full-fledged war economy. Production goals set for 1942 included sixty thousand warplanes, forty-five thousand tanks, and twenty thousand antiaircraft guns. Administration officials made decisions on resource allocation so that critical industries would have adequate amounts of steel, rubber, aluminum, and other important materials. Large corporations received most of the government contracts for

Impregnable:
Unconquerable; incapable of being taken by assault.

Ocean-girt: Being surrounded by vast oceans.

war production because they had large research staffs and their assembly lines were already in production; therefore, they could produce the most war materials in the shortest amount of time. These corporations were located in densely populated urban areas, so the pool of available workers was large. However, thousands of additional workers were needed to meet the government's production goals, so many Americans from rural areas flocked to the cities for war industry jobs.

People who remained in rural areas farmed and prospered. Fewer farms existed in the early 1940s than had existed prior to the Great Depression, but those that survived grew larger and were able to supply enough food for Americans on the home front and for Allied soldiers and civilians abroad. Union leadership promised that no strikes would occur during wartime, and the number of work stoppages dropped dramatically by the end of 1942.

Did you know . . .

- American industrial leaders demanded that the way industries mobilize for war production be controlled by the private corporations, not by government agencies. They wanted to avoid the types of government control that Roosevelt placed on business during the Great Depression, even though such measures were designed to strengthen the U.S. economy. Hoping to build increased support from business for the war, Roosevelt agreed to let business leaders take the lead in mobilization. As a result, private corporations forged strong working alliances with the U.S. military services in order to meet production goals. This alliance, which became known as the military-industrial complex, would greatly influence U.S. foreign policy and economy into the twenty-first century.

- Unemployment virtually disappeared once mobilization went into full swing. Anyone who wanted to work—including women and minorities—could find a job.

- Cities struggled with the influx of thousands of new residents who came to find employment. As a result, severe housing shortages developed, public transportation was overcrowded, and there was a lack of recreational facilities, such as public parks.

- Millions of men joined the military and crowded onto rapidly expanding military bases. Their wives and children followed them across the country to live near the bases.

Consider the following . . .

- As large corporations converted to producing war armaments, they gobbled up materials such as metals and rubber. Predict what happened to many small companies trying to produce civilian products.

- Mobilization changed American society dramatically. Identify and discuss several of those changes.

- In his "Arsenal of Democracy" speech and in "Proclamation No. 2487" President Roosevelt asked workers not to disrupt production efforts with strikes (work stoppages); he wanted employers and workers represented by labor unions to cooperate for the sake of the war effort. What was the overall response of unions and management from 1942 to 1945?

- Reread the final portion of this excerpt, beginning with "We have learned a terrible lesson. . . ." Discuss the similarities and differences between America's response to the Pearl Harbor attack and the nation's reaction to the September 11, 2001, terrorist attacks on the U.S. mainland.

For More Information

Books

Harris, Mark J., Franklin D. Mitchell, and Steven J. Schechter, eds. *The Homefront: America during World War II*. New York: Putnam, 1984.

Ketchum, Richard M. *The Borrowed Years, 1938–1941: America on the Way to War*. New York: Random House, 1989.

Roosevelt, Franklin D. *The Public Papers and Addresses of Franklin D. Roosevelt, 1941 Volume*. New York: Harper & Brothers, 1950.

Civil Defense

As war spread through Europe and Asia in 1940 and 1941, President Franklin D. Roosevelt (1882–1945; served 1933–45) issued a call for war mobilization among U.S. industries. He also asked U.S. communities to begin organizing civil defense plans. Civil defense refers to a system of defensive measures designed to protect civilians and their property from enemy attack. In the twenty-first century, after the September 11, 2001, terrorist attacks against American civilians on the U.S. mainland, government officials began to refer to civil defense as "homeland security."

On May 20, 1941, President Roosevelt established the Office of Civilian Defense (OCD), replacing the inactive Council of National Defense created by Congress in 1916. The purpose of the OCD was to help states and communities set up civil defense councils. Roosevelt also hoped the OCD would spur civilians' awareness of and support for the nation's war efforts. However, the general public exhibited little enthusiasm for civil defense; many people clung to the hope that the United States would not be drawn directly into the hostilities.

American attitudes toward civil defense changed on Sunday, December 7, 1941. Huddled around their radios, Americans listened in shock and disbelief as grim-voiced announcers reported that Japanese bombs had killed several thousand U.S. servicemen at Pearl Harbor, Hawaii. On December 8 President Roosevelt signed a declaration of war against Japan, and in the next few days Germany and Italy declared war on the United States. Although thousands of local civil defense councils were in place, they did not have many volunteers before the Pearl Harbor attack. However, after the bombing of Pearl Harbor, Americans realized that more attacks might be launched by air and sea—against any U.S. community. Overnight, Americans' shock turned into anger and then into unified resolve and action. Suddenly OCD was flooded with volunteers and requests for information on how to become involved.

The first excerpt is the complete text of a booklet titled *What to Do in an Air Raid,* published by the **Office of Civilian Defense** in 1942. The booklet was widely available and gave clear and precise instructions about individual and family protection in an air raid. The second excerpt, **"Thomas A. Scott,"** is an account of a U.S. citizen involved in numerous volunteer civil defense activities. The third excerpt, "Are America's Civilians Ready for Attack?," written by **Helena H. Smith and William Sloane** describes the civil defense preparations of two U.S. communities.

Office of Civilian Defense

Complete text of What to Do in an Air Raid

Published by the U.S. Office of Civilian Defense, Washington, D.C., 1942.

"Await *official* information before taking any action. When the Air Raid Warden comes to your home, do what he tells you. He is for your protection. He is your friend."

Before World War II (1939–45) the United States felt effectively protected by the vast oceans to its east and west. However, by the late 1930s, bomber planes became a major component of Germany's and Japan's military strategy, and America's shores suddenly seemed vulnerable to attack. As long as the Allies (those nations, including the United States, Great Britain, and Soviet Union, who united in the fight against Germany, Italy, and Japan during World War II) controlled the Atlantic and the Pacific and any bases within possible striking distance of the United States, a sustained enemy attack on American soil was not possible. However, sporadic raids launched from aircraft carriers or by dirigibles (balloon airships, like blimps) or by long-range bombers coming from Europe were possible. Americans feared that enemy pilots might bail out over the countryside or a city and wreak havoc until captured. Enemy bombers could be shot down by the U.S. military while crossing the ocean or over America, but plans had to be made should an enemy plane actually reach the skies over America safely. Civil defense leaders assumed large cities and industrial areas on the East Coast and West Coast would be the primary targets of an air attack.

The Office of Civilian Defense (OCD) advised communities to begin planning for possible attacks. OCD informed Americans that there were two essential actions that would minimize damage during air attacks: seeking protective shelter and blacking out or camouflaging potential targets. OCD set up specific air raid signals and initiated air raid and blackout drills that the public practiced in earnest. The national OCD published booklets explaining civil defense procedures in clear and precise terms. It also published booklets listing volunteer opportunities for civil defense. Booklet titles included "You and the War," "Protection of School Children and School Property," "The Neighborhood in Action," "A Handbook for Air Raid Wardens," "How to Organize Civilian Protection in Your Neighborhood," and "How Do I Go About Aiding Civilian Defense?."

On the subject of air raid protection the OCD had Americans' undivided attention. To educate the public on this popular and important topic, OCD published "What to Do in an Air Raid" and printed fifty-seven million copies of the booklet. (The U.S. population at the time was approximately 130 million.) The cover of the publication gave Americans this frank advice: "Read and Keep This Pamphlet. It May Save your Life."

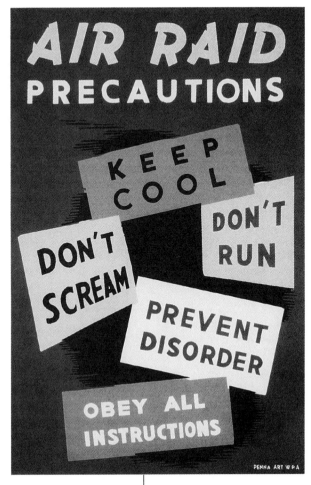

Posters such as this one offered advice to American citizens on how to behave in the event of an air raid. *The Library of Congress.*

Things to remember while reading
What to Do in an Air Raid . . .

- During the winter of 1940–41, German bombers carried out intense, devastating air raids over London, England. Accounts of these attacks were fresh in the memories of American citizens.

- Precautions against attack were in everyone's minds but most Americans were at a loss as to how they should most effectively proceed in a unified way that would make a difference, such as dimout and blackout procedures, community warning systems, and safe places to go to if a raid occurred. Ordinary citizens had no knowledge of bomb types (such as the difference between explosive and incendiary bombs) or how to deal with them, so they committed the instructions in the pamphlet to memory.

What to Do in an Air Raid

1. KEEP COOL

Above all, keep cool. Don't lose your head.

Do not crowd the streets; avoid chaos, prevent disorder and havoc.

You can fool the enemy. It is easy. If planes come over stay where you are. Don't phone unnecessarily. The chance you will be hit is small. It is part of the risk we must take to win this war.

Until an alarm, go about your usual business and recreation in the ordinary way.

Think twice before you do anything. Don't believe rumors— spreading false rumors is part of the enemy's technique. Don't let him take you in.

Know your air-raid warning. In general, it is short blasts or rising and falling pitch, on whistles or horns. The "all clear" is a steady tone for 2 minutes. (This is subject to change.)

Await official information before taking any action. When the Air Raid Warden comes to your home, do what he tells you. He is for your protection. He is your friend.

He will help you do your part to whip the enemy.

We can do it. We will do it, if we stay calm and cool and strong and alert.

2. STAY HOME

The safest place in an air raid is at home.

If you are away from home, get under cover in the nearest shelter. Avoid crowded places. Stay off the streets.

The enemy wants you to run out into the streets, create a mob, start a panic. Don't do it!

*If **incendiary bombs** fall, play a spray from a garden hose (never a splash or stream) of water on the bomb. Switch to a stream to put out any fire started by the bomb. Switch back to a spray for the bomb. The bomb will burn for about 15 minutes if left alone, only about 2 minutes under a fine water spray. A jet splash, stream or bucket of water will make it explode.*

If you have a soda-and-acid extinguisher (the kind you turn upside down), use it with your finger over the nozzle to make a spray. Don't use the chemical kind (small cylinders of liquid) on bombs. It is all right for ordinary fires.

But above all, keep cool, stay home.

Choose one member of the family to be the home air-warden—who will remember all the rules and what to do. Mother makes the best.

3. PUT OUT LIGHTS

*Whether or not **black-out** is ordered, don't show more light than is necessary. If planes come over, put out or cover all lights at once—don't wait for the black-out order. The light that can't be seen will never guide an enemy. Remember, a candle light may be seen for miles from the air.*

*If you have **portieres** or curtains, arrange a double thickness over your windows. Blankets will do. If you have heavy black paper, paste it on your windows. Don't crowd or stampede stores to get it, however. You probably have everything you need at home. Be ingenious—**improvise**.*

This type of air raid alarm siren sounded out warning tones that could be heard for several miles. Many sirens like these were placed on roofs of firehouses.
The Library of Congress.

Incendiary bombs: Bombs designed to start fires.

Black-out: Turning off all lights or completely concealing them from outside view.

Portieres: Curtains that hang across doorways.

Improvise: Be creative with materials you already have.

Should you get an air-raid warning, remember to shut off gas stoves and gas furnaces. Bomb explosions may blow them out from blast effect. Gas that collects may be explosive later.

Prepare one room, the one with the least window glass, in the strongest part of your house, for a refuge room. Put food and drinking water in it. Put a sturdy table in it. Put mattresses and chairs in it. Take a magazine or two, and a deck of cards, into it. Take things like eyeglasses and dentures with you when you go into it. Take toilet facilities, paper, a screen. If you have a portable radio, take that too. Above all, keep calm. Stay at home. Put out lights.

4. LIE DOWN

If bombs start to fall near you, lie down. You will feel the blast least that way, escape fragments or splinters.

The safest place is under a good stout table—the stronger the legs the better.

A mattress under a table combines comfort with safety.

The enemy may use **explosive bombs** *or incendiary bombs, or both. If incendiaries are used, it's more important to deal with them than to be safe from blast. So defeat the incendiary with a* spray *(never a splash or stream) of water, then go back to safety under a table in a refuge room.*

Most raids will likely be over in your immediate neighborhood *in a short time. However, stay under cover till the "all clear" is sounded.*

Know your raid alarms. Know the all clear. Official news of these will come to you from your Air Raid Warden. Don't believe rumors. Ask the warden when he comes.

Should your house be hit, keep cool. Answer tappings from rescue crews if you are trapped. (You most likely won't be either hit or trapped, but if you are, you can depend on rescue squads to go after you.) Again—keep cool, and wait. Don't yell after you hear them coming to you, unless they tell you to. Keep cool!

Just keeping cool hurts the enemy more than anything else you can do. Keep calm. Stay at home. Put out lights. Lie down.

5. STAY AWAY FROM WINDOWS

Glass shatters easily, so stay away from windows.

Don't go to windows and look out, in an air raid. It is a dangerous thing, and helps the enemy. The Air Raid Warden is out

Explosive bombs: Also called demolition bombs; heavy bombs that detonate on surface impact and can destroy buildings and create flying debris.

there watching for you. Again we say, get off the street if planes
come over.

At night, there is danger of being caught in blast from explosives.

Antiaircraft fire means falling **shrapnel.** You are safe from it
indoors, away from windows. It's more important to shell a plane
than it is to see it from a window. Do not say—we are repeating;
we would rather repeat until we bore you than have you forget.

Shrapnel: Shell fragments.

Stay in your refuge room, away from windows. That is the safest place. Go there at the first alarm; stay there until the all clear.

Above all, keep calm. Stay home. Put out lights. Lie down. Stay away from windows.

You can do all those things without any special equipment, other than what you have now in your home.

You can help lick the enemy with your bare hands, if you will do just those few simple things.

Be a good fellow and follow instructions and keep well.

Do not be a wise guy and get hurt.

6. YOU CAN HELP

Strong, capable, calm people are needed to man the volunteer services. If you want to help, there are lots of opportunities.

If you know first aid, and have a certificate, there is an immediate job for you. If you are a veteran, or a former volunteer or regular fireman, or policeman, there is work for you. If you have no special skills but are strong and husky, there is a job for you in rescue squads, road-repair units, or demolition and clearance squads. If you have and can drive a car, you may be needed for drivers' corps. Older Boy and Girl Scouts over 15 can help as messengers. Both men and women are needed.

Here's how to get started:

If there's a Civilian Defense Volunteer Office in your community, call there and ask where to report. If not, call your local Defense Council or Committee, or the Chamber of Commerce. Phone and ask where to report, rather than going in person.

THERE ARE PEOPLE NEEDED FOR . . .

AIR RAID WARDENS (men and women)

AUXILIARY FIREMEN (men)

AUXILIARY POLICE (men and women)

FIRE WATCHERS (men and women)

NURSES' AIDES (trained women)

EMERGENCY MEDICAL FORCES (men and women with Red Cross First Aid Certificates)

RESCUE SQUADS (men)

ROAD REPAIR UNITS (strong, husky men)

DEMOLITION AND CLEARANCE SQUADS (strong, husky men)

ELECTRICAL REPAIR UNITS (trained electricians)

DECONTAMINATION SQUADS (strong men and women)

EMERGENCY FOOD AND HOUSING UNITS (women who can cook and serve)

ABOVE ALL . . .

KEEP COOL

STAY HOME

PUT OUT LIGHTS

LIE DOWN

STAY AWAY FROM WINDOWS

. . . YOU CAN HELP!

What happened next . . .

By the end of January 1942 more than 5 million citizens had volunteered for OCD forces nationwide, including 671,000 volunteering as air raid wardens, 335,000 as auxiliary police, and 266,000 as emergency medical personnel.

The only enemy aircraft that managed to drop bombs on the U.S. mainland was a small Japanese floatplane flown by Nobuo Fujita (1912–1997). A Japanese submarine transported the plane in a watertight compartment to a point just off the Oregon coast. On September 9, 1942, Fujita flew the plane to the mountains in southwestern Oregon and dropped incendiary bombs on a forest about 10 miles from the tiny town of Brookings; he then returned to the waiting submarine. The Japanese scheme was to set off massive forest fires that would distract the United States from its war missions in the Pacific. However, the forest was damp from recent storms, so the fires that were started were small and the overall damage was insignificant. Fujita made another attempt, equally unsuccessful, a few days later. Because of wartime censorship policies, these attacks did not receive much coverage from the U.S. news media. No other similar attacks were ever carried out.

Did you know . . .

- The many different civil defense squads and units all adopted insignia so they could be easily identified by civilians and other emergency aid groups. Each civil defense insignia featured a blue circle surrounding a white triangle. Within the triangle was a distinct symbol for the person's squad or unit, such as rescue squad or medical force. The insignia were proudly worn on armbands and helmets, and schoolchildren enjoyed learning to identify the symbols.

- By July 1943 over twelve million Americans were registered OCD volunteers. However, in 1944 and 1945 interest waned as victory appeared probable and enemy attack on U.S. soil seemed less and less likely.

Consider the following . . .

- This excerpt stresses in-home protection from air raids. Why do you think the government favored this approach rather than the construction of public air raid shelters? Hint: For one possibility, think in terms of the availability of building materials.

- According to the booklet, which civil defense volunteer was supposed to provide guidance during an air raid? What qualities of character would you hope that person possessed?

- Check the list of needed volunteers. Which group might you have joined?

For More Information

Books

Fujita: Flying Samurai. Medford, OR: Webb Research Group, 2000.

Hoopes, Roy. *Americans Remember the Home Front: An Oral Narrative*. New York: Hawthorne Books, 1977.

Jeffries, John W. *Wartime America: The World War II Home Front*. Chicago: I. R. Dee, 1996.

Lingeman, Richard R. *Don't You Know There's a War On? The American Home Front, 1941–1945*. New York: G. P. Putnam's Sons, 1970.

Web sites

American Civil Defense Association. http://www.tacda.org (accessed on July 28, 2004).

Civil Air Patrol. http://www.cap.gov/about/history.html (accessed on July 28, 2004).

U.S. Department of Homeland Security. http://www.dhs.gov (accessed on July 28, 2004).

Thomas A. Scott

Complete text of "Thomas A. Scott"

Reprinted from *The Homefront: America during World War II*. Published in 1984.

> "One of our responsibilities as an air raid warden was to make sure everybody had their lights turned out at night and that people weren't wandering around without any place to go."

Thomas A. Scott, a young American stockbroker, was eager to serve his country in the military during World War II (1939–45). However, after a required physical examination, he received the classification of 4-F. Doctors usually gave the 4-F classification to people who had a medical condition or physical disability that would make it difficult for them to perform military duties. In Scott's case, he had a circulatory blood flow problem in his legs. Anyone with this classification would not be accepted into military service. Thomas Scott's classification did not dampen his patriotic desire to participate in the war effort. Like most Americans, he was determined to take part in the nation's push for victory.

Scott had a very personal reason motivating his volunteer efforts. In 1939, before the United States had officially entered the war, Scott encouraged his younger brother to see the world as a serviceman in the U.S. Army. Unfortunately Scott's brother was in the Philippines when the United States declared war on Japan, and he was taken prisoner by the Japanese.

The United States depended heavily on home front volunteers like Scott. Millions of American civilians, including

Scott, took on civil defense responsibilities. Scott volunteered for four different types of duty. In the first part of the following excerpt he describes his duties as an Office of Civilian Defense (OCD) air raid warden in Philadelphia, Pennsylvania.

In the next part of the excerpt Scott shares his experiences as part of the Volunteer Port Security Force. President Roosevelt established this force in February 1942 to aid the Coast Guard in the protection of U.S. seaports, port warehouses, piers, and other waterfront facilities. The Volunteer Port Security Force worked in close cooperation with the Coast Guard Auxiliary, an organization made up of private boat owners who volunteered to assist the regular Coast Guard in many capacities, including patrolling U.S. coastlines.

Turning his vigilance skyward, Scott volunteered with another OCD organization, the Civil Air Raid Warning Service, also known as the Aircraft Warning Service (AWS). OCD formed AWS in 1941 to protect the U.S. mainland, especially coastal regions, from foreign attacks by air. Ultimately more than one and a half million people volunteered to scan the skies for enemy aircraft.

Air raid wardens were a vital part of home front civilian defense during World War II.
The Library of Congress.

Scott's fourth volunteer activity was serving as a speaker for the War Finance Committee's war bond drives. The U.S. government sold war bonds to the public to help pay for the costs of warfare. Bonds were available in denominations ranging from $25 to $10,000. Selling bonds is actually a way of borrowing money. For example, if a factory worker purchased a $25 war bond, he was essentially lending the money to the government. The government would eventually buy back the bond, paying the factory worker $25 plus interest. The government sponsored seven major bond drives during the war years, and the drives raised a total of $135 billion. Thomas Scott was one of the volunteer speakers who encouraged Americans to purchase war bonds.

Things to remember while reading "Thomas A. Scott" . . .

- Many Americans were convinced that an enemy air or naval strike would eventually hit the U.S. mainland.

- German submarines lurked all along the eastern U.S. coastline during the early 1940s, and Japanese submarines skulked in the waters off America's western coast.

- Rumors abounded that German saboteurs aboard the submarines landed on U.S. coasts under cover of darkness. Therefore a key task of volunteers, such as the Volunteer Port Security Force, was to watch for suspicious activity along the coast including the ports.

"Thomas A. Scott"

*I was classified 4-F because of **a circulatory condition** in my legs. Because I was 4-F I couldn't be a general and I couldn't work down to a private, so I figured what else can I do? Anybody who was rejected for the service was conscious of the fact that he wasn't doing what other guys his age were doing. Going around in civilian clothes wasn't exactly a comfortable feeling. And since I felt I had a duty and a responsibility towards the war effort, I went into civilian defense as an air raid warden.*

Our mission was to protect the homefront. If it hadn't been for air raid wardens in Britain they would have been in a hell of a way. Right? We didn't know whether the Germans would come over here. Their newer planes had the capability to do it. In World War I [1914–18] the United States didn't have to worry about that. All they had to worry about was submarines. In World War II, we had to worry about airplanes coming into Philadelphia.

One of our responsibilities as an air raid warden was to make sure everybody had their lights turned out at night and that people weren't wandering around without any place to go. After dark, to make certain there were no lights burning anywhere, we used to climb onto the roofs to see if there were any skylights illuminated. A lot of people would leave the light on in the bathroom instead of

A circulatory condition: A problem with blood flow.

anywhere else in the house. That was the worst thing you could let happen, because often there was a skylight in the bathroom. One time we ran into a very suspicious incident when we caught three skylights, one right in our post, one up at the western end of Overbrook, and one up in North Philadelphia, which made a direct arrow to the navy yard. Well, we jumped quickly on that and got the civilian-defense people to take a plane and check it out.

Another of our duties was to have one or two wardens on alert at all times to watch for anything that might happen in the neighborhood—like suspicious strangers wandering around. In addition to that, of course, we had other responsibilities in the event of an air raid.

Our post organized the first full-scale **mock air raid** in the area. It covered roughly a two-block-square neighborhood in which we had approximately eleven hundred residents. In April of '42 we had a full-scale demonstration, showing what air raid wardens actually did. We had trucks running around throwing Fourth of July flares to imitate magnesium bombs. Then we had people

Air raid wardens for a Washington, D.C., neighborhood gather before their shift. Each warden controls a specific section of the neighborhood, and it is his or her job to clear the streets at night, prevent panic, and get help quickly when needed.
The Library of Congress.

Mock air raid: A practice session that simulated what might occur during an actual air raid.

Rapid delivery of vital messages, in the event of telephone disruption during an air raid, was one of the jobs for young people in the civilian defense organization. *The Library of Congress.*

pretend that they were hurt and faint. It was up to us to take care of them until a medic came along. Several thousand spectators lined the porches all around the area to watch. People from all over Philadelphia came.

Everybody participated, tailors and grocers and **druggists**, people in all kinds of occupations, because it was a mixed area. There was a job for everybody from ten years old on up. We had air raid wardens and volunteer police and volunteer firemen. We even set up a messenger service for the kids. So everyone felt they were actively participating in the war effort. We had over a hundred persons out of eleven hundred who were actively involved.

During the war I was also involved with the Volunteer Port Security Force, which was organized to man the port of Philadelphia with volunteers to relieve the military of that responsibility. There were over seven thousand volunteers, from all walks of life, lawyers, cabdrivers, stockbrokers, which I was at the time, anyone who had flexible hours. We served eight hours a day, every

Druggist: One who owns or manages a drugstore.

sixth day, around the clock. We would alternate from the A to the B to the C watch. Our job was to board the ships in port and patrol them. We had to buy our own uniforms and report an hour before our shift to headquarters to get our guns and equipment. The force was so successful that we reduced the accident and **pilferage** rate in the port below the peacetime rate, which was amazing. Service was later extended to other ports across the country.

As the war went on and more and more men were called into the service, our ranks began to thin. So I suggested that we set up recruiting headquarters for the Port Security Force in the army induction center at Thirty-second and Lancaster where all the draftees were taken for examination. The result was that anybody who was rejected was automatically sent over to us. We told them, "You're lucky. You don't have to go into active service. You can join the 4-F's and other rejectees." We got a hell of a lot of recruits that way.

I also became involved in the Civil Air Raid Warning Service through a partner in one of the stock exchange firms who learned I was interested in civilian defense of all kinds. He asked me to head up the Civil Air Raid Warning Service for the First Air and Third Service Command, which covered practically the Eastern **seaboard** as far as Ohio. We worked four-hour shifts, one day a week, all around the clock. There was always a Philadelphia policeman, one of our people, and an air force officer on duty at all times. It was our responsibility, anytime a threat appeared, like an unidentified airplane, to send out the air raid warning signals—yellow, blue or red, as the case indicated—all the way out to Ohio, up to New York, and down to North Carolina. As the war progressed, and more people were drained off into defense work or the service, we had to recruit more volunteers here too, and I organized another successful recruiting campaign among the graduating classes of the Philadelphia-area high schools.

A volunteer aircraft spotter scans the skies for unidentified aircraft. Any information is relayed from a secret telephone and radio network to the Aircraft Warning Service center.
The Library of Congress.

Pilferage: Small amounts of goods stolen again and again.

Seaboard: The country along a coastline.

"Thousands Watch Skies for Enemy Planes"

During World War II civilian volunteers on the home front watched the skies for enemy aircraft around large cities and ports and in remote areas as well. Spotters in the Pacific Northwest saw planes more frequently than spotters in other areas did. Here is a firsthand account of the activity at an Oregon watchtower. The author, Frederick Simpich, interviewed the spotters who were on duty and published his account in the October 1942 issue of *National Geographic Magazine*.

On a wooded Oregon hilltop we came to a high tower. Up in its lookout box were three high school girls with telephone and binoculars.

"We're aircraft watchers," they said. "The Army appoints a chief aircraft observer and he names us local spotters. There are 200 in this area; each one serves free, a few hours a week. They say there are half a million in the whole country."

"Isn't it lonely up here?"

"The boys say it is at night, when the cougars howl."

"What do you do when you see a plane?"

"Call the operator, say 'Army flash,' and she connects us right away with the Army's regional Fighter Command filter board. Somebody at the center says 'Army, go ahead, please,' and we report what we see."

Later I sat in such a center, earphones on, and heard reports coming in. One woman's voice said: "A big plane with four motors. Flying 10,000 feet up. Going fast southwest. Anna two."

The last words, "Anna two," were the code words for the location of that woman's lookout station. Local maps are laid out in squares, with each square identified by a girl's name and a number, just as various sections on National Geographic Society maps are designated as F4, G2, etc.

All over the Pacific Northwest, as all over the country, this simple system is at work.

Volunteer watchers are on duty day and night. Their lookout posts may be shacks on a beach, village water towers, roofs of skyscrapers, or a tower out in the hills, such as that used by the three girls.

*I was also one of the top speakers for the War Finance Committee in every one of its drives. During the war we all had a common objective. It gave us the **impetus** to work together and show we were all on the same team. When President Roosevelt was re-elected to his fourth term and they asked me again to speak for the War Finance Drive, I said I'd come but only on one condition, that I work with a union organizer, because "these damn union people, they've put Roosevelt in, let them pay for it." So I got tied up with one of the union leaders, and we went out to the factories to*

Impetus: Driving force, incentive.

Reports from them flow in to filter centers, where other volunteers watch the local map and push small painted blocks about to show the movements of aircraft as reported. Next comes an information center, where all data are coordinated. Here is a big map which shows the location and movement of all Army, Navy, or commercial planes and their changing locations, either in the air or on the ground.

Air Minutemen Ready for Action

Officers from both branches of the armed services are on duty here, telephones at their ears. Movements of every plane are carefully followed by using long sticks to push symbolic blocks about on the table map.

Quickly sifted and sorted, all such data are then sent to yet another big room, the operations center, which shows the distribution of air and ground forces.

Normally, the Army and Navy men on duty know at once, say when "Anna two" reports a four-motored ship going southwest exactly what ship (an alternative term for airplane) it is, when and where it started, and where it's going.

But if it's unidentified, or there's doubt, interceptor planes go up to investigate. At the nearest convenient field they're waiting, engines all warmed up.

But what would happen, you ask, if a fleet of enemy planes should suddenly be reported coming in from the sea?

Plenty would happen. Automatic range finders, listening devices, searchlights if needed, antiaircraft guns, Army Signal Corps, Navy and Army gathers and interceptors, barrage balloon (a network of balloons, steel cables, and nets placed over a town or city to protect against attacking enemy aircraft) crews— every device for repelling an air raid would get set for action.

Also, warnings would be flashed to any city or town that might seem in danger of enemy bombs. There civilian defense groups, also on duty day and night (Seattle alone has enrolled more than 50,000), would watch their signal board. A yellow light means a warning; a blue means "Black out at once; danger threatens." A red light means "A raid is coming; get busy!"

Then firemen, policemen, air-raid wardens, Red Cross—all the machinery for civilian defense gets under way.

sell bonds together. They would introduce him, and they'd all give him a big hand. He'd say, "Now, he's a stockbroker. We don't like each other, but doggone it, he's got a message for you, too." Then he'd introduce me, and then I'd come back and say, "I don't like him either, but doggone it, we're in this together and both sides are fighting: **capital is fighting, labor is fighting, we're all fighting on the same team.** Now let's see how much money we can raise." And it worked out beautifully. The union organizer and I became good friends and we conducted a very successful campaign.

Capital is fighting, labor is fighting, we're all fighting on the same team: Meaning the wealthy who hold money (capital) as well as the working class were working toward the same goal of victory.

Female civilian defense workers, trained to handle trouble calls and dispense help as needed, at a message center in Washington, D.C., April 1943.
The Library of Congress.

During the war I saw that in a crisis you could get everybody to work together. I think that's one of the things that we learned during the Depression, and it was borne out again in World War II. When people are up against it, they have a tendency to be more tolerant and to help each other. When you get into a crisis the humanity comes out in most of us. During the war we had a specific objective. Everybody had certain obligations, and doggone it, they fulfilled them. But the minute the war was over and that objective disappeared, of course, it all fell apart.

Depression: Reference to the Great Depression, a major economic crisis lasting from 1929 to 1941 leading to massive unemployment and widespread hunger.

Borne out: Proven.

What happened next . . .

Scott's brother was a prisoner of war for three and a half years. He eventually returned to the United States. Scott commented, "I sent him over. I had to bring him back. Mission accomplished."

Opportunities to volunteer for civil defense duty helped promote home front support for the war effort. People who were unable to serve in the military found a niche in civil defense and helped contribute to the Allied victory.

Did you know . . .

- One of the air raid warden's chief responsibilities was enforcing blackouts. The enemy could not carry out a successful nighttime sneak attack if he could not see his target.

- The Aircraft Warning Service was one of the first large-scale OCD organizations that accepted volunteers. Aircraft spotters were essential because radar technology in 1941 was still in the experimental stage and did not effectively cover coastal areas.

- As Scott mentions, even teens and preteens volunteered for civil defense duty. The OCD created the Junior Citizens Service Corps for youngsters.

Consider the following . . .

- Scott says that "Going around in civilian clothes wasn't exactly a comfortable feeling." Why do you think he felt that way? Since World War II (1939–45), has there been a time when American men might have had similar feelings?

- According to Scott, Americans seem to work together best during a crisis. He cites the Great Depression (1929–41) and World War II as examples. Think of examples from the twenty-first century that support Scott's theory.

For More Information

Books

Harris, Mark J., Franklin D. Mitchell, and Steven J. Schechter, eds. *The Homefront: America during World War II*. New York: G. P. Putnam's Sons, 1984.

Lingeman, Richard R. *Don't You Know There's a War On? The American Home Front, 1941–1945.* New York: G. P. Putnam's Sons, 1970.

Terkel, Studs. *"The Good War": An Oral History of World War II.* New York: Pantheon Books, 1984.

Periodicals

Simpich, Frederick. "Wartime in the Pacific Northwest." *National Geographic Magazine.* (October 1942) pp. 422–426.

Helena H. Smith and William Sloane

Excerpt from "Are America's Civilians Ready for Attack?"
Reprinted from the *Saturday Evening Post*.
Published June 6, 1942.

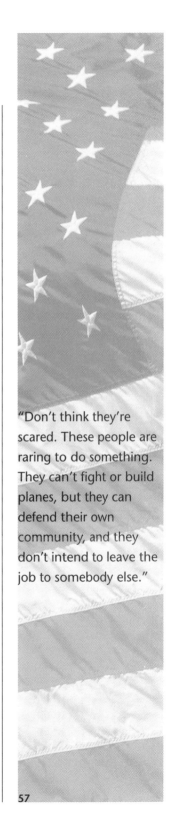

After the Japanese attacked Pearl Harbor on December 7, 1941, the United States officially entered World War II, and U.S. citizens eagerly sought civil defense volunteer opportunities. Americans on the eastern and western coasts felt most vulnerable to enemy attack, but civil defense volunteers came forward nationwide. Midwestern cities practiced for air raids and carried out blackout rehearsals as meticulously as coastal cities did. Air raid survival classes were popular, and hundreds of thousands of U.S. citizens completed Red Cross first aid classes.

Small towns across the country set up their own civil defense councils and took pride in strong community participation. Newspapers and magazines frequently reported on the nation's progress in civil defense preparedness. One such report is excerpted here. It comes from the June 6, 1942, edition of the *Saturday Evening Post,* a popular, nationally distributed magazine. The article is titled "Are America's Civilians Ready for Attack?" It focuses on two very different communities: one in Sheridan County, Wyoming, a ranching region in the West, and the other in Rockland County, New York, a rural area on the outskirts of New York City.

"Don't think they're scared. These people are raring to do something. They can't fight or build planes, but they can defend their own community, and they don't intend to leave the job to somebody else."

Things to remember while reading the excerpt from "Are America's Civilians Ready for Attack?" . . .

- The surprise attack on Pearl Harbor outraged U.S. citizens. Their outrage soon transformed into a patriotic desire to participate in the war effort. People channeled their energies into civil defense preparedness in their communities.

- Women were caught up in the patriotic fervor as much as men were, and they took a central role in civil defense planning such as serving as nursing aides, emergency cooks, or as neighborhood block leaders guiding community preparations.

Excerpt from "Are America's Civilians Ready for Attack?"

Two widely separated communities report on how civilian defense is working today.

SHERIDAN COUNTY, WYOMING

by Helena Huntington Smith

The town of Sheridan, Wyoming, is 1700 miles from the Atlantic seaboard and 900 from the Pacific. Set in the middle of the sparsely settled plains, it is far from the great industrial centers and the great training camps. Its people never see a ship, a military plane, nor even a soldier, unless he is home on leave. Few spots in the United States are farther, geographically, from the center of this country's war effort. None is closer to it in spirit. In the zeal and thoroughness of its preparation, Sheridan could serve as a model for many communities much nearer the front line of probable attack; for here is one American town that has taken to heart the grim lessons of Pearl Harbor and **Singapore.**

A few years ago Sheridan County, stretching from the foothills of the Big Horn Mountains to the sunburned prairies along Powder River, was the real Wild West. Today it is a thriving, irrigated cattle and sheep region, a county of cowboys and "horseback farmers"

Singapore: The author is referring to the invasion of China by Japan in 1937.

where the rich are not very rich and the poor are not poverty-stricken. Its favorite **side line** is raising fine saddle horses; another is **dudes**, some of whom settle here permanently.

But it takes more than a few well-to-do Easterners to account for the fact that recently this Wyoming county led all the other counties in the United States in **per-capita contribution** to **Bundles for Britain.** Coal miners in Monarch, as well as ranchers on Big Goose, Clear Creek, Beaver, Prairie Dog and a dozen other creeks also had a share in that.

Of a total population of 19,000 in Sheridan County, 3000 have enlisted in civilian-defense activities. The little town of Ranchester, with a population of 153, has signed up 100 percent. The 153rd man was sick in bed, so they brought the papers to him there.

The civilian-defense-volunteer office was organized on January sixth, and has operated without benefit of Federal funds—which it feels is only proper, since these funds are being and should be spent in areas of greater danger. The director, an officer of World War I, is W. Paxton Roberts, a ranchman from over the line in Montana who has a winter home in Sheridan. The city has donated an office in the city hall. An air-raid protection system has been set up in accordance with the blueprint issued by the Office of Civilian Defense. It is almost ready to function, its personnel all chosen and most of them well on their way through the prescribed courses of training.

More than 700 people will soon have finished the standard Red Cross first-aid course of twenty-two hours, and there is a waiting list of four or five hundred more. Nine instructors are being kept busy. In addition, the post office, the telephone company and the beet-sugar-refining plant has each had its own course for employees; and every community from Ranchester, under the mountains, to Arvada, beside the quicksands of Powder River, has each given one. Men and women on remote ranches have waked up to their own potential helplessness. . . .

Moreover, foreseeing a shortage of trained nurses sooner or later, 250 women are taking up home nursing in order that they can look after their own families in case of illness, or help in emergency hospitals. About 300 people are taking or have already taken the five-hour course in **gas first aid** given by Sheridan's Dr. O.L. Veach; among those who have completed it are the employees of the electric company, the nine city firemen and the mayor. . . .

Side line: An activity in addition to the main activities of the area.

Dudes: People from the city who move to the country ranching life.

Per-capita contribution: The total dollar amount contributed by a community divided by the number of people in that community.

Bundles for Britain: Boxes of supplies put together by volunteers and sent to Britain to help in their survival in the war against Germany.

Gas first aid: Preparations for possible event of bombs filled with poisonous or toxic gases.

A Red Cross canteen unit provides food and drink during civilian defense exercises. This particular unit is equipped to feed 500 people in the event of a disaster.
The Library of Congress.

Raring: Very eager.

Canteen: A place where food, rest, and companionship are available, usually operated by volunteers.

*Don't think they're scared. The emotion out here is the opposite of fright. These people are **raring** to do something. They can't fight or build planes, but they can defend their own community, and they don't intend to leave the job to somebody else.*

*A large number of women who signed up for civilian defense put down "canteen work" as one of the things they wanted to do. Many did this under the impression that canteen work meant handing out doughnuts and coffee. Actually, under the current hard-boiled interpretation, it calls for a stiff training in how to run a **canteen**. All those who signed up were invited to join a twenty-hour nutrition course given by Miss Katherine Bailey, the county home-demonstration agent, and a ten-hour course in large-scale cookery and institutional management under the cafeteria teacher at the high school.*

"We thought they'd drop out when they discovered how much work it was," said Miss Bailey. "Instead, they kept on coming until we hardly know what to do with them." Seventy women are taking the full course. A few will be picked to run the kitchens in

emergency hospitals; meanwhile, all are learning food facts of benefit to their families.

A Stitch in Time

*As to air raids, it is Sheridan's private opinion that no enemy in his senses would bomb it. There is always the remote chance, however, that a flock of **Jap** raiders, being chased away from some big industrial objective and scuttling for home, might unload their bombs on anything showing lights. **Not being in the confidence of** the Axis High Commands, Sheridan figures that its job is to pre-pare. Accordingly, a post-office employee, Harold Bryce, and his aides have drawn up a detailed plan for the evacuation of Sheridan's entire population up into the mountains in case of con-tinued bombing or invasion. A civil air patrol, **serving as an adjunct to** the office of civilian defense, was organized February third. . . . At the time of organization, the Sheridan group con-sisted of ten pilots and boasted four planes, but enlistments in the regular forces have since reduced this to three pilots and two planes. In addition, there are approximately twenty ground-crew members.*

*Meanwhile, as Sheridan is more likely to have to receive evacuees than be evacuated itself, the civilian-defense office has mapped out what to do in the event that this inland community is ever called upon to receive a large number of women and children from the Pacific coast. With twin requirements of food and hous-ing in mind, the following steps have been taken: Real-estate men have been put on file as the people most familiar with housing facilities. All vacant houses have been listed. Restaurant cooks have been registered, as well as a former chief **steward** in the Navy and a half dozen old Army mess sergeants. The dude ranches can also be called upon. . . .*

But when all is said and done, Sheridan County's biggest con-tribution to the nation's war effort is to go on producing its $1,260,000 output of beef cattle each year; its $690,000 worth of lambs and wool; its oats and alfalfa and wheat; its $379,000 crop of sugar beets. It must produce for its own requirements, too, and not draw on the nation's food stocks.

*As in most Western states, there is a shortage of farm labor here. But the county war board, functioning under the Department of Agriculture, has made a survey of labor requirements; schools are speeding up their schedules, so that children can go home early in June and help. One thing is certain—whatever **makeshifts** and*

Jap: A derogatory term for the Japanese.

Not being in the confidence of: Not expecting to be forewarned by.

Serving as an adjunct to: An assistant to.

Steward: Manager of food and other supplies.

Makeshifts: Quick, temporary changes.

extra hours are required, next fall will see the loaded stock cars roll out as usual.

*The idea that rural sections lag behind urban areas in awareness of world events has been **exploded** in this year of crisis, 1942. By doing all that has been asked of it, and more, Wyoming's Sheridan County has proved that it is wide awake and determined to fight this war to a finish.*

ROCKLAND COUNTY, NEW YORK

by William Sloane

Rockland County, New York, is country, not city, in character. The greater part of its area is composed of small, stony farms. Its towns are not large and seldom well-to-do, its public services not highly developed. . . .

*On the afternoon of December seventh I happened to drop in on a playwright whose house is about a mile below mine on the road. He was not home, but his wife made me somewhat frantically welcome and asked me if I knew the **Japs** were bombing Pearl Harbor.*

*That was a Sunday. By Tuesday night the residents of the area had organized a town meeting at the local schoolhouse. The meeting was thoroughly spontaneous; no one group in the area had more to do with it than the others. Its temper was far from hysterical; the people felt that we should act as quickly and as wisely as possible, and the meeting appointed Mrs. Maxwell Anderson a temporary chairman to survey the situation and **render** a report on what was best to be done.*

*Throughout the week that followed there was much activity in our area. The civilian-defense-volunteer cards, as I remember it, were distributed in that week by a corps of captains, and **laboriously** copied, so that when we filed the originals at the courthouse we still had a useful basic record of every adult in our area. This job was so well done by Betty Heiffel and a dozen others that it has been a clerical asset to us ever since.*

A little later the same sort of job was done with the housing-survey cards. All of us feel that it is vital for civilian defense to know your area and the people in it on a house-to-house and person-to-person basis.

Exploded: Dramatically changed.

Japs: Derogatory term for the Japanese.

Render: Give.

Laboriously: Involving a hard effort.

By December twenty-second we were ready for the second town meeting. Our informal organization had drawn up **enabling resolutions**, a suggested permanent committee, and a concrete group of proposals for action. In doing so, I think we succeeded in preserving the momentum of the civilian-defense effort.

Our **tentative** committee was at pains to make its proposed committee membership truly representative of all districts and groups within our area, knowing that success would depend upon mobilizing the whole population. This has worked so well that today we have nearly 30 per cent of the entire adult winter population enrolled in the protective services. . . .

Our first job was to find a site for the **disaster depot.** We also began to organize ourselves into various subcommittees which have gradually settled into the pattern of the protective services authorized by the Office of Civilian Defense. . . .

At this point the story becomes complicated. My own part of it consisted of general organizational work and the frequent issuing of a publication called The Bulletin. This sheet proved of the utmost value. It gave authoritative and sensible information to the local householders about such topics as incendiary bombs, air-raid precautions, **salvage of waste materials**, blackouts and community activities. It told the residents who was who in civilian defense, and how to donate services and goods to the cause. It told why the volunteer cards were being distributed and why the housing survey was being made. It tried to be long on facts and short on **preachment.** It gave them a feeling of knowing what went on each week. This is of vital importance to civilian defense in any area. Unless people know what is being done, and why, they will begin to speculate. Rumors will spread and mistrust will spring up on every hand.

We found the site for our depot in the abandoned chicken house on a large estate. It was a chicken house in the Hollywood tradition, with three main rooms before you got to where the chickens were supposed to be. It had electric light, cold running water, plastered walls and a concrete floor. All kinds of people contributed to refurbishing that building. One room we made into an office, stocked with borrowed typewriters, old desks and a heavy golden-oak file case that had been retired years before. We built in a desk shelf along one wall, installed a stove, two telephones, a control board, cleaned and painted and put up blackout curtains. This room is now a local control and message center in the approved OCD manner; it is the brain of our defense organization.

Enabling resolutions: Authorization to take certain actions.

Tentative: Not yet fully developed.

Disaster depot: Slang reference to a central location to organize activities and store supplies needed for civil defense.

Salvage of waste materials: Collecting and recycling materials needed for the war effort, such as metals and rubber.

Preachment: Preaching; in other words, the newsletter tried to be helpful, not pushy.

Wartime Plant Protection

While individual households and communities prepared to defend the home front, U.S. businesses and industrial plants also were expected to develop civil defense plans. In its January 3, 1942, issue *Business Week* magazine published a brief article titled "Wartime Plant Protection: An Engineering Problem," which offered the following advice for plant operators:

> *Don't write, wire, or phone the Washington Office of Civilian Defense for advice on blackouts or related problems. If you are an important Army or Navy supplier and your plant is considered vulnerable to air attack, you have already received your instructions. If not, get in touch with your city or county Defense Committee.*
>
> ***Working by States**—If your local authorities can't give you the answers, go to your State Defense Council. OCD has already* supplied the states with more information than they can use for many months to come, and the state councils have organized more than 4,000 local committees.
>
> *If you wish to read up on the fine points of air-raid protection, send 50¢ to the Superintendent of Documents, Washington, with a request for three official booklets: "Blackouts" (25¢); "Civilian Defense—Protection Construction, Structures Series, Bulletin No. 1" (25¢); "Protection of Industrial Plants and Public Buildings" (gratis).*
>
> ***Camouflage**—A booklet on protective industrial camouflage, promised since early fall, may be ready when you write, but you will be wise to attempt no camouflage without full military consent and cooperation.*
>
> *Don't permit yourself to be rushed into half-baked air-raid precautions. Protection for your establishment is definitely an engineering problem (that is, a physical change*

The Lord Helps Those—

Next to that we established a Red Cross room, which contains canvas cots, blankets, emergency medical supplies, crutches, basins, surgical instruments, an examination and dressing table, a sterilizer, and much other stuff that we bought from . . . a country doctor. It has its own outer door, to which we have built a ramp for stretcher cases. It is heated.

*Our third room is as large as the other two combined. It is the general meeting room. We have stocked it with food and dishes and a cookstove. It already had a sink. It is our future **canteen** for refugees or people in our own area who are rendered homeless.*

Canteen: A place where food, recreation, and companionship are available.

of some sort to the structure will be required). Some firms in coastal cities are already finding it more expensive to remove the wrong kind of blackout paint than to put it on.

Pick the Right Man—You will do well to designate a level-headed employee as defense boss or coordinator, preferably one with intimate acquaintance with your plant and personnel. Give him full authority to cooperate with civil and military authorities. If yours is a large establishment, follow the OCD organization plan (set forth in the free booklet) and give him four competent assistants to organize and supervise your private fire, police, health, and maintenance services.

The first assignment for your new defense boss should be to study (1) the chances of your being bombed at all, (2) the kinds of bombs that might be used against you. If the chances are one in a thousand that you will ever be visited by a 1,000-lb demolition bomb (largest yet carried by any plane operating from an aircraft carrier), it would be a misuse of time, money, and material to prepare against it. On the other hand, if there is a reasonable probability that you may have to contend with 2-lb magnesium-thermic incendiary bombs, prepare accordingly. The cost of special fire protection equipment—stirrup pumps, dry sand, smothering powder, "fog spray" nozzles—would be nominal (very small, insignificant).

Watch the Details—Next assignment for the defense boss will be to plan, set up, and maintain every protective measure for personnel and plant that is justified by the preliminary analysis. Above all, insist that he keep watching every detail. British experience indicates that the want of a spare ladder, or pail of sand, or adequate ventilation in an air-raid shelter, can lead to more loss of life and property than the inadequate sandbagging of a store or factory façade (the front of a building).

Everything in this room was donated to us. All our training courses and first-aid classes are held here. The furniture is old, shabby, sometimes rickety. But we have tested it, and it works, and when the people of our area come into this room they see their own donations in use, and they know that civilian defense in North Clarkstown means their own defense.

Another major activity has been our training program. You may or may not be familiar with the training requirements of the Office of Civilian Defense, but they involve an average of three courses for each volunteer in each service. No professional instructors were available to us for a long time. But we have finished **Gas-Defense A** at last, are well along in First Aid, have our **Fire-Defense** course arranged for next week, and other courses under way.

Gas-Defense A and **Fire-Defense:** Examples of training in protection against toxic chemical and incendiary bombs.

We think, now, that if anything happens in our area, we know enough to be able to help ourselves and our fellow citizens.

What happened next . . .

Sheridan and Rockland maintained their civil defense readiness throughout the war years, but they were never called upon to initiate emergency actions. In mid-1945 they and the rest of the nation celebrated the war's end.

Did you know ...

- Sheridan's population was made up of real cowboys as well as "dudes," people who had moved there from urban areas to take up ranching life. Rockland's residents were small farmers, artisans, and transplants from New York City's professional groups.

- Sheridan County and Rockland County operated their civil defense programs without federal tax money. They were proud to handle the finances themselves so that the tax money could go directly to the war effort.

Consider the following . . .

- Compare and contrast the organizational approaches of the two communities.

- What activities did each community consider most important for civil defense preparedness?

- Check the rate of participation in each community. If the United States faced a crisis similar to World War II during the twenty-first century, do you think American communities would achieve such high levels of participation in civil defense? Give supporting reasons for your answer.

For More Information

Books

Lingeman, Richard R. *Don't You Know There's a War On? The American Home Front, 1941–1945.* New York: G. P. Putnam's Sons, 1970.

O'Brien, Kenneth P., and Lynn H. Parsons, eds. *The Home-Front War: World War II and American Society.* Westport, CT: Greenwood Press, 1995.

Winkler, Allan M. *Home Front U.S.A.: America during World War II.* Arlington Heights, IL: H. Davidson, 1986.

Periodicals

Smith, Helena H., and William Sloane. "Are America's Civilians Ready for Attack?" *Saturday Evening Post* (June 6, 1942): pp. 19, 38, 39, 42.

"Wartime Plant Protection: An Engineering Problem," *Business Week* (January 3, 1942): p. 16.

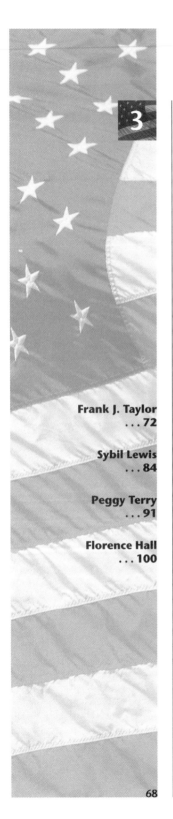

Working Women
on the Home Front

At the beginning of World War II (1939–45) approximately 50 million women over the age of fourteen lived in the United States. Ninety percent were white, 9 percent were black, and the other 1 percent included American Indians, Japanese Americans, Hispanic Americans, and other ethnic minority groups. Between 12 million and 14 million of these adult women were part of the U.S. labor force; they made up roughly 25 percent of the nation's total workforce. Most white working women were relatively young: They generally had just graduated from high school and would work only a year or two as retail salespeople, clerks, or typists until they married. College-educated women worked as teachers, secretaries, nurses, and librarians. Working black women of all ages took jobs in domestic services—the only jobs available to them at that time—serving as maids, cooks, and laundry workers. When the United States officially entered World War II in December 1941, this employment picture would drastically change.

When the United States entered the war, millions of American men left the labor force to join the armed services.

The more **WOMEN** at work the sooner we **WIN!**

WOMEN ARE NEEDED ALSO AS:

FARM WORKERS	WAITRESSES	TIMEKEEPERS	LAUNDRESSES
TYPISTS	BUS DRIVERS	ELEVATOR OPERATORS	TEACHERS
SALESPEOPLE	TAXI DRIVERS	MESSENGERS	CONDUCTORS

—and in hundreds of other war jobs!

SEE YOUR LOCAL U.S. EMPLOYMENT SERVICE

Proclaiming "The More Women at Work, the Sooner We Win!" this 1942 poster encourages women to enter the war industry.
The Library of Congress.

At the same time, U.S. industries were mobilizing to produce massive quantities of war materials, so they needed to replace these workers quickly. Women were the single largest untapped labor resource in the country, and they began to fill almost every type of job left vacant by men departing for the military. Every week thousands of working women—clerks, maids, and even a large number of teachers—shifted into higher-paying war industry jobs. Many housewives entered paid employment for the first time. Over the next few years approximately five million women joined the U.S. labor force. By 1944, when U.S. industries were in full wartime production, women made up 36 percent of the total U.S. workforce. Women became proficient in jobs that had previously been held exclusively by men. They became welders, riveters, mechanics, and electricians. They drove trucks and buses and operated heavy machines. They also took jobs in the rapidly expanding departments of the U.S. government. These so-called government girls were not only secretaries, clerks, and telephone operators; some assembled artillery shells, ground lenses for gun sights and bombsights, manufactured gas masks, or repaired parachutes. Much less publicized, but doing equally important work, many women became farm laborers to help meet the nation's wartime agricultural goals.

The first excerpt, "Meet the Girls Who Keep 'Em Flying," authored by **Frank J. Taylor**, was originally published in the *Saturday Evening Post* on May 30, 1942. It tells about several working women—or "Rosies," as they were known—in Southern California aircraft plants. "Rosie the Riveter" was the symbolic image of the female war industry worker. Clad in overalls and showing off strong muscles, Rosie appeared on posters and magazines nationwide, inspiring millions of women to take jobs in the war industry.

The second excerpt, **"Sybil Lewis,"** is an account of a black woman who left Oklahoma for Los Angeles to find better-paying work. "Sybil Lewis" was first published in *The Homefront: America during World War II* (1984). The third excerpt, **"Peggy Terry,"** comes from Studs Terkel's *"The Good War": An Oral History of World War II* (1984). Terry tells of leaving the rural backwoods for war manufacturing jobs. In their reminiscences, both Sybil Lewis and Peggy Terry describe how their new employment opportunities broadened their vision of the world.

The fourth excerpt, "They're Getting In the Crops," published in the July 1943 issue of *Independent Woman*, was written by **Florence Hall**, the head of the Women's Land

Army, an organization that recruited women from the cities to help harvest crops on farms, where workers and perhaps even the farmer himself had left for war or work in the war industries. Although generally overlooked in World War II history, women who joined the farm labor force played a crucial role in the home front war effort.

Frank J. Taylor

Excerpt from "Meet the Girls Who Keep 'Em Flying"
**Reprinted from the *Saturday Evening Post*.
Published on May 30, 1942.**

"Mechanics in fancy work pants will be doing up to 60% of this country's airplane building by the end of the war."

"The foreman asked if I could run a lathe, and I said, 'I can, if you'll show me how.' He did, and I've been at it ever since." These words were spoken by Mrs. Francis DeWitt and recorded in "Meet the Girls Who Keep 'Em Flying," an article printed in the May 30, 1942, issue of the *Saturday Evening Post*. Mrs. DeWitt, a San Diego wife and mother, had tired of "keeping house and playing bridge," so she joined millions of other women on the home front who went to work in the war industries. She became one of Consolidated Aircraft's best lathe operators. A lathe is a machine used for shaping parts.

In "Meet the Girls," women such as Mrs. Clover Hoffman, "Jerry" Patterson, and Mrs. Mary Rozar are introduced. Mrs. Hoffman, the wife of a machinist's mate stationed on a destroyer at Pearl Harbor and the mother of three-and-a-half-year-old twins, helped build bombers at Consolidated Aircraft Company. "Jerry" Patterson, whose husband was called into the service in 1941, went to Southern California and took a job putting together electrical-control assemblies in an aircraft plant. Every night she wrote to her husband, who

Donating Typewriters to the War Effort

Many women found work as secretaries during the war. At that time, a secretary's most valued tool was her typewriter. When the U.S. government called for a typewriter drive to round up a large number of typewriters for government work, secretaries and the businesses they worked for proudly donated to the cause. Margaret Fishback wrote the following poem to support the typewriter drive. Titled "Take a Letter from Uncle Sam," the poem was published in the March 1943 issue of *Independent Woman*.

Dear Secretaries of the Nation:

Your middle name's Cooperation . . .

You've purchased bonds, you've purchased stamps,

You've sent your dream men off to camps,

And now the sacrifice supreme

Will also find you on the beam.

You'll help to win this ghastly war

By yielding one of every four

Typewriters to your Uncle Sammy.

Our soldiers, sailors, and marines

Take orders typed upon machines

To speed the war to its conclusion.

That's why I seek your contribution.

And though your eyes with tears grow wet

When you give up your faithful pet,

I know you'll still contrive to type

And call your loss a service stripe.

was stationed in the Philippines on the Bataan Peninsula, telling him what she had done that day at work. Mrs. Rozar, a forty-four-year-old mother of a young serviceman killed in the Pearl Harbor attack, smoothed rough edges of various parts that were used to build B-17s, giant bombers designed by Boeing Aircraft.

These women wanted to contribute directly to the war effort. "Every time I finish a piece for a bomber," Mrs. Rozar says, "I feel that we're that much closer to winning the war." However, male supervisors and coworkers were originally skeptical about women's ability to perform industrial jobs. Nevertheless, women quickly won approval and acceptance on the job because they excelled in a variety of manufacturing tasks, especially jobs that required a high degree of dexterity and fine motor skills. Women were speedy and patient and could focus on certain assembly line tasks much longer than men could.

Things to remember while reading the excerpt from "Meet the Girls Who Keep 'Em Flying" . . .

- At the beginning of World War II most Americans believed that a woman's proper role was to stay at home and care for her husband and children.

- Historically, in the United States, people had generally assumed that women had no ability to do mechanical or technical jobs.

- As twelve million American men left the labor force for the military, women became a vital resource for U.S. industry, stepping in to fill vacant positions and keep war mobilization on track.

Excerpt from "Meet the Girls Who Keep 'Em Flying"

Mechanics in fancy work pants will be doing up to 60% of this country's airplane building by the end of the war.

*Fuming over the sneak bombing of Pearl Harbor, Mrs. Clover Hoffman, diminutive and spirited mother of Cliff and Charlotte, twins aged three and one half, reached a decision important in the task of defeating the **Japs** and the Nazis. Resigning her job as waitress in a San Diego restaurant, and parking the twins with her mother, Mrs. Hoffman presented herself at the employment office of the Consolidated Aircraft Corporation.*

"I want to work on a bomber," she told Mrs. Mamie Kipple, assistant employment director in charge of hiring the women who work in the company's two sprawling plants.

"Why do you want to work on a bomber?" asked Mrs. Kipple.

Japs: Derogatory term used for the Japanese.

Jumperalls: Loose fitting, one-piece work outfits.

Jigs: Tools that hold two pieces of work together or hold a piece steady that is being worked on.

Lathes: A machine that rotates a piece that is being worked on.

"That's something I can do to help bring Harry back."

"Who is Harry?"

"My husband. He's machinist's mate on a destroyer at Pearl Harbor."

"Have you ever worked at a factory?"

"No, but I can learn, if you'll give me a chance."

Like other aircraft manufacturers of Southern California, where half the country's bombers and fighters first take wing, the Consolidated management, which began employing women for factory work last September, had a soft spot for Pearl Harbor wives and widows. The following day, Mrs. Hoffman, in trim blue **jumperalls**, was busily sorting and testing small parts in the blister department. A blister is a transparent plastic turret from which gunners aboard the huge flying boats and heavy-bombardment bombers fight off enemy attackers.

A female factory worker spends her days at an aircraft factory doing her part to keep the war industry moving forward. *The Library of Congress.*

Within a month, with nimble fingers and a will to learn, Mrs. Hoffman was rated as a veteran factory hand among the thousands of "Keep-'Em Flying girls" helping to build planes in West Coast aircraft plants, strictly a man's world until eight months ago. When they first appeared on the assembly benches, the **jigs** and the **lathes**, the **women were "the lipsticks" to the men**. Workers and bosses alike said, as did hard-boiled Bert Bowler, plant manager for Consolidated, "The factory's no place for women."

Now Bowler says, "They're better than men for jobs calling for finger work. They will stick on a **tedious** assembly line long after the men quit. Women can do from twenty-two to twenty-five percent of the work in this plant as efficiently as men."

At the Inglewood plant of North American Aviation, Inc., with 1100 women on the pay roll, M.E. Beaman, industrial-relations director, goes further than that. "Women can do approximately fifty percent of the work required to construct a modern airplane," he estimated. Douglas Aircraft, which started late in

Women were "the lipsticks" to the men: A demeaning perspective; the men felt that women were only "window dressing," with no ability to meaningfully contribute to industry.

Tedious: Long and dull.

the employment of women in the factory, expects to have 40,000 on the pay rolls of its four plants by the end of 1942. After a study of British plants, Douglas engineers think women may have to do 60 percent of the building of planes before the aircraft plants reach all-out production. Lockheed and Vega, with 2000 women filtered into groups working on everything from radio wiring to tubing-detail assemblies—plumbing, in plain English—are hiring and training housewives and girls fresh out of school at the rate of 200 a week. Vultee, which pioneered the use of women in aircraft building one year ago, rates them as indispensable. At Seattle, the Boeing Aircraft Company launched courses for women factory hands on the first of the year. In Midwestern cities all the major Pacific Coast plane builders except Lockheed and Vega are rushing supplementary plants in which approximately 50 per cent of the work will be handled by women. By the end of the year, it is estimated that 200,000 housewives will have left their homes for the aircraft factories. . . .

When the President called for 60,000 planes this year, 125,000 more in 1943, the aircraft builders began frantically breaking up the building of one big bomber into 1000 little jobs, each simple enough for workers who had never before seen the inside of a factory. The most readily available labor was that of women, knocking at the factory doors for a chance to do something **tangible** to help win the war. . . .

I talked with dozens of them above the din of the riveting and stamping machines. It was an eye opener, not only in wartime industrial readjustment but in devotion to purpose. In every plant, foremen who once dreaded the influx of "the lipsticks" told with enthusiasm how mixing women workers in the teams had stepped up both morale and the output of planes.

Kitchen Technique

"The main problem with women," one foreman told me, "is to get them to take it easy for a while and not rush and worry about the work. So I tell 'em, just imagine you're in a kitchen baking a cake instead of in a factory building a bomber."

"Women workers handle the repetitive jobs without losing interest or a letdown in efficiency," he continued. "I guess it's because this is win-the-war work for them, while men are eager to get ahead personally. We team the women with the men because they learn faster from men than from women."

Tangible: Something that is real, such as can be touched or seen.

American Home Front in World War II: Primary Sources

In the Vega sheet-metal department, I watched Mrs. Mary Rozar, barely five feet tall, dressed in slacks and blouse, protected by a leather apron, absorbed in smoothing the edges of odd-shaped parts for **Flying Fortresses.** Mrs. Rozar appeared at the employment office when the Vega management announced it would give preference to wives and widows of men in service at Pearl Harbor and in the Philippines.

"I'm not a Pearl Harbor widow," she told Miss Carmichael, apologetically, "but I'm a Pearl Harbor mother. My Johnny boy lost his life on **the Arizona.** I have another son, Earl, somewhere in Alaska with the United States Army. I want to help build planes."

"Have you worked in a factory?"

"No, but I know how to work. I'm a widow and I've worked in a laundry to put my boys through school."

At the Vega and Lockheed plants, women applicants as well as men must pass stiff temperament, intelligence, manipulative and physical tests. At forty-four, Mrs. Rozar passed these with ease.

Women and men work side by side making parts for bomber planes.
Courtesy of the FDR Library.

Flying Fortresses: B-17 bombers.

The Arizona: Refers to the U.S.S. *Arizona*, one of the battleships destroyed in the Pearl Harbor bombing.

The **manipulative test** revealed that the spunky little Pearl Harbor mother had an unusual **aptitude** for tools. She was a natural for the sheet-metal department.

"Every time I finish a piece for a bomber," Mrs. Rozar told me earnestly, "I feel that we're that much closer to winning the war."

Upstairs, where hundreds of girls **deftly** connect and mark wires for the electrical-control assemblies, I noticed an attractive young woman with much poise who came in with the second shift and hit her stride in nothing flat. The foreman introduced her— "Jerry" Patterson.

"You don't look like a factory worker, " I said.

"Maybe I don't, and maybe I'm not, but I can put these assemblies together," she replied.

Her husband, Capt. Russell Patterson, was on Bataan Peninsula under General Wainwright, she said. The young Pattersons were living in Chicago, where he was an attorney when called to the service early in 1941.

"I tried working in a dentist's office first," she said. "That gave me no satisfaction, so I came out here, took the tests, and they put me to work on these assemblies. I haven't heard from Russell, and I can't get word to him, but every night I write half a page of a letter to tell him what I did that day to help finish a plane. I'm saving the letters for the day when **General MacArthur** goes back to the Philippines."

Downstairs on the bomber assembly line where the engines are lowered to be fastened to the wings, I encountered "Hank," who is the plant's star woman mechanic. Hank's full name is Henrietta Sumner Plume. Before the war, she ran a flying school, held the unofficial women's upside-down flight record and was runner-up for the women's endurance flying record. When the Army closed private flying schools on the Pacific Coast, Hank applied for employment as a **ferry pilot**, but accepted a job working on bomber assemblies while she studied engine installation, in which course she rated third in a class of twenty-five men.

"What's your reason for being here?" I asked. . . .

"I want to fly," replied Hank. "If I can't be a ferry pilot, I'll be a flight inspector. That's checking planes on their test flights. I just got word that I passed my examination."

Manipulative test: Evaluation of a person's skill with their hands.

Aptitude: Ability to learn.

Deftly: Skillfully.

General MacArthur: General Douglas MacArthur, the military commander in charge of military operations on the Pacific front.

Ferry pilot: A pilot who delivers airplanes by flying them to an appointed destination.

American Home Front in World War II: Primary Sources

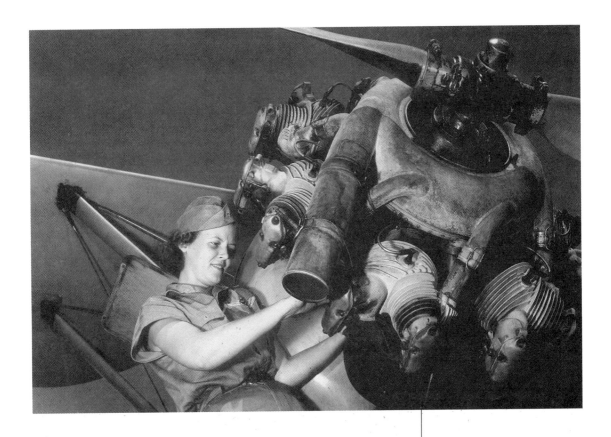

*In aircraft factories, the work is done by groups, each under a lead man who is a combination instructor and **straw boss**. Personnel managers assumed, when women came into the plants, that they would work best under male lead men. But in several plants women have worked up to lead positions. The first on record was Toni Baumeister, twenty-two, who joined the Douglas pay roll several years ago as file clerk, then became a **stenographer**. "The factory was a regular magnet for Toni," her former boss recalled. She applied for a shop job where she could work with her hands long before the Douglas management considered employing women in the factory, and by sheer persistence talked the personnel manager into transferring her two years ago. For a time she rattled around in the big plant built for men only, an orphan in jumperalls, working in the toolroom while she studied blueprint reading at night school. Next she became a **riveter**. By last fall, when women poured into the plant in hundreds, Toni Baumeister's experience qualified her for Douglas' first female lead man, in charge of instructing twenty women in the use of rivet*

A uniformed female mechanic rebuilds an airplane engine.
Courtesy of the FDR Library.

Straw boss: One who has supervisory authority under guidance of another supervisor.

Stenographer: One who takes notes in shorthand for later typing.

Riveter: One who fastens airplane or ship parts with flattened metal bolts.

guns. *This spring she moved up the ladder to a better job—**liaison** for Chief Inspector Leo Provost.*

"Toni's demonstrated that a lead woman is better than a man over women," said her former superior regretfully. "Women can't put anything over a woman, but they can over a lead man."

"What do they try to put over?" I asked.

*"Oh, little things. Time out for a smoke, which is against the rules. They'll do it, where men won't. Or powdering their noses on company time just before quitting. A woman lead man puts a stop to that in a hurry. But it's funny about women—they are more conscientious than men on the **testing machines**," Provost added. "Nothing gets by them unless it is right. . . ."*

There are astonishingly few aircraft jobs that women fresh out of the kitchen can't master. Newcomers start on simple jobs—sorting small parts or testing them with machines while they learn welding, riveting, trimming sheetmetal parts on band saws, bending tubing, spray painting, connecting electrical and pipe assemblies, running punch and drill presses. Consolidated has eighty women inspectors, all of them girls with two years of college, and 300 with trade-school training.

Mrs. Francis DeWitt, thirty-one, wife of a candy salesman and mother of a thirteen-year-old son, is one of Consolidated's best lathe operators.

*"I never did anything more mechanical than replace a blown-out fuse," she said. "But after the war broke out, I wasn't satisfied with keeping house and playing bridge, so I enrolled in the craft school run by the city in Balboa Park. In three weeks, the school recommended me for a job down here. The foreman asked if I could run a lathe, and I said, 'I can, if you'll show me how.' He did, and I've been at it ever since. **I've put every pay check into War Savings Bonds, so I'm hitting the Japs two ways** every week I work here. . . ."*

Consolidated turned to women workers last fall when surveys revealed that San Diego and environs had no more places to sleep for the hundreds of newly arrived men workers. In two years, as the plant's pay roll had jumped from 2000 to 20,000, incoming workers and their families, largely from the Midwest, spewed over the surrounding area, occupying every available house, room, tent, trailer and barn. Federal housing projects threw prefabricated homes together by the thousands; still there were not enough places to sleep. When the U.S. Defense Plant Corporation

---

Liaison: One who aids communications between individuals or organizations.

Testing machines: Equipment used to test the electrical equipment installed in the aircraft before they are delivered for use.

I've put every pay check into War Savings Bonds . . . : She is contributing to the war in two ways: first by producing war materials and, second, by contributing part of her income to help finance the war by buying war bonds.

American Home Front in World War II: Primary Sources

A female lathe operator machining parts for transport planes at the Consolidated Aircraft Corporation plant, 1942.
The Library of Congress.

completed the tremendous new parts plant, doubling the company's pay roll again, the executives reluctantly concluded that there was but one answer—to start hiring local women whose housing problems were already solved.

Of the first batch of 500 women signed up by Mrs. Kipple, 90 percent were wives of workers, or of Army and Navy men stationed at San Diego. The city opened its trade school to women enrollees, and the company hired them as rapidly as they learned the names of the tools and how to handle them. By April first of this year, the two Consolidated plants had 3200 women working in twenty-six factory departments. As in other aircraft plants, the bottom age limit was eighteen, and there was no top. Women in their fifties found jobs on the sub-assembly lines putting together the **electrical harnesses** that control the big bombers and flying boats.

Electrical harnesses: Numerous electrical wires bundled together as they run through the aircraft from the controls to the various parts of the plane.

What happened next . . .

In November 1941 a woman was rarely seen in a factory room. Yet by early 1942 a monumental attitude change had occurred: Employers realized that they would have to employ women to fill positions left vacant by male workers who had joined the military. They began to hire women by the thousands and discovered that these new workers were dependable, skillful, and highly efficient. By late 1943, 35 percent of industry workers were women. At Douglas Aircraft and Boeing Aircraft plants at least 45 percent of workers were women. By 1944 more than two and a half million women were employed in war industries.

Did you know . . .

• At the start of World War II women who were already employed and women in high school and college were the first war industry recruits. When this resource was used up, the federal government mounted a massive advertising campaign to encourage married women to enter the workforce.

• High-paying war industry jobs lured thousands of female teachers away from the classroom, leaving ten to fifteen thousand teaching vacancies.

• Factories seeking women workers advertised their jobs in glamorous terms and promoted women's factory attire—including slacks—as a fashionable new look. (Before World War II, most American women did not wear slacks.)

Consider the following . . .

• In this excerpt, the author reports that male factory workers used to refer to female coworkers as "lipsticks" and grumble that a factory was "no place for women." According to the author, in what way and why did male attitudes change?

• Examine how the author of the excerpt characterizes women workers. What does it have to say about the male attitudes or general stereotypes of the war years? How would the piece be written in the twenty-first century?

- How did factories change manufacturing procedures so that inexperienced workers could build complicated aircraft?

- Predict what happened to women workers when the war ended and soldiers returned to civilian life on the home front.

For More Information

Books

Coleman, Penny. *Rosie the Riveter: Women Workers on the Home Front in World War II*. New York: Crown, 1995.

Cott, Nancy F., ed. *No Small Courage: A History of Women in the United States*. New York: Oxford University Press, 2000.

Sinott, Susan. *Doing Our Part: American Women on the Home Front during World War II*. New York: Franklin Watts, 1995.

Zeinert, Karen. *Those Incredible Women of World War II*. Brookfield, CT: Millbrook Press, 1994.

Periodicals

Taylor, Frank J. "Meet the Girls Who Keep 'Em Flying." *Saturday Evening Post* (May 30, 1942): pp. 30, 31, 57, 58.

Web sites

Rosie the Riveter and Other Women World War II Heroes. http://www.u.arizona.edu/~kari/rosie.htm (accessed on July 28, 2004).

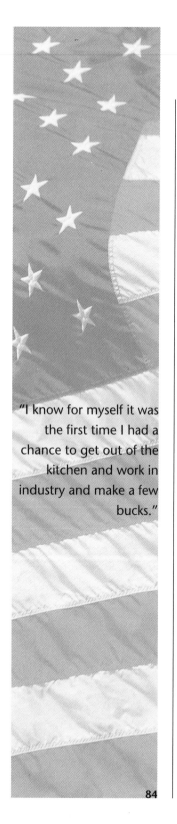

Sybil Lewis

Complete text of the essay "Sybil Lewis"

Reprinted from *The Homefront: America during World War II*. Published in 1984.

In 1941 between 40 and 50 percent of all black American women worked outside their home. They mainly worked as poorly paid maids and cooks, the only jobs widely available to them. As war industry jobs became available, thousands of black women migrated to industrial urban areas on both coasts and in the Great Lakes region, searching for better-paying work. Many went from earning $2 to $3 a week to $40 and more a week. Sybil Lewis, a black woman from a small town in Oklahoma, moved to Los Angeles and found a job as a riveter at Lockheed Aircraft. For the first time in her life she had money in her pocket and expectations of a better life. She later went to work at Douglas Aircraft, and eventually she became a welder in a shipyard. For Sybil Lewis and many other black women, the wartime economy and job market opened up opportunities and experiences that had previously been closed to them.

Things to remember while reading "Sybil Lewis" . . .

- In the South, where 75 percent of black Americans lived, racial discrimination was severe, and segregation (the separation of whites and blacks) was the norm in almost every part of daily life.

- When war industry jobs first became plentiful, most employers still avoided hiring blacks. However, in June 1941 President Franklin Roosevelt (1882–1945; served 1933–45) issued Executive Order 8802, which banned racial discrimination in the war industries. Companies that violated this order risked losing profitable government defense contracts.

"Sybil Lewis"

When I first arrived in Los Angeles, I began to look for a job. I decided I didn't want to do maid work anymore, so I got a job as a waitress in a small black restaurant. I was making pretty good money, more than I had in Sapulpa, but I didn't like the job that much; I didn't have the knack for getting good tips. Then I saw an ad in the newspaper offering to train women for defense work. I went to Lockheed Aircraft and applied. They said they'd call me, but I never got a response, so I went back and applied again. You had to be pretty persistent. Finally they accepted me. They gave me a short training program and taught me how to rivet. Then they put me to work in the plant riveting small airplane parts, mainly gasoline tanks.

The women worked in pairs. I was the riveter, and this big strong white girl from a cotton farm in Arkansas worked as the bucker. The riveter used a gun to shoot rivets through the metal and fasten it together. The bucker used a bucking bar on the other side of the metal to smooth out the rivets. Bucking was harder than shooting rivets; it required more muscle. Riveting required more skill.

I worked for a while as a riveter with this white girl, when the boss came around one day and said, "We've decided to make some changes." At this point he assigned her to do the riveting and me to do the bucking. I wanted to know why. He said, "Well, we just interchange once in a while." But I was never given the riveting job back. That was the first encounter I had with **segregation** *in California, and it didn't sit too well with me.*

Segregation: Meaning here refers to discrimination based on skin color.

A black woman and a white woman work together on an assembly line at the Douglas Aircraft Company in Long Beach, California.
© Corbis. Reproduced by permission.

It brought back some of my experiences in Sapulpa—you're a Negro, so you do the hard work. I wasn't failing as a riveter— in fact, the other girl learned to rivet from me—but I felt they gave me the job of bucker because I was black.

So I applied to Douglas Aircraft in Santa Monica and was hired as a riveter there. On that job I did not encounter the same prejudice. As a matter of fact, the foreman was more **congenial.** But Maywood, where Lockheed was located, was a very segregated city. Going into that city, you were really going into forbidden territory. Santa Monica was not as segregated a community.

I worked in aircraft for a few years, then in '43 I saw an ad in the paper for women trainees to learn arc welding. The salary sounded good, from a dollar to a dollar-twenty-five an hour. I wanted to learn that skill and I wanted to make more money, so I answered the ad and they sent me to a short course at welding school. After I passed the trainee course, they employed me at the shipyards. That was a little different than working in aircraft, because in the shipyard you found mostly men. There I ran into another kind of discrimination: because I was a woman I was paid less than a man for doing the same job.

I was an arc welder, I'd passed both the army and navy tests, and I knew I could do the job, but I found from talking with some of the men that they made more money. You'd ask about this, but they'd say, "Well, you don't have the experience," or "The men have to lift some heavy pieces of steel and you don't have to," but I knew that I had to help lift steel, too.

They started everyone off at a dollar-twenty an hour. There were higher-paying jobs, though, like **chippers** and crane operators, that were for men only. Once, the foreman told me I had to go on the skids—the long docks alongside the hull. I said, "That sounds pretty dangerous. Will I make more than one-twenty an

Congenial: Friendly or agreeable.

Chipper: A worker who cuts with a sharp-edged tool.

hour?" And he said, "No, one-twenty is the top pay you'll get."
But the men got more.

It was interesting that although they didn't pay women as much as men, the men treated you differently if you wore slacks. I noticed, for example, that when you'd get on the bus or the streetcar, you stood all the way, more than the lady who would get on with a dress. I never could understand why men wouldn't give women in slacks a seat. And at the shipyards the language wasn't the best. Nobody respected you enough to clean up the way they spoke. It didn't seem to bother the men that you were a woman. During the war years men began to say, "You have a man's job and you're getting paid almost the same, so we don't have to give you a seat anymore, or show the common courtesies that men show women." All those little niceties were lost.

I enjoyed working at the shipyard; it was a unique job for a woman, and I liked the challenge. But it was a dangerous job.

Female factory workers, such as this welder, were paid less than male workers for doing the same job.
The Library of Congress.

Some jobs first considered to be for men only—such as chippers, shown here—were soon turned over to women, who proved they were just as skilled as men in the workplace.
The Library of Congress.

Interim period: A space of time between events.

The safety measures were very poor. Many people were injured by falling steel. Finally I was assigned to a very hazardous area and I asked to be transferred into a safer area. I was not granted that. They said, "You have to work where they assign you at all times." I thought it was getting too dangerous, so I quit.

*The war years had a tremendous impact on women. I know for myself it was the first time I had a chance to get out of the kitchen and work in industry and make a few bucks. This was something I had never dreamed would happen. In Sapulpa all that women had to look forward to was keeping house and raising families. The war years offered new possibilities. You came out to California, put on your pants and took your lunch pail to a man's job. In Oklahoma a woman's place was in the home, and men went to work and provided. This was the beginning of women's feeling that they could do something more. We were trained to do this kind of work because of the war, but there was no question that this was just an **interim period**. We were all* *told that when the war was over we would not be needed anymore.*

What happened next . . .

Sybil Lewis tired of defense work, but she stayed on in California, waiting for her husband in the army to return home. Intrigued by Hollywood's movie industry, she took a well-paid position as a maid at Paramount Studios. She was still working there when the war ended in 1945. Lewis said to herself, "You came to California to earn money to go back to Oklahoma, and now you're going back and complete your education." That is exactly what both she and her husband did. After graduating from college, Sybil Lewis returned to California and pursued civil service work (jobs with the federal government). Looking back on the war years, she later stated that "the impact of war changed my life, gave me an opportunity to leave my small town and discover there was another way of life."

Did you know . . .

- Black women were eager to get jobs in the war industries because the work paid well. However, employers often assigned them to the most uncomfortable and most dangerous jobs and required them to work night shifts.

- Some black women achieved considerable career success in prosperous black communities that sprang up around war industry plants, such as the shipbuilding community of Richmond, California. For example, one black woman, Margaret Starks, saw a different type of opportunity in the war industry. As thousands of black Americans migrated to Richmond, California, to work in the Kaiser shipyards, she recognized a potential market for entertainment and established the most popular nightclub in North Richmond, Tappers Inn, for the growing black community.

Consider the following . . .

- Sybil Lewis often worked with a white woman on a two-person riveting and bucking team. She stated they opened up, talked, and learned from each other. Think of some important lessons they might have learned from each other.

- Women workers, both blacks and whites, were the first to be laid off after the war. How do you think they felt about giving up their wages and returning to their previous lifestyles?

For More Information

Books

Gluck, Sherna Berger. *Rosie the Riveter Revisited: Women, the War, and Social Change.* Boston: Twayne Publishers, 1987.

Harris, Mark J., Franklin D. Mitchell, and Steven J. Schechter, eds. *The Homefront: America during World War II.* New York: G.P. Putnam's Sons, 1984.

Honey, Maureen, ed. *Bitter Fruit: African American Women in World War II.* Columbia: University of Missouri Press, 1999.

Terkel, Studs. *"The Good War": An Oral History of World War II.* New York: Ballantine Books, 1984.

Web sites

Rosie the Riveter Trust. http://www.rosietheriveter.org (accessed on July 29, 2004).

Peggy Terry

Excerpt from the essay "Peggy Terry"
**Reprinted from *"The Good War": An Oral History of World War II*.
Compiled by Studs Terkel.
Published in 1984.**

Peggy Terry was eighteen years old when she took a job in a munitions factory in Viola, Kentucky. Unlike women factory workers in war industry boomtowns, she was barely aware that a war had started and certainly did not understand its implications. Peggy Terry's job—putting explosive powder into shells—was hazardous. Some of the material she worked with was harmful to her health, but the job paid the rent and bought food and clothes, so she never asked questions about the risks of working in the factory.

By the time Peggy Terry moved to a job in Michigan, she had begun to learn about a bigger world. She worked with people of different ethnic backgrounds and began to see that the ideas she had been raised with about other people, particularly minorities, were untrue. They were people just like her. Meanwhile, her husband went off to Europe and North Africa as a paratrooper (troops trained to parachute into combat areas), leaving her to provide for herself and her family.

"We made the fabulous sum of thirty-two dollars a week. To us it was just an absolute miracle. Before that, we made nothing."

Things to remember while reading the excerpt from "Peggy Terry" . . .

- Peggy Terry grew up in the 1930s—the decade of the Great Depression, the worst economic downturn in U.S. history. She knew life only as a struggle to survive.

- After a decade of scarce jobs, scarce food, and little money, many Americans viewed war industry jobs, even the hazardous ones, as their ticket to a more financially secure life.

Excerpt from "Peggy Terry"

*The first work I had after the Depression was at a shell-loading plant in Viola, Kentucky. It is between Paducah and Mayfield. They were large shells: anti-aircraft, **incendiaries**, and **tracers**. We painted red on the tips of the tracers. My mother, my sister, and myself worked there. Each of us worked a different shift because we had little ones at home. We made the fabulous sum of thirty-two dollars a week. (Laughs.) To us it was just an absolute miracle. Before that, we made nothing.*

You won't believe how incredibly ignorant I was. I knew vaguely that a war had started, but I had no idea what it meant.

Didn't you have a radio?

Gosh, no. That was an absolute luxury. We were just moving around, working wherever we could find work. I was eighteen. My husband was nineteen. We were living day to day. When you are involved in stayin' alive, you don't think about big things like a war. It didn't occur to us that we were making these shells to kill people. It never entered my head.

*There were no women foremen where we worked. We were just a bunch of hillbilly women laughin' and talkin'. It was like a **social**. Now we'd have money to buy shoes and a dress and pay rent and get some food on the table. We were just happy to have work.*

*I worked in building number 11. I pulled a lot of gadgets on a machine. The shell slid under and powder went into it. Another level you pulled tamped it down. Then it moved on a conveyer belt to another building where the **detonator** was dropped in. You did this over and over.*

Incendiaries: Bombs designed to start fires.

Tracers: Bullets or projectiles that leave bright trails through the air.

Social: A pleasant meeting with friends.

Detonator: A small explosive device in a bomb that triggers the larger bomb explosion.

Tetryl was one of the ingredients and it turned us orange. Just as orange as an orange. Our hair was streaked orange. Our hands, our face, our neck just turned orange, even our eyeballs. We never questioned. None of us ever asked, What is this? Is this harmful? We simply didn't think about it. That was just one of the conditions of the job. The only thing we worried about was other women thinking we had dyed our hair. Back then it was a disgrace if you dyed your hair. We worried what people would say.

We used to laugh about it on the bus. It eventually wore off. But I seem to remember some of the women had breathing problems. The shells were painted a dark gray. When the paint didn't come out smooth, we had to take rags wet with some kind of remover and wash that paint off. The fumes from these rags—it was like breathing cleaning fluid. It burned the nose and throat. Oh, it was difficult to breathe. I remember that.

Nothing ever blew up, but I remember the building where they dropped in the detonator. These detonators are little black things about the size of a thumb. This terrible thunderstorm came and all

Women factory workers line up to punch their timecards at the end of a long shift. Many female workers experienced hazardous working conditions in their factories, but most just accepted it as part of their job. *The Library of Congress.*

Tetryl: An explosive chemical substance.

the lights went out. Somebody knocked a box of detonators off on the floor. Here we were in the pitch dark. Somebody was screaming, "Don't move, anybody!" They were afraid you'd step on the detonator. We were down on our hands and knees crawling out of that building in the storm. (Laughs.) We were in slow motion. If we'd stepped on one . . .

Mamma was what they called terminated—fired. Mamma's mother took sick and died and Mamma asked for time off and they told her no. Mamma said, "Well, I'm gonna be with my mamma. If I have to give up my job, I will just have to." So they terminated Mamma. That's when I started gettin' nasty. I didn't take as much baloney and pushing around as I had taken. I told 'em I was gonna quit, and they told me if I quit they would **blacklist** me wherever I would go. They had my fingerprints and all that. I guess it was just **bluff**, because I did get other work.

I think of how little we knew of human rights, union rights. We knew Daddy had been a hell-raiser in the mine workers' union, but at that point it hadn't rubbed off on any of us women. Coca-Cola and Dr. Pepper were allowed in every building, but not a drop of water. You could only get a drink of water if you went to the cafeteria, which was about two city blocks away. Of course you couldn't leave your machine long enough to go get a drink. I drank Coke and Dr. Pepper and I hated 'em. I hate 'em today. We had to buy it, of course. We couldn't leave to go to the bathroom, 'cause it was way the heck over there.

We were awarded the navy E for excellence. We were just so proud of that E. It was like we were a big family, and we hugged and kissed each other. They had the navy band out there celebrating us. We were so proud of ourselves.

First time my mother ever worked at anything except in the fields—first real job Mamma ever had. It was a big break in everybody's life. Once, Mamma woke up in the middle of the night to go to the bathroom and she saw the bus going down. She said, "Oh, my goodness, I've overslept." She jerked her clothes on, throwed her lunch in the bag, and was out on the corner, ready to go, when Boy Blue, our driver, said, "Honey, this is the wrong shift." Mamma wasn't supposed to be there until six in the morning. She never lived that down. She would have enjoyed telling you that.

My world was really very small. When we came from Oklahoma to Paducah, that was like a journey to the center of the earth. It was during the **Depression** and you did good having bus

Blacklist: A person who is routinely avoided by employers for work.

Bluff: To deceive or trick another person.

Depression: The Great Depression was a major economic crisis that lasted from 1929 to 1941. During the Depression unemployment and hunger were widespread.

fare to get across town. The war just widened my world. Especially after I came up to Michigan.

My grandfather went up to Jackson, Michigan, after he retired from the railroad. He wrote back and told us we could make twice as much in the war plants in Jackson. We did. We made ninety dollars a week. We did some kind of testing for airplane radios.

Ohh, I met all those wonderful **Pollacks**. They were the first people I'd ever known that were any different from me. A whole new world just opened up! I learned to drink beer like crazy with 'em. They were all very union-conscious. I learned a lot of things that I didn't even know existed.

We were very patriotic and we understood that the Nazis were someone who would have to be stopped. We didn't know about **concentration camps**. I don't think anybody I knew did. With the Japanese, that was a whole different thing. We were just ready to wipe them out. They sure as heck didn't look like us. They were **yellow little creatures that smiled when they bombed our boys**. I remember someone in Paducah got up this idea of burning everything they had that was Japanese. I had this little ceramic cat and I said, "I don't care, I am not burning it." They had this big bonfire and people came and brought what they had that was made in Japan. Threw it on the bonfire. I hid my cat. It's on the shelf in my bathroom right now. (Laughs.)

In all the movies we saw, the Germans were always tall and handsome. There'd be one meanie, a little short dumpy bad Nazi. But the main characters were good-lookin' and they looked like us. The Japanese were all evil. . . .

I believe the war was the beginning of my **seeing things**. You just can't stay uninvolved and not knowing when such a **momentous** thing is happening. It's just little things that start happening and you put one piece with another. Suddenly, a puzzle begins to take shape. . . .

The war gave a lot of people jobs. It led them to expect more than they had before. People's expectations, financially, spiritually, were raised. There was such a beautiful dream. We were gonna reach the end of the rainbow. When the war ended, the rainbow vanished. Almost immediately we went into **Korea**. There was no peace, which we were promised.

I remember a woman saying on the bus that she hoped the war didn't end until she got her refrigerator paid for. An old man

Pollacks: A derogatory term referring to people of Polish descent or from Poland.

Concentration camps: Places where German soldiers gathered people they considered enemies, such as Jews, Gypsies, and political opponents.

Yellow little creatures that smiled when they bombed our boys: Derogatory reference to Japanese pilots who bombed U.S. military bases at Pearl Harbor, Hawaii, on December 7, 1941.

Seeing things: She was introduced to parts of the country and people she had never seen before, changing her preconceived ideas and stereotypes she had grown up with.

Momentous: Very important.

Korea: The Korean War (1950–1953) began only five years after the end of World War II.

"While Their Parents Build Planes"

The following text is from "While Their Parents Build Planes," an article written by Frances Duncan and published in the March 1943 issue of *Woman's Home Companion*. The article makes daycare centers sound very desirable, but in the early 1940s most Americans viewed them as highly detrimental to child development. Most women frowned on mothers who left children behind in order to enter the workforce. Most working mothers preferred to leave their children with a nonworking relative.

The children have a wonderful time at this combination nursery and playground in Burbank, California, which two women, Nina Killgore and Frances Duncan, had the wit and gumption [willingness, drive] to start when they saw how badly it was needed.

With mother driving rivets instead of being home when a fellow comes in from school, it's a dislocated world for youngsters. At this playground (just a fenced-in vacant lot) there's always something to do . . . about forty children . . . are taken care of here.

A working mother drops off her children at a daycare center. *Courtesy of the FDR Library.*

Much of the nursery play equipment is improvised. This merry-go-round is just an

Bomb dropped on Hiroshima: The atomic bomb the United States dropped on the Japanese city of Hiroshima on August 6, 1945, immediately killing over seventy thousand people.

Hirohito: The emperor of Japan from 1926 until his death in 1989.

hit her over the head with an umbrella. He said, "How dare you!" (Laughs.) . . .

I knew the **bomb dropped on Hiroshima** was a big terrible thing, but I didn't know it was the horror it was. It was on working people. It wasn't anywhere near the big shots of Japan who started the war in the first place. We didn't drop it on them. **Hirohito** and his white horse, it never touched him. It was dropped on women and children who had nothing to say about whether their country went to war or not.

old wagon wheel, its axle imbedded in cement, and it goes by boy power. Play areas are divided so that the children may be grouped by ages. On the high board fence on one side of the yard the children helped paint story murals.

Every morning the flag is raised over the playhouse which the children built from a Lockheed engine crate and which takes turns being a fort, a Red Cross hospital or a pony express station. Nearby the boys have rigged an antiaircraft battery (two-by-fours mounted on a bench and camouflaged with eucalyptus boughs). Elsewhere on the playground is the Victory garden [small fruit and vegetable gardens grown by individuals or families, planted in their own yards and public places, such as parks], where the Shetland pony helps with the plowing. For this pony the boys built a barn. Said eight-year-old Wally as he sawed the boards of the barn roof, "I like to do something that is something when I get it finished!" The nursery encourages constructive ability.

Time for lunch which is usually served out of doors under the trees. Other meals are served too, for this is a twenty-four-hour nursery. Night shift parents leave Johnny at three in the afternoon on the way to work and pick him up at ten the next morning. This gives the parents a chance to sleep late. When dad goes to work at five-thirty, A.M., mother at seven, the twins are fetched at six-thirty in the morning to spend the day. A father in working togs [clothes] brings in his baby just finishing her bottle at seven-thirty. One mother brings her baby on a bicycle. At nine-thirty the Killgores' big car brings in a load of children collected from a wide area.

After luncheon come naps. Cots are unfolded and cribs set up . . . One of the most useful of the nonprofessional helpers is a fourteen-year-old boy who comes afternoons to give pony-rides and make model airplanes. Help is a problem. Part-time assistance from older women might be the solution. As in any place where people care for children, county authorities check up at intervals.

To take care of these children whose fathers and mothers work day and night turning out war materials is vitally important. For it is to keep them free and happy under the American flag that we are fighting. Your community can do just as well as Burbank does if you're intelligent, energetic and interested in children.

I was happy my husband would get to come home and wouldn't be sent there from Germany. Every day when the paper came out, there'd be somebody I knew with their picture. An awful lot of kids I knew, went to school and church with, were killed.

No bombs were ever dropped on us. I can't help but believe the **cold war** started because we were untouched. Except for our boys that went out of the country and were killed, we came out of that war in good shape. People with more money than they'd had in years.

Cold War: The Cold War was an intense political and economic rivalry from 1945 to 1991 between the United States and the Soviet Union falling just short of military conflict.

No, I don't think we'd have been satisfied to go back to what we had during the Depression. To be deprived of things we got used to. Materially, we're a thousand times better off. But the war turned me against religion. . . . I don't know how chaplains can call themselves men of God and prepare boys to go into battle. If the bible says, Thou shalt not kill, it doesn't say, except in time of war. They'll send a man to the electric chair who in a temper killed somebody. But they pin medals on our men. The more people they kill, the more medals they pin on 'em. I was just so glad when it was over, because I wanted my husband home. I didn't understand any of the implications except that the killing was over and that's a pretty good thing to think about whether you're political or not. (Laughs.) The killing be over forever.

What happened next . . .

At war's end, Peggy Terry's husband returned home. He had been severely traumatized by his combat experiences, and he had nightmares, drank too much alcohol, and became abusive to his family. Peggy Terry became a much more introspective person and began to question the values she had been taught to live by, such as discriminatory perspectives toward minorities and ethnic groups.

Did you know . . .

- War industry jobs were often dangerous or harmful to workers' health, and there were rarely safety precautions in place to protect factory employees. Many accidents and illnesses occurred, but employees had no rights to file official complaints or request compensation. They were generally satisfied if they received a few cents extra each hour as hazard pay.

- Labor unions provided some protection for employees of large factories by organizing and placing demands for better working conditions before management. But smaller war factories, numbering in the thousands, operated without any restrictions or rules regarding pay, hours, and other working conditions.

Consider the following . . .

- Study Peggy Terry's comments on the portrayal of Germans and Japanese people in movies. Discuss what she meant by "being manipulated." Does the motion picture industry still "manipulate" its audience today? Think of examples from recent movies you have seen to back up your answer.

- Consider Terry's thoughts on the Hiroshima bombing. Do you agree with her views or not? Take sides and debate with classmates.

For More Information

Books

Harris, Mark J., Franklin D. Mitchell, and Steven J. Schechter, eds. *The Homefront: America during World War II*. New York: G. P. Putnam's Sons, 1984.

Hartmann, Susan M. *The Home Front and Beyond: American Women in the 1940s*. Boston: Twayne Publishers, 1982.

Lingeman, Richard R. *Don't You Know There's a War On? The American Home Front, 1941–1945*. New York: G. P. Putnam's Sons, 1970.

Terkel, Studs. *"The Good War": An Oral History of World War II*. New York: Ballantine Books, 1984.

Web sites

What Did You Do in the War, Grandma? http://www.stg.brown.edu/projects/WWII_Women/tocCS.html (accessed on July 29, 2004).

Women and the Home Front during World War II. http://www.teacheroz.com/WWIIHomefront.htm (accessed on July 29, 2004).

Florence Hall

Excerpt from "They're Getting In the Crops"
Reprinted from *Independent Woman*.
Published July 1943.

"This year millions of farm women and girls will be doing farm work to help meet the wartime goals. But this will not be enough. They must have help from their sisters in the towns and cities."

By mid-1942 there was an acute shortage of workers on U.S. farms. Millions of farmers and their hired hands left the land to join the military or to take war industry jobs. Agriculture officials predicted that 75 percent of farmers would incur severe labor shortages by 1943. However, women willingly stepped forward to fill the need for workers, just as they had in the war industries. Wives, daughters, and sisters of farmers jumped in to take over farming responsibilities, but they needed more help as there were more farming chores to accomplish than they could tackle themselves. The U.S. Department of Agriculture (USDA), the U.S. Extension Service (which provided educational assistance on the latest farming methods), and the U.S. Employment Service all looked to nontraditional workers, including urban women and students, to rescue the crops. Women's volunteer groups formed in various states, mostly in New England and on the West Coast, and began tending and harvesting crops in the summer and fall of 1942.

In April 1943 the USDA announced the formation of the Women's Land Army (WLA); senior home economist Florence Louise Hall (1888–1952) was appointed the head of the new agency. Hall immediately began a recruitment campaign for WLA. She oversaw the recruitment and organization of hundreds of thousands of women volunteers who would alleviate the wartime farm labor shortage.

Hall wrote an article called "They're Getting In the Crops" for the July 1943 issue of *Independent Woman*. In the article Hall explained how nonfarm women were aiding farm communities, and she encouraged businesswomen to spend their vacation time helping out on U.S. farms. Hall chose to publish the piece in *Independent Woman* because it was the official magazine of the Business and Professional Women's Clubs, a group that she hoped would help recruit more WLA volunteers.

Things to remember while reading the excerpt from "They're Getting In the Crops" . . .

- At first, farmers were very skeptical that city women with only a few weeks of training could be of any help.

- By December 1942 thousands of women volunteers had proved their ability to get farmwork done. However, the secretary of agriculture, Claude R. Wickard (1893–1967), still believed that women did not belong in the fields. It was Meredith L. Wilson, director of the U.S. Extension Service (a department within the USDA), who charged ahead with the idea of using urban women to solve the farm labor shortage.

- Women who worked as farm laborers on the home front during the war did not receive as much publicity as women working in war industry factories, but they were indispensable to the war effort.

Excerpt from "They're Getting In the Crops"

*This year millions of farm women and girls will be doing farm work to help meet the **wartime goals**. But this will not be enough. They must have help from their sisters in the towns and cities.*

Wartime goals: To not only feed U.S. troops, but Allied troops as well since European agriculture was greatly disrupted by the war.

A Women's Land Army volunteer harvests beans at a Massachusetts farm.
National Archives photo no. 016-G-323 (28).

A Women's Land Army volunteer harvests beans at a Massachusetts farm.
National Archives photo no. 016-G-323 (28).

Many city women came from the farm or from a small town, where, as young girls, they learned enough about farm work to fill in, at least, on emergencies when labor was scarce. These women—and many others too—are now needed in the Women's Land Army. Women who can contribute a month or two, women who are willing to spend their vacations working on a farm—even women who can give only weekends or holidays—can be used from now until harvest time in the new Women's Land Army of the United States of America. . . .

*College girls are making a good name for themselves in the Women's Land Army. From the Ohio State University fifty YWCA girls are spending ten weeks on farms in Erie County, thinning peaches, picking fruit and vegetables. They are **billeted** in an old school building and are paying $15 for an instructor. These girls spend their evenings studying. About one hundred college girls are working on Maine farms. Some of these girls have developed into skillful rogueing crews, which weed out diseased plants, to help Maine farmers keep their seed potato industry up to its high*

Billeted: Assigned to living quarters.

American Home Front in World War II: Primary Sources

standards. The girls were given special training in large commercial potato fields learning to detect and remove potato plants affected with **leafroll, mosaic, and blackleg**. These girls are assuring Maine potato growers of competent roguers this season.

Most of the **seasonal jobs** done by the Women's Land Army working from labor camps can be learned quickly by inexperienced women with a little instruction on the job. Picking berries, cutting asparagus, transplanting tomatoes, and harvesting fruits and vegetables require some skill which can be mastered on the job, plus considerable physical conditioning for women unaccustomed to work in the open. Women who plan to spend their vacations in this way could make their path easier by taking regular exercise outdoors. Walking is particularly good as a muscle conditioner. . . .

A member of the Women's Land Army working on a poultry farm.
© Hulton-Deutsch Collection/ Corbis. Reproduced by permission.

The year-round worker is given a short course of from two to six weeks in the state agricultural college or similar institution. At the Farmingdale Agricultural Institute at Farmingdale, N.Y., for example, three such courses of four weeks each, were conducted during the winter and spring months. Girls and women from every walk of life were enrolled—girls from offices, factories, beauty parlors, shops—girls who never before had done any form of work at all. Professional women, school teachers, housewives of all ages were also found in the classes. Thirty-four graduates are now at work on farms in New York State and in Connecticut, and making good in a big way.

At first the farmers were somewhat **chary** about accepting the services of these city-bred, book-taught feminine farm hands. They were inclined to suspect that the girls and women would get hurt, be afraid of—or spoil!—the farm animals, ruin expensive—and now priceless—machinery, stand around asking silly questions, and generally prove themselves more trouble than they were worth. Instead they are finding that women and girls have been able to take over most of the lighter farm chores so that the

Leafroll, mosaic, and blackleg: Plant diseases.

Seasonal jobs: Jobs done in-season. Spring planting and fall harvesting, for example.

Chary: Hesitant.

farmers themselves may be free for the heavier work of the field. They are discovering that even in a short four weeks' course these women have not only learned not to be afraid of cows but to milk and otherwise handle cows expertly. They know now that women are teachable, that they do a thorough job, that they are reliable, hard working, conscientious and completely in earnest about farm work. Accordingly year-round women farm workers are in demand, to the full number which can be recruited and trained, for poultry, dairy and general produce farms throughout the country; and for the services of these women, when *trained, the farmers will gladly pay the same wages they would expect to pay to a man for the same type of work.*

*During the spring, the University of Maryland trained twenty-six women in a three-weeks' course. The enrollees proved themselves women of serious purpose, eager to learn, and strongly motivated by patriotism. Some of them had husbands in **North Africa,** and felt that, by growing food, they were performing the best service they could for their men on the battle fronts.*

*A similar course was offered by the University of Maryland the previous spring and felt to be an unqualified success. But this spring a new and greatly heightened spirit of devotion and earnestness was noted in the students. They **quailed** at nothing—however hard or however strange to them. The **docking** of lambs, for example, might well be expected to strike women as a mean sort of job. Nevertheless the students faced up to it without a squeal. Shearing of sheep might be thought a task to awaken feminine squeamishness. The students went right to work and practiced until they could shear their sheep with the sure touch of experts.*

Desiring to talk with one of last year's graduates who I had heard was doing exceptionally well both for herself and for her country, I went to call on Mrs. Yochelson. Mrs. Yochelson now has a chicken farm in the vicinity of Washington [D.C.]. When Mrs. Yochelson came out of her chicken house to greet me dressed in blue overalls and rubber boots, I thought to myself, "Why, this is one of the women I saw last year who was afraid *of a chicken." She told me her story. She had been an active **club woman** in town, but after Pearl Harbor had determined to go into some sort of war service. Farming seemed the most **feasible.** She and her husband lived outside the city, and her husband suggested that she grow chickens. She joined the Women's Land Army and attended the course at the University of Maryland, buying 5,000 baby chicks before the course*

North Africa: At the time, the main battlefront in the campaign against Germany was in North Africa; the women believed they were contributing at least something while their husbands contributed a lot by being overseas in the military.

Quailed: Faltered or recoiled in fear.

Docking: Removing part of the tail.

Club woman: Slang for reference to a person who spends much time in social activities, such as country clubs or book clubs.

Feasible: The most suitable for her.

American Home Front in World War II: Primary Sources

*was over. Last year she sold 11,000 chickens and handled 11,200 dozen eggs which she had **candled**, weighed and packed herself. "Last year," she smiled, "I was afraid of chickens. Now I love them. It's such fun to watch them grow. If you watch them and talk to them, they eat more and grow faster—and I have the satisfaction of feeling that I am doing something essential for victory." . . .*

*The American Women's Land Army is growing, but many more serious-minded recruits are needed. Most of the states report that they have **more calls** than they can fill. Women's organizations are proving very helpful in recruiting women for the Land Army. Many more women would be glad to do this type of war service, if they knew about it. To get the necessary information to city women we need the cooperation of just such organizations as the Business and Professional Women's Clubs. Clubs that wish to help can get in touch with the local county agricultural agent, usually located in the County Court House, or in the offices of the U.S. Employment Service.*

*The members of the Women's Land Army, in common with the **WAACS, the WAVES, the SPARS, the WAFS** and other women's groups serving their country in this time of war, have their own special uniform. A highly practical, and at the same time **becoming**, work outfit has been designed for them. It consists of well-fitting dark blue denim overalls, light blue shirt and cap with sun visor. The cap bears on its front the red, white and blue insignia of the Women's Land Army. A matching denim jacket is also obtainable to give extra warmth in the chill of the early morn.*

The outfit is optional and is bought by the women themselves with their own earnings. It is reasonably priced and distributed by a non-profit organization. For those who do not wish to buy the uniform because they already have a satisfactory working outfit, or for other reasons, an arm band bearing the Women's Land Army insignia is available.

What happened next . . .

Between mid-1943 and the end of 1945 approximately one and a half million women joined WLA, and an equal number found farmwork on their own. By 1945, 22.4 percent

Candled: Visually examined for growth and fertility by holding the egg up to a light.

More calls: More requests from farms needing assistance.

WAACS, WAVES, SPARS, WAFS: The various organizations created for women to assist the military services, including the Women's Army Auxiliary Corps, Women Accepted for Volunteer Emergency Service, Semper Paratus—Always Ready, and Women's Auxiliary Ferrying Squadron.

Becoming: Attractive.

of all agricultural workers were women, up from 8 percent in 1940. Women hoed, weeded, thinned, and harvested all sorts of crops. They cared for sheep, cattle, dairy cattle, and chickens. With their help, farmers were able to increase overall production and meet the wartime agricultural goals called for by the federal government.

Did you know . . .

- Articles published in popular magazines such as *McCall's, Time, Saturday Evening Post,* and *Country Gentleman* promoted the idea of city women going to work as farm laborers during the war years. Agricultural publications also printed favorable reports about women's contributions.

- Pay for farmwork was supposed to be at least 30 cents an hour, but it varied regionally. It was much higher in the Pacific Northwest at 60 to 95 cents an hour, but in the Southeast workers made only 20 cents an hour.

- The formation of the Women's Land Army was inspired by the British Land Girls in Great Britain and similar programs in Australia, New Zealand, and Canada.

- Eleanor Roosevelt (1884–1962), a longtime strong supporter for improved job opportunities for women in America, gave her support to the WLA.

Consider the following . . .

- What do you think were the major reasons behind so many women going into the fields, even spending their vacation time as farm laborers?

- Through the Victory Farm Volunteers (VFV) program, students between the ages of eleven and seventeen helped harvest crops during the war years. Find out more about the VFV and how schools helped organize and prepare students to work in the fields.

- Research the role of women in federal, state, and county extension services, particularly their participation in "home demonstrations."

For More Information

Books

Carpenter, Stephanie A. *On the Farm Front: The Women's Land Army in World War II.* DeKalb: Northern Illinois University Press, 2003.

Periodicals

Hall, Florence. "They're Getting In the Crops." *Independent Woman* (July 1943): pp. 194–216.

Litoff, Judy B., and David C. Smith. "'To the Rescue of the Crops': The Women's Land Army during World War II." *Prologue* (Winter 1993): pp. 347–361.

Web sites

United States Department of Agriculture (USDA). http://www.usda.gov (accessed on July 29, 2004).

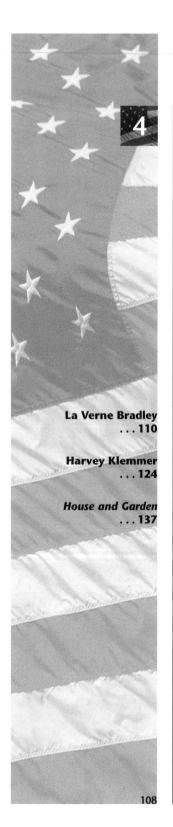

Home Front Communities

For the United States, World War II (1939–45) officially began on December 8, 1941, and ended September 2, 1945. During this almost four-year period, every community in America changed in some way as it adjusted to wartime. Some communities, and the regions surrounding them, experienced drastic economic changes and population growth as they became war industry centers and staging areas for servicemen en route to overseas battle zones. Cities on the west coast and the east coast and in the upper Midwest-Great Lakes region underwent the greatest changes. Among the cities most affected by the war were San Diego, Los Angeles, and San Francisco in California; the Seattle-Tacoma area in Washington State; Mobile, Alabama; Charleston, South Carolina; Norfolk, Virginia; Washington, D.C.; and Detroit, Michigan.

The first two excerpts in this chapter come from *National Geographic Magazine,* a popular monthly publication (both in the early 1940s and into the twenty-first century). The first excerpt, "San Francisco: Gibraltar of the West Coast," describes wartime San Francisco as both a military hub from which thousands of army and navy men departed and a war industry center that drew in thousands of civilian war workers. The second excerpt, "Michigan Fights," describes the push toward full mobilization by U.S. industrial manufacturers. The final excerpt, "Houses for Defense," was originally printed in *House and Garden,* a widely read home decorating and gardening magazine that continues to be popular in the twenty-first century. The article addresses the chief problem encountered by the war industry and the military in urban areas: housing. Housing was scarce, so war workers and military personnel lived in extremely overcrowded conditions. To solve the housing shortage, builders introduced prefabricated houses (houses whose parts were built in a factory and then assembled on-site) and rapidly built entire subdivisions full of such homes. The U.S. government provided funding for this "defense housing" through the Lanham Act, which passed in October 1940.

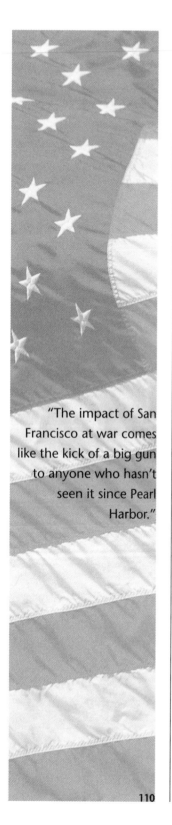

La Verne Bradley

Excerpt from "San Francisco: Gibraltar of the West Coast"
Written by La Verne Bradley.
Published in *National Geographic Magazine*,
March 1943.

In "San Francisco: Gibraltar of the West Coast," wartime San Francisco, California, comes alive as the author describes the sights, sounds, and bustle of a war industry center and military hub. Navy sailors and pilots and army soldiers by the thousands crowded the city. San Francisco was a premier staging area for the war in the Pacific. Thousands of military ships loaded with men and supplies moved in an almost continuous line under the Golden Gate Bridge, setting out across the vast Pacific for Japan and the Philippines. The port and the entire coastline were heavily guarded, and many roads and areas surrounding sensitive facilities, such as military or power plants, were closed to the public. North of Oakland, at Mare Island in San Pablo Bay, was the largest naval shipbuilding and repair yard in the West. Also in the Bay Area were Henry Kaiser's (1882–1967) shipyards, which turned the previously sleepy community of Richmond into a throbbing city where businesses operated on a round-the-clock schedule.

Author La Verne Bradley states that "San Francisco is the same enchanting thing it ever was." However, she stresses that physical changes and military restrictions were the rule during wartime.

Things to remember while reading the excerpt from "San Francisco: Gibraltar of the West Coast" . . .

- Gibraltar is a small country in southwest Europe controlled by Britain. Its main landform is a large rocky ridge, known as the Rock, considered to be one of the Pillars of Hercules in Greek mythology noted for its strength. Gibraltar similarly is noted as a symbol of British naval strength.

- The influx of money from military paydays and war industry paydays provided a major boost to San Francisco's economy. After a decade of high unemployment during the Great Depression (1929–41), virtually anyone who wanted a job could find work.

- Residents of San Francisco believed the city and its facilities might well come under Japanese attack. Blackouts and dimouts occurred nightly and were taken very seriously.

- San Francisco had an ethnically diverse population, including many thousand Chinese, Japanese, and Italian immigrants.

- Between San Francisco and Oakland along the connecting Bay Bridge was man-made Treasure Island. The World's Fair Golden Gate International Exposition took place on Treasure Island in February 1939; the event was designed not only to attract tourists but to provide employment. It closed in September 1940, and when the United States entered the war, the navy took over the entire island to expand its facilities.

Excerpt from "San Francisco: Gibraltar of the West Coast"

The impact of San Francisco at war comes like the kick of a big gun to anyone who hasn't seen it since Pearl Harbor.

*Fighting men have taken over the city. . . . They have **geared its life**, colored its streets, inspired its people.*

*Troops, guns, bayonets, motor units, ships, supplies—on the move. Soldiers, marines, mines, nets, bayonets, barrages, barbed wire—on guard. "It is absolutely forbidden to cross this line." "No cameras or **field glasses**, please." "Men in uniform—welcome!"*

If for a moment you lose yourself in old smells, sounds, memories, fighter planes come screaming down the skyline and, lifting you right up on your toes, almost clip off the top of the old Ferry Building to remind you that this is 1943—and a city at war!

Helmeted, bullet-belted patrols guard every bridgehead, river mouth, slip landing, seemingly harmless road entrances, tunnels, railroad crossings, barren hills. . . .

You feel the electric thrill of an area charged with action.

*You hear the **rivet guns** and **hammer presses** of shipyards; the screech of braked wheels grating on steel rails as oil moves in thousands of tank cars from refineries; the roar of blast furnaces; the thunder of Army trucks speeding by under guard—10, 20, 30— filled with soldiers.*

You see hills being leveled as giant shovels slap at their sides like fly swatters. You see new towns rising from reclaimed swamps and dust holes.

*You look across fields of **barrage balloons** suspended awkwardly in midair like tail-heavy sausages.*

Finally, you look across to the Golden Gate where, against a low sun, a line of blue, heavily burdened ships is slowly steaming out.

Threshold of Pacific Theater of War

*San Francisco is the administrative headquarters for the Army's Western Defense Command and 4th Army, and the Navy's Western Sea Frontier and 12th Naval District. From here command extends to the whole Western **Theater of War**.*

*The city's magnificent, wave-washed **Golden Gate** is the most strongly fortified spot in America.*

*The Navy has here the Mare Island Navy Yard, the new Alameda Naval Air Station, a blimp base, supply depots, **drydocks**, and training centers.*

Geared its life: Speeded up the pace of life.

Field glasses: Binoculars.

Rivet guns: Tools that thrust a bolt of metal through two or more pieces of metal.

Hammer presses: Large machines that fasten metal pieces together by driving them together by high pressure.

Barrage balloons: Balloons from which nets and wires are hung to protect against attacks by enemy aircraft.

Theater of War: Region of war operations.

Golden Gate: The Golden Gate Bridge, which connects San Francisco to the California coastline to the north.

Drydocks: Docks where ships are kept out of the water, either for construction or repair.

An aerial photograph of the Mare Island Naval shipyard in San Francisco, California, shows a fleet of submarines docked in their berthing area. © *Bettmann/Corbis. Reproduced by permission.*

All other activities are **subordinated to** the moving of troops and supplies, defending the harbor, maintaining port facilities, and supporting new war industries. During the early months of the war San Francisco **cleared** more military supplies than all other United States ports combined. . . .

For the thousands of men who pass through that Golden Gate, it is their last glimpse of America for many months; it holds all their parting memories.

Subordinated to: Treated as less important than.

Cleared: Shipped out.

For these men, and the thousands of families, sweethearts, and friends who are here because of them, San Francisco has a tradition to maintain, and she knows her job. . . .

To the West Lies the Enemy

Here as strongly as in any other place in America people are aware of what defeat by Japan could mean and they are ready for any emergency.

You get the sense of this, and of the confidence behind it, as you travel from the big guns of the coastal defense, across the tallest bridge in the world, and drop down over old Fort Point into the Presidio, the largest military post in the United States built entirely within the limits of a city.

In normal times the Presidio lies in quiet parklike detachment, with the Pacific curling in great white waves at its feet. But now it bristles with war activity.

On a bouncing, bounding jeep we drove from one **barricaded extremity** to the other. On every parade ground, in every available clearing, clusters of men were drilling, exercising, holding bayonet practice on rows of stuffed dummies, or running over Commando obstacle courses.

We roared down to the "Old Fort," or Fort Point, **sequestered** beneath the massive **girders** of the bridge. Here, looking out from Civil War **casemates** which once mounted 10-inch **columbiads** (and never fired a hostile shot), we watched the return of the busy fishing fleet which each day comes and goes grandly under naval escort.

We went by hospital buildings . . . up and down hills past historic guns and live ones.

At each crossing **sentries** appeared out of the mist to ask for identification.

Through shady eucalyptus and cypress and along green parade grounds today there is a constant thunder of trucks, troop **lorries**, armored scout cars, jeeps, and **prime-movers**; an endless coming and going of more soldiers than the Presidio has ever seen at one time in all its long, romantic history.

Coast Artillery on Guard

The security of San Francisco lies in the hands of the Coast Artillery, whose Harbor Defense headquarters are at Fort Winfield

Barricaded extremity: A border of the military post, fortified with obstructions to halt the advance of an enemy.

Sequestered: Secluded.

Girders: Horizontal beams that support loads.

Casemates: Armored enclosures.

Columbiads: Guns.

Sentries: Guards.

Lorries: Trucks.

Prime-movers: Power sources that put other machines in motion.

Scott, on the bluff overlooking the Golden Gate. The **defenses** themselves are distributed about the Bay among Forts Scott, Barry, Baker, Funston, Miley, and Cronkhite—and stretch for miles up and down the coastline. . . .

They watch the fog roll in, night fall. The coast turns black and silent. **Combers** break over the shore, but no other sound is heard as barren hills and shorelines settle in for a lonely watch. As huge guns point out to sea, night stations are manned, and men fall back to watching and waiting!. . . .

Mare Island

Mare Island was the first spot in America to get the news about Pearl Harbor. With its powerful radio station it intercepted **Kimmel's** historic message to the Pacific Fleet which ended with "This is no drill." The news was flashed to Washington [D.C.] and read to President Roosevelt by **Secretary Knox** before an official **communiqué** reached the Navy Department.

When the U.S.S. Shaw limped home from the attack, Mare Island gave it a new **nose** and sent it back to fight.

When from 500 to 600 Pearl Harbor wounded arrived on Christmas Day, 1941, Mare Island went to work patching up their hurts and has already discharged 99 percent of them. It is still mending ships and men, and turning out new ships besides. . . .

A **medley of unholy discords** rises from the shipyards, machine shops, drydocks, warehouses, and other centers of shipbuilding and ship-repair activity on this small Manhattan-like island in the north end of the Bay. Shipfitters, pattern makers, molders, painters, **flange turners**, electricians mill about in purposeful confusion, eventually losing themselves in the crushing crowds of a changing shift.

Sprinkled throughout the thousands of civilian workers are the white caps of sailors passing from barracks to headquarters, hospital to recreation center, destroyer to **corvette**, ship to shore.

Ordinarily about seven or eight thousand people are employed here. It is the largest naval construction yard in the West. The extra 30,000 or so have charted a production curve which is almost **vertical**.

Besides the construction and repair of naval vessels, **merchant ships** are being converted to war use—cargoes to refrigerator ships, and **liners** to cargoes.

Defenses: Military installations providing security to the Bay area.

Combers: Long curling waves.

Mare Island: An island near Vallejo, California, north of San Francisco Bay.

Kimmel: Admiral Husband Kimmel (1882–1968), commander of the Pearl Harbor navy base at the time of the surprise Japanese attack.

Secretary Knox: Frank Knox (1874–1944), secretary of the navy during World War II.

Communiqué: Communication.

Nose: Bow, or front, of the ship.

Medley of unholy discords: A great range of loud sounds.

Flange turners: Workers who create rims or collars on metal parts to create attachments or give greater strength.

Corvette: An armed ship smaller than a destroyer.

Vertical: Going straight up.

Merchant ships: Ships carrying cargo to be delivered and sold.

Liners: Passenger ships.

Workers leaving a San Francisco shipyard by the thousands at the end of their shift. *The Library of Congress.*

Tenders: Vessels that supply other ships.

Lathe: A machine that rotates a piece that is being worked on.

Pincers: A gripping tool with two long projections that grasp another object.

We drove up to a channel dock and stepped out to look at a damaged submarine in from the sea. . . .

Lined up in wooden cradles in another section were the half-formed shapes of escort vessels for both the United States and Great Britain. In other precise rows were corvettes, **tenders**, destroyers, subs.

No part of Mare Island looks familiar any more. What construction hasn't done, camouflage has. Bomb shelters cover the island, and on every turn you see the poison-gas attack warning signals—iron-bar triangles to be rung like the dinner gongs used in old mining and lumber camps.

The shipfitter's shop with a crew of 10,000 is the largest in the United States. Here and in the machine shops we found girls and gray-haired women in blue jeans and bandannas bending over **lathes** of all sizes.

Men were picking up hot slabs of steel with long **pincers** and tossing them across a passageway for cooling. Huge blocks of red-hot metal were being smashed with 2,000-ton drop hammers and taking new shape as if they were wax.

The screaming of giant **planers** followed by the rattling of rivet guns sounded like fighter planes pulling out of power dives with all machine guns hammering. The noise was deafening—but its vibrating strength was magnificent.

In their overalls and goggles the shipyard women look rough, but they are doing a job. Their talk has **tang**, too. To them "pickling" means washing steel plates with acid to eliminate rust and scale; "counterbore" is a form of drilling, not something you do over a **bridge** table; and they don't eat a "**rabbet**," they caulk it.

Three hundred special buses carry thousands of Mare Island workers to and from the mainland and neighboring Bay cities. Workers commute from as far away as Sacramento and San Jose. Noncommuters are housed in barracks and emergency dwellings sprawled all over the dusty hills surrounding Vallejo. Rows and rows of new buildings file up and down the **undulating** landscape. They look like cookie boxes with holes punched in them.

On **sidings**, in special clearings, behind billboards—wherever room can be found—trailers are bunched together like frightened beetles.

Vallejo, "The Naval City," and Richmond, with its petroleum industry and shipyards, have caught the main overflow of new war worker residents. Normal suburban towns before the **emergency**, they now operate on a stepped-up 24-hour schedule. Rippling rayon banners around movie houses announce, "Open all night." Workers give parties by the shift. Bands frequently begin to play at five and six o'clock in the morning.

Old sections of Vallejo's main street, usually quiet at night, now twinkle with lights and entertainment. Jeeps piled high with sailors and soldiers go roaring up the street, as civilians crowd and cheer—and try to get on, too. New restaurants and hot-dog stands along the highway advertise the boom. We passed the "Hunk-a-dory" somewhere along the way.

Berth of the "Flying Navy"

In 1938 the United States had seven naval air stations handling the maintenance and overhaul of our Navy's **heavier-than-air craft**. Today there are many more than 20.

Planers: Tools for smoothing or shaping a surface.

Tang: Pointed and brief speech.

Bridge: Bridge is a card game; this is a reference to bidding and counterbidding in bridge games.

Rabbet: A deep notch in a board made to join with another board.

Undulating: Wavy.

Sidings: Along railroad lines.

Emergency: Bombing of Pearl Harbor by Japanese.

Heavier-than-air craft: Manned reconnaissance (information-gathering) balloons; blimps.

One of the largest of these new bases is the Alameda Naval Air Station, directly across the Bay from San Francisco. Called the *"shore hope"* of many Navy officers, it spreads out like an architect's dream with streamlined barracks, mess halls, theater, recreation centers, and **dispensary**. Here, too, is located one of the largest airfields in the world, with shining new runways, hangars, machine shops, and training schools. . . .

Following a marching line of sailors to the mess hall, we skirted one company and entered the galley. Steaming hot, twenty 80-gallon soup **coppers** were lined up along the center of the room; a chef was stirring one with an oar.

"Court of Pacifica" Seems Ironic Now

Huge refrigerator rooms held mountains of vegetables, fruits, and dairy products. In the bakery, which also is a training school, we saw part of the 750 pies and 1,500 loaves of bread turned out daily. . . .

Across Treasure Island's **"Court of Pacifica,"** where lights once played on a dancing fountain and melody drifted from a screen of stars, **bluejackets** now march to gunnery practice or patrol duty. "Pacifica," raised in tribute to the peace and **comity** of Pacific nations, looks down on strange goings-on these days, for Treasure Island is today an active unit of the Navy's war program.

Based here are naval patrol forces, a large boot camp for raw naval recruits, and the West Coast Armed guard, which, while awaiting assignment to merchant ships, devotes its time to **signal study** and gunnery tactics.

In the former Science Building of the **Fair** we found sailors straddling small two-man benches taking **code**.

The original Administration Building houses Naval Head-quarters and the offices of Pan American Airways; the Hall of Air Transportation is Pan Am's hangar; and the Palace of Fine Arts is the Navy machine shop.

The mess hall here is now the biggest in the Navy. An average of 6,000 men can be fed in 40 minutes. They get all the milk they can drink, and that week it was 25,000 gallons. . . .

Chinatown Since Pearl Harbor

San Francisco's crowded Chinatown has changed since Pearl Harbor. On the surface this is hardly noticeable, except for the **empty**

Shore hope: A desired military assignment.

Dispensary: Health care facility.

Coppers: Large copper cooking pots.

Court of Pacifica: A part of the San Francisco 1939 World Fair that looked into the future regarding architectural design and other aspects of life.

Bluejackets: Military servicemen.

Comity: Courtesy and respect between nations.

Signal study: The study of naval light and flag communication signs.

Fair: San Francisco World Fair in 1939 held on Treasure Island in San Francisco Bay.

Code: Using secret codes for communications.

Empty stores of the Japanese: Businesses left behind by Japanese Americans when evacuated to internment camps after the bombing of Pearl Harbor.

*stores of the Japanese. The same old scents of **musty sandalwood** and potent perfume still **waft** from ornate, lacquered doors. . . .*

But underneath the old familiar scenes there have been far-reaching changes. Traditions have gone overboard with the rise of a new wartime generation.

Some six thousand men have left their old jobs in Chinatown to go into shipyards. Being a race of craftsmen with small agile hands, they have taken to precision-tool work as ducks to water.

*As for the armed services, more than three thousand boys from Chinatown have either been called up or have enlisted, and about three-fourths of the **colony's doctors and dentists are on their way**. . . .*

*Before their **evacuation** the Japanese in the San Francisco area were found mainly in the big shipping lines, in banking, in the export-import business.*

They had nurseries, truck farms, goldfish and marine-plant aquariums. They were merchants, photographers, gardeners, house servants.

*They played an **extravagant** role in the business of shipping out an annual $16,000,000 worth of cut flowers.*

*But **they did not fish**! This is one of the strangest circumstances in their relations with the city, and nobody seems to know the answer.*

*The larger fishing craft down along the water front were owned by **Slavs**; the smaller ones by Italians. No Japanese owned fishing boats, and few, if any, were employed on them.*

Italians Loyal to U.S.A.

*International colonies have been part of San Francisco since the first **windjammers raked in** through the Golden Gate. It does not surprise a San Franciscan even now to turn his radio to an Italian program and hear men of an **enemy tongue** selling **bonds** for American defense.*

*Now that **alien restrictions** have been lifted, the Italian colony goes on its normal Italo-Americano way, hoping the war will end as soon as possible so it can get on with its fishing—and send money home to the "**poor ones who have been so misled**."*

The impassioned loyalty of many local Italian leaders to the war cause has made a good impression on the city. They have

Musty sandalwood: Incense.

Waft: Lightly carried in the air.

Colony's doctors and dentists are on their way: Asian American doctors sent overseas for military duty.

Evacuation: Forced removal of Japanese Americans from the West Coast.

Extravant: Beyond what was necessary.

They did not fish: Stereotypical perception of the Japanese as fishermen, since their homeland is an island and fishing is a traditionally important economy of Japan.

Slavs: Immigrants and their descendants from Eastern Europe, such as Poland, Czechoslovakia, and the Ukraine.

International colonies: Many distinct ethnic neighborhoods.

Windjammers: Sailing ships.

Raked in: Leaning in the ocean breeze while entering the bay.

Enemy tongue: Italy was part of the Axis fighting against the Allies.

Bonds: Reference to war bonds.

Alien restrictions:
Immediately after the bombing of Pearl Harbor, President Roosevelt signed an order classifying aliens in the United States from Germany, Italy, and Japan as enemy aliens with limits on their movement; the restrictions on the Italian and German aliens were soon lifted.

Poor ones who have been so misled: Italian citizens who supported Italian dictator Benito Mussolini as he led them into an alliance with Nazi Germany.

Unsparingly: Tirelessly.

Hospitality work: Providing comfort and support to servicemen before leaving or upon returning from overseas, or located on military bases distant from family.

City at play: Servicemen on leave and war industry workers away from their long shifts enjoyed recreating in the city.

Decentralization plan: Plan to move power or control from the federal government to regional or local communities.

Embarcadero: Landing places for boats along the bay shoreline.

Congress: Coming together.

Kodachroming: Taking colored photographs of.

Bronzed fisherfolk: Sun-weathered fishermen.

worked **unsparingly** that there would be no doubt as to the sympathies of their people.

War work, **hospitality work**, volunteer service work, and a wartime **city at play** have made changes in San Francisco's old way of life. Business is not going on as usual.

The Government in its **decentralization plan** has sent many important war boards and agencies to this area. Bring in 250,000 people as a resident war population, and watch the natives warm up for action. Tell the tourist to "See California AFTER the War!" and notice the transformation in a land which in one year absorbed $200,000,000 in transient trade.

The problem now is to keep everyone away from San Francisco who hasn't a direct connection with the war effort. Railroads plead with people not to waste space, not to expect the usual service, not to come at all unless they have to.

Change and no change. San Francisco is the same enchanting thing it ever was.

Physical changes tell mainly of military restrictions.

Panorama from Telegraph Hill

No more **Embarcadero** for the civilian; no more the disorganized **congress** of freight trains, trucks, vans, taxies whirling in confusion along the water front. No more **Kodachroming** red lobsters, pink shrimps, and **bronzed fisherfolk** along Fisherman's Wharf.

No pictures of bridges, buildings, skylines, communications, military movements, ships, supplies, natural resources.

No driving out through the Presidio along El Camino del Mar to the Palace of the Legion of Honor; you go by way of town now, perhaps past Sea Cliff with its beautiful homes boarded up or blacked-out, or frequently "For Sale." No sitting in a window at the Cliff House watching the moonlight play on huge waves breaking against Seal Rocks.

By Army proclamation everything visible from the sea has been totally blacked out and every bright light for 150 miles inland has been dimmed.

Street lights are painted black on the top and seaward sides. From San Francisco you can scarcely make out where the city of Berkeley lies across the Bay. Crescents of metal shield the orange **sodium-vapor lights** strung like amber beads above the bridges.

*Beach **concessions** look ghostly in their abandonment, and still worse, the huge Ferris wheel moves around silently without lights! At night barely a handful of cars, their lights dimmed to less than an eightieth of their normal strength, fumbles along that magnificent shore highway.*

*You will be chilled by the dimout gloom of Market Street, unless you join the spirited crowds and forget the past. In a city famous for its **luminous fog-banked brilliance**, the Army dimout has worked some **eerie** changes.*

A man sprays black paint on his car's headlights, making the car compliant with blackout restrictions. Only a small circle is left unpainted, so that the amount of light put out is dramatically reduced. © *Bettmann/Corbis. Reproduced by permission.*

Sodium-vapor lights: Electric lamps that contain sodium vapor used to light roadways.

Concessions: Small businesses catering to recreationists at the beach.

What happened next . . .

In 1945 San Francisco's population reached approximately 827,000, up from 634,000 in 1930. Also in 1945 delegates

Luminous fog-banked brilliance: City lights showing through the frequent San Francisco fog.

Eerie: Strange.

from fifty countries met in San Francisco for several months to establish the United Nations, an international organization that was set up to maintain peace among its member nations.

In 1945 and 1946 the Golden Gate welcomed home hundreds of thousands of sailors and soldiers who had served in battle zones in the Pacific.

Did you know . . .

- Industrial mogul Henry Kaiser (1882–1967) crisscrossed the country in search of workers for his Richmond shipyards. He found thousands of black American men and women in the South eager to go to Richmond. They were trained as welders, drillers, crane operators, and ship-fitters, and they were paid well in their new positions.

- Kaiser built a hospital to provide health care for his shipbuilders and their families. That hospital was the beginning of Kaiser Permanente Health Care, a giant company that still serves people throughout much of the nation.

- Many of the spots mentioned in the article, including the Presidio, Fort Point, and Cliff House (a restaurant), are still in operation in the twenty-first century.

Consider the following . . .

- List the types of jobs that Japanese Americans in San Francisco held before the United States entered World War II. Research what happened to Japanese Americans during the war years.

- Of all the sites mentioned in this excerpt, how many can you locate on a current map of the Bay Area?

For More Information

Books

Bailey, Ronald H. *The Home Front, U.S.A.* Alexandria, VA: Time-Life Books, 1977.

Lutz, Catherine. *Homefront: A Military City and the American Twentieth Century*. Boston: Beacon Press, 2001.

Warren, James R. *The War Years: A Chronicle of Washington State in World War II*. Seattle: University of Washington Press, 2000.

Periodicals

Bradley, La Verne. "San Francisco: Gibraltar of the West Coast." *National Geographic Magazine* (March 1943): pp. 279–308.

Harvey Klemmer

Excerpt from "Michigan Fights"
Written by Harvey Klemmer.
Published in *National Geographic Magazine*,
December 1944.

"Detroit is producing more munitions than any other city in the world. The rest of the State piles record output on record output. Tanks. Trucks. Planes. Ships. Guns. Ammunition. And, most important of all, engines."

After the Pearl Harbor attack in December 1941, U.S. war mobilization shifted into high gear. Industry's ability to retool assembly lines was the key to making a rapid changeover from mass production of civilian goods to mass production of war materials. Michigan's automobile industry had highly efficient assembly lines, which could be readily transformed into war industries. When the federal government banned production of civilian automobiles in early 1942 (to conserve metal and rubber for the manufacture of war materials), auto manufacturing plants were able to switch, by retooling (changing their machinery) and changing their production layout, to the production of aircraft, aircraft parts, military trucks, tanks, and marine equipment including amphibious landing craft called "DUKWs."

Some automobile manufacturers had to build larger facilities to accommodate their new, larger products. Henry Ford (1863–1947) of Ford Motor Company oversaw the construction of the giant Willow Run plant west of Detroit, Michigan. This massive facility produced B-24 bombers in classic Ford assembly line fashion. Thousands of small manufacturers supplemented the production of Ford, Chrysler, General Motors, and other auto manufacturing giants. Some worked from garages; others operated out of mere shacks, like the one Harvey Klemmer mentions in this excerpt, "Michigan Fights."

The federal government and private contractors built some housing near Willow Run to prevent over-crowding among the thousands of new workers who poured into the area. However, the housing supply could not keep up with demand, and many of the workers had to live in trailers or in rented rooms in private homes. Like other war industry centers across the nation, Michigan communities were bursting at the seams.

Equipment at a Ford automotive plant is retooled to stamp out metal parts for U.S. Army jeeps during World War II. *The Library of Congress.*

Things to remember while reading the excerpt from "Michigan Fights" . . .

- Approximately 13,500 new residents moved into Detroit each month in 1943 and 1944. The population of the greater metropolitan area increased by 600,000 during the war years.

- When the United States entered World War II, war production—and the need for war industry workers—dramatically increased. However, at the same time, thousands of Michigan men joined the military and shipped out for overseas battle zones. This left many factory jobs open for women and for black Americans who had not joined the armed services.

Excerpt from "Michigan Fights"

*A workman in one of Detroit's great automobile plants lowers a **battery** of drills onto a block of gleaming metal. The drills bite into the block with fierce precision, throwing off **rivulets** of white*

Battery: A grouping of drills designed to operate at the same time.

Rivulets: Small streams.

A 1942 poster announcing employment opportunities for farm and industrial laborers in Michigan. So many workers poured into the Detroit area in the early 1940s that the housing supply could not keep up with demand. *The Library of Congress.*

fluid and littering the floor with bits of tortured metal. Wisps of smoke, blue and bitter, rise from the deepening holes. The drills reach the end of their journey, pause, extract themselves.

The workman carefully inspects the holes. He smiles grimly, pushes back his cap with oil-stained hands.

"Hitler should have known better," he grins. "He made a great mistake in putting this war on wheels."

Yes, Hitler made a great mistake when he tried to conquer the world with machines. Michigan has helped see to that.

"Powerhouse of Victory"

One-eighth of the weapons now speeding the day of victory are the production of Michigan factories. These weapons have been pouring from the **forge** and the machine shop and the assembly line at the rate of millions of dollars worth a month.

Detroit is producing more munitions than any other city in the world. The rest of the State piles record output on record output. Tanks. Trucks. Planes. Ships. Guns. Ammunition. And, most important of all, engines.

"Boss" (Charles F.) Kettering, of General Motors, said at the beginning of the war: "**Horsepower** is war power." Detroit and Michigan have the horsepower. They probably have more of what it takes to keep planes flying, tanks rolling, and ships sailing than all of Hitler's **domain**. A war of movement is right down our alley.

General Brehon B. Somervell expressed it thus: "When Hitler hitched his wagon to an internal-combustion engine, he opened up a new front, commonly called Detroit."

The citizens of Detroit **concur**. They adopted a new slogan for their city. It is "Powerhouse of Victory."

It does not take long—in Michigan—to realize that you are on a real battle front. The industrial sections roar with machinery. The sky by day is dark with smoke and it glows by night with the reflections of countless **retorts**.

Waves of workers advance on the various plants, tend their machines, retreat to the sanctuary of home. This State and this city, which gave us the technique of **mass production**, mobilized that technique in irresistible force to crush our enemies.

The bulk of Michigan's war production is accounted for by the automobile industry. Automobile, truck, parts and accessory plants are now working on war orders. They have filled about 20 billion dollars in war orders since Pearl Harbor—more than 8-1/2 billions in 1943. The country's automotive industry entered 1944 with a **backlog** of nearly 14 billions.

About half the contracts were in aircraft, including helicopters and gliders, engines, and parts. The remainder consisted principally of military vehicles, tanks, ammunition, artillery, and marine equipment.

Forge: A machine from which melted metal is poured for producing a desired shape of object.

Horsepower: Powerful machines that energize factories.

Domain: Arsenal of weapons.

Concur: Agree.

Retorts: Chambers heating materials for manufacturing that give off glow from fires.

Mass production: The manufacture of goods in large quantities, made possible by assembly line processes.

Backlog: Orders for war materials waiting to be filled.

A former Oldsmobile automobile factory converts to machine gun manufacturing during World War II, Lansing, Michigan. *The Library of Congress.*

War production has been rolling off the assembly lines at the rate of a million dollars an hour. The same energy and materials applied to peacetime production would yield 16,500,000 cars and trucks a year—more than three times the record 1929 output of 5,358,000 units.

In Engines, Michigan shines

In engines, Michigan shines: here the automotive industry has really gone to town. Michigan motors have gone to war by the tens of thousands—in the air, on the land, and at sea. War is horsepower, and when it comes to horsepower the Detroit area can outproduce the entire **Axis world**. . . .

Michigan's other industries also have run full blast on war production.

The building of ships has been resumed. One of the most interesting operations is the building of destroyer escort vessels at Bay City. They are built up-side down and roll over in launching.

In the field of small powerboats, Michigan is **pre-eminent**. . . .

Axis world: Nations who fought against the Allies in World War II including Germany, Italy, and Japan.

Pre-eminent: Highly important in its production.

The factories of Michigan also turned out radios for the armed forces, steel, chemicals, armor plate, parachutes, pharmaceuticals, gun carriages, and plastics.

*Aircraft production, especially engines, is **prodigious**.*

*Detroit is today the leading **tool and die center** of the country.*

Some amazing conversions have been undertaken. Thus a company which normally turns out vacuum cleaners is today making gas masks; lumberjacks are producing gliders.

*Chrysler is making **gyrocompasses**; General Motors spark-plug division, machine guns; and its Buick Division, engines for the famed **Liberator bombers**.*

*Little plants have sprung up all over the State to supplement the work of established **concerns**. Garages, stores, even branch banks have been converted into factories.*

Driving along Lake St. Clair, I saw a shack with ship propellers piled outside. A little farther along, in a field, was a sign and an arrow pointing into a neighboring wood lot. The sign said: "Thermo-Plastics." Look sharply before you enter a store in Michigan. It may look like a butcher shop but when you get in you are likely to discover that it is a machine shop.

Encountering an old friend in the western part of the State, I asked him how he was getting on with his law practice.

"Not so good," he replied. "I'm making munitions."

He had rented an old garage, rounded up a few workers, and become a manufacturer of antiaircraft shells.

Another friend, also a lawyer, organized a small firm of toolmakers.

*Great Lakes shipping has, for the third season, won a desperate race with ice, fog, and time. Prodigious quantities of the materials required for victory have been moved—coal, grain, limestone, and crumbly red **hematite** from the famed Mesabi, Menominee, and other ranges of the Lake Superior region.*

*Ninety million tons of iron ore, one of the most vital materials of modern warfare, were scheduled for delivery to the **arsenals of democracy** this year.*

Day and night, for more than seven months, a fleet of some 300 vessels has shuttled over the 800-mile route between the

Prodigious: Enormous in quantity.

Tool and die center: Machines created to make products.

Gyrocompasses: Compasses equipped with a gyroscope; useful in flying.

Liberator bombers: B-24 four-engine bombers built by the thousands during World War II.

Concerns: Larger businesses already well established.

Hematite: Iron ore.

Arsenals of democracy: Reference to war industries using President Roosevelt's famous phrase.

B-24 bomber airplanes are lined up inside the production area of Henry Ford's Willow Run manufacturing plant.
© Bettmann/Corbis. Reproduced by permission.

upper and the lower Lakes. It is one of the transportation miracles of the world. The vessels load in two or three hours, **discharge** in six or eight. . . .

The great **locks** at **Sault Ste. Marie** have throbbed with activity. The **Soo Canal system**, even before the war, was by far the busiest waterway on earth, in some years passing more tonnage than the Suez and Panama Canals combined. For the past three years, it has been one of the most vital life lines of the war. Eighty-five percent of the iron ore required by American industry must pass through this channel. It is no wonder that Sault Ste. Marie has become one of the most closely guarded spots in the United States. . . .

A Bomber an Hour at Willow Run

A major war enterprise is the fabulous bomber plant **built for Henry Ford** by the Government at Willow Run. It is no secret that at Willow Run they can turn out a bomber every working hour if military needs require it.

I used to visit friends on a farm which once occupied this site. It gave me a queer feeling to go back. Willow Run just staggers the imagination. There is no other way to put it. Everything about the place is "supercolossal."

It is so big that workers must be careful to enter the right gate or they may have to walk for half an hour to reach their spot in the assembly line. The buildings seem to go over the horizon and out of sight. Highways complete with **cloverleaves and grade separations**, cluster about the gates like **skeins** of tangled yarn.

Willow Run is a **bone of contention** for the surrounding countryside. Building such a factory in an area where there was neither housing nor transportation was bound to result in plenty of headaches.

Housing in Willow Run, as elsewhere in wartime Michigan, is the principal difficulty. Neighboring communities, especially Ypsilanti, have been crowded to the point of explosion. Housing developments were put in by the Federal Government, including dormitories for single workers. Still there were not enough accommodations to go around.

Workers commute from as far away as Adrian, a distance of 43 miles. Many come 40 miles from the east, including 20 miles through Detroit traffic. Trailer camps dot the fields for miles around. People live in anything with a roof on it—barns, garages, stores. One family found refuge in a chicken coop.

Private contractors have attempted to take up some of the slack. There is a new sub-division near Dearborn with an enormous sign on the highway:

"Houses! $100 down. No **red tape**. Move in."

Discharge: Unload.

Locks: Enclosed canals with gates on both ends built to raise and lower ships passing from one water level to another.

Sault Ste. Marie: A town in Ontario, Canada, near Lake Superior on the Saint Mary's River.

Soo Canal system: A Canadian canal system connecting Lake Superior and Lake Huron for ship passage.

Built for Henry Ford: One of many plants built for war industries by the government as part of industrial mobilization at the beginning of the war.

Cloverleaves and grade separations: Modern-day freeway designs with circling interchanges and divided lanes.

Skeins: Loose coils.

Bone of contention: Controversial topic.

Red tape: Excessive administrative paperwork.

The doubling and quadrupling of populations has naturally created problems in near-by communities. Hospitals are inadequate; nor are there enough doctors and dentists.

The people have pitched in, however, and somehow or another have managed to get along. The bombers are rolling—that is the important thing. . . .

Women's Part in Michigan Industry

*Women have always played an important part in Michigan industry. They are doing even more in the war. Consider Eleanor Hardy, mother of 14, who went to work in a Detroit war plant. Mrs. Hardy's mother-in-law looks after the children. Mrs. Hardy spends ten hours a day, six days a week at a **lathe.***

Wages have been good. Weekly factory earnings have averaged around $62 in the Detroit area, $56 for the State as a whole. . . .

The war towns are definitely getting shabby. The streets are not kept up, rubbish lies loose in the alleys, and the buildings grow grimier by the day. People are philosophical about it all. There is a job to be done: our men need weapons: we can't worry about a little dirt in the streets.

*The air in the war centers definitely is that of a boom town. Night clubs are crowded; money flows freely; the streets are **thronged** with shoppers. Because they work around the clock in these towns, a curious kind of night life has evolved.*

Workers who finish at, say, 3 a.m. go out for a few hours of recreation before turning in. Detroit city ordinances have been amended to permit bowling alleys to stay open.

*Young women war workers are now permitted, by ordinance amendment, to attend all-night movies. Going to work in the morning, you see **queues** before places of amusement.*

Two Billion Telephone Calls

*The **indices** of city life continue to climb. The Michigan Bell Telephone Company reports that calls hit the two-billion mark in 1943. Mail, power consumption, spending, saving, and wages have risen to all-time peaks. Detroit's population has been increasing at the rate of 13,500 persons a month for the past two years. The population of the **city proper** is now 1,650,000; of the metropolitan area, 2,455,000, an increase of 600,000 over the prewar figure.*

Lathe: A machine in which the piece being worked on is rotated while a fixed tool shapes it.

Thronged: Crowded.

Queues: Lines of people

Indices: Various numbers that serve as a measure or indicator of change (in prices or traffic volume, for example).

City proper: Heart of the city, not including suburbs and surrounding rural areas.

Idle: Neglectful.

Creeds: Different sets of values and beliefs.

A preponderance of men: The presence of considerably more men than women.

No one knows where it will all end. The important thing now is to win the war; later on we will worry about conveniences and comforts. . . .

*It would be **idle** to deny that the war has brought serious problems to the people of Michigan. The influx of several hundred thousand people representing many **creeds**, and shades of political opinion, has set up stresses and strains which many regard as dangerous. Students of the situation believe that Detroit and Michigan will solve their problems, but they do not dodge the fact that these problems are serious.*

*The principal difficulty, of course, is over-crowding. Other problems are lack of recreation, **a preponderance of men** in the population, and the drift of young people **away from the land**.*

*Finally, the mass-production technique, with its **monotonous** repetition of a single motion, contains certain dangers. In peacetime the monotony of the assembly line is balanced by shorter hours. Today, overtime work has removed the safety valve of leisure.*

Factory workers leaving the Dodge truck plant in Detroit, Michigan, after an eight-hour shift, circa early 1940s. Shifts let out at all times of the day and night, forcing local shops and recreation facilities to stay open almost twenty-four hours a day. *The Library of Congress.*

Away from the land: Part of the general U.S. population shift from rural farming communities to industrial cities.

Monotonous: At the same level or intensity.

*Notwithstanding the abnormal conditions of wartime life, the authorities say there has been no serious deterioration of morals in Michigan. The boom towns are not "wide open." **Organized vice** has been kept well under control.*

Health conditions generally have been good despite war conditions. The year 1943 set a new record in the number of babies born, the highest since 1915.

However, authorities now are concerned over a shortage of hospital beds. A probate judge in Detroit, after investigating conditions at the Receiving Hospital, said the load was so great that patients had to be "piled in like cordwood."

Problem of "Latchkey Children"

The authorities are worried about juvenile delinquency. Working mothers are blamed, and the Governor has asked plants to refrain from hiring mothers with young children. Schoolteachers characterize the children from homes where the mother has gone into a war plant as "latchkey children." They carry house keys around their necks. . . .

*One social worker with whom I talked **decried** the discussion which has gone on about juvenile delinquency. She declared that in her opinion the problem is greatly misunderstood, that delinquency has not been increased to any marked extent by the war, and that the public is just more conscious of it than in peacetime.*

Meanwhile, the State and city governments and private agencies are doing everything they can to give young people an opportunity to grow up in a healthful environment.

*Constructive measures which have been undertaken include the establishment of **canteens** in schools, the opening up of school gymnasiums and swimming pools, and the encouragement of clubs and recreation centers throughout the State. . . .*

Social services, both public and private, have been stepped up to cope with wartime conditions. Special emphasis has been placed on the maintenance of nursery schools for the children of working mothers. . . .

Education has suffered in wartime Michigan. There is an acute shortage of teachers: the colleges and universities have been devoting themselves largely to the training of men for the armed

Organized vice: Moral crimes such as prostitution.

Decried: Expressed strong disapproval.

Canteens: Centers for recreation and snacks.

Social services: Assistance for disabled, poor, and aged.

Drill ground: An area where military trainees are taught discipline.

American Home Front in World War II: Primary Sources

services. The campus at the University of Michigan looks like a **drill ground.**

What happened next . . .

At the end of the war in September 1945, Detroit's automobile industry ceased its production of tanks, aircraft, and other military equipment. It quickly reverted back to production of automobiles. Wartime production had brought full employment and hence prosperity to Michigan. The financial hardships endured during the Great Depression (1929–41) were gone for good. During the war years wages were high, but few consumer goods were available for purchase. At the end of the war Americans were eager to spend their savings on Detroit's new cars and many other consumer goods produced in Michigan. As a result the state's economy continued to prosper through the rest of the 1940s.

Did you know . . .

- Detroit and surrounding war industry towns operated around the clock. Lines formed outside movie houses at the end of shifts, even at odd times such as 8 A.M.

- Before the war, people living in the Detroit area drove their own cars to get to work. This lifestyle pattern changed with gasoline rationing (limits placed on fuel, and also on rubber, which was used in car tires). Suddenly public transportation, such as buses and streetcars, were overwhelmed with daily riders.

- The black American population in Detroit grew from 150,000 in 1940 to 200,000 in 1944. Overcrowded housing, job discrimination, and lack of recreational activities contributed to race riots in June 1943.

- Many people who had never before been outside the rural surroundings of Kentucky and Tennessee migrated north for Michigan's war industry jobs. At the war's end, a good number of them returned home—with more money and a greatly expanded view of the world.

- Throughout the United States college men left school for the military, but the universities soon filled back up with soldiers attending training programs. As the author of this excerpt notes, the University of Michigan looked like a military "drill ground."

Consider the following . . .

- By the late 1930s Adolf Hitler (1889–1945), the leader of Nazi Germany, had developed a military that possessed advanced technological equipment such as tanks and warplanes; the German army was better equipped than any other army in the world. Why did the Michigan workman say that it was "a great mistake" for Hitler to put the war "on wheels"?

- According to the author of this excerpt, what did local governments and private agencies do to alleviate the problem of "latchkey children"? Since the end of World War II, "latchkey children" have become the norm in American society. Does your community have facilities and programs for children of working parents? Are they similar to the ones mentioned in this excerpt?

For More Information

Books

Capeci, Dominic J., and Edward Jeffries, eds. *Detroit and the "Good War": The World War II Letters of Mayor Edward Jeffries and Friends.* Lexington: University Press of Kentucky, 1996.

Rubenstein, Bruce A., and Lawrence E. Ziewacz. *Michigan: A History of the Great Lakes State.* 3rd ed. Wheeling, IL: Harlan Davidson, 2002.

Periodicals

Atwood, Albert W. "The Miracle of War Production." *National Geographic Magazine* (December 1942): pp. 693–715.

Klemmer, Harvey. "Michigan Fights." *National Geographic Magazine* (December 1944): pp. 676–715.

House and Garden

Excerpt from "Houses for Defense"
Published in *House and Garden*,
February 1942.

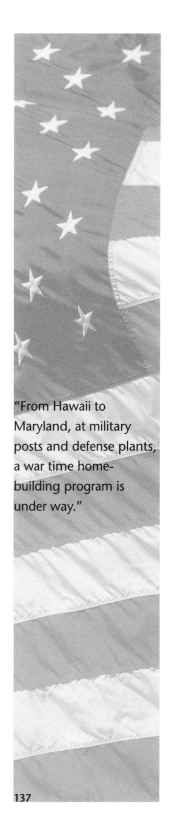

"From Hawaii to Maryland, at military posts and defense plants, a war time home-building program is under way."

As war industry regions and military hubs experienced an ever increasing influx of workers and military personnel, the housing shortage became acute. Recognizing that the problem could become even more severe as the war continued, the House Public Buildings and Grounds Committee, a group in the U.S. House of Representatives, discussed housing needs. Under the leadership of Fritz G. Lanham (1880–1965), the group introduced a potential solution, which became known as the Lanham Act when it was passed by Congress in October 1940. The act appropriated $750 million to the Federal Works Agency for the construction of large housing projects in crowded war industry centers, also referred to as "defense" centers. Created exclusively for war industry workers and military families, these housing projects were called "defense housing." The federal government built approximately 625,000 defense housing units between 1940 and 1944.

Although many of the units were styled like dormitories, builders also constructed whole subdivisions of one- and two-bedroom single-family and duplex-style homes. Linda Vista, in San Diego, California, began as this type of subdivision. The original plan for Linda Vista called for the construction of

A construction crew raises the framework for houses at a defense housing project called Franklin Terrace in Erie, Pennsylvania, July 1941. *© Corbis. Reproduced by permission.*

three thousand houses for Consolidated Aircraft Company employees. Construction began in early 1941, and the entire subdivision was scheduled to be completed in three hundred days. The first homes opened on March 6, and ultimately the number of new homes exceeded the initial goal of three thousand. By April 1943, 4,416 families—about 16,245 people—lived at Linda Vista. It had a daycare center, a high school, a Safeway grocery store, and a department store.

Atchison Village in Richmond, California, also came into existence as a defense housing project. Construction was managed by Richmond Housing Authority, the first housing authority to manage a project under the Lanham Act. Housing authorities are public agencies concerned with seeing that sufficient housing in adequate condition is available to local population. Atchison provided housing for people who worked at the massive Kaiser shipyards in Richmond. Eventually twenty-one thousand units were built. Most were torn down after the war, but the original Atchison Village survived.

Broad Creek Village, another well-known defense housing project, was built on 507 acres along the present Virginia Beach Boulevard in Norfolk County, Virginia. It was designed for military families. The village had an elementary school, a police and fire station, a shopping center, and recreation areas.

Other housing projects mentioned in this excerpt include Indian Head, Maryland, built for naval powder (producing gun powder under contract with the U.S. Navy) factory workers; units in Baltimore, Maryland, created for employees of the Glenn L. Martin Company, which built bombers; and units in Forest Glen, Maryland, constructed to house employees of the Army Medical Center in Forest Glen.

Things to remember while reading the excerpt from "Houses for Defense" . . .

- Government-funded defense housing projects were built rapidly out of economical materials.

- The government favored prefabricated, demountable housing. A prefabricated house is built in sections and assembled in a factory; then it is demounted (disassembled), transported to a housing development, and put back together on-site. The government hoped that at war's end many units could be disassembled again and moved to areas in need of low-cost housing.

- Population shifts to war industry centers and military hubs involved about 25 percent of the U.S. population. People who moved in order to take war-related jobs needed housing in their new locations.

Excerpt from "Houses for Defense"

From Hawaii to Maryland, at military posts and defense plants, a war time home-building program is under way.

*Our enormously expanded defense industries have brought to the **fore** the need for hundreds of thousands of new small homes*

Fore: Forefront of attention.

ABOVE, INDIAN HEAD, MARYLAND, ON THE BANKS OF THE POTOMAC. BELOW, FIVE OF THE PREFABRICATED UNITS

Aerial shot of prefabricated houses at Indian Head, Maryland. Also included are five up-close examples of prefabricated homes.
House & Garden.

to provide modern, comfortable accommodations for defense workers and their families. The tremendous defense housing program has been energetically sponsored by the Government and the results are already miraculous. Of special interest to HOUSE & GARDEN *are the new ideas in planning and in the technique of construction which, applied to these little homes today, may well be instrumental in bringing about vast improvements in homes of every size after the war.*

STEPS IN THE ASSEMBLING OF THIS HOUSE ARE SHOWN ON THE COVER

EACH HOUSE RESTS ON CONCRETE PIERS JOINED BY PRECAST CONCRETE RAILS

WALLBOARD PANELS ARE NAILED QUICKLY TO THE WOOD FRAME

*The following . . . pages are devoted to a variety of new techniques and designs, some of which are already in service in military establishments or near defense plants, while others are now in process of construction. The **air view** is Indian Head, Maryland, where the Public Buildings Administration [PBA] has been active in building homes for married workers employed by the Naval powder factories at Indian Head. All of the units used are prefabricated*

Prefabricated house circa World War II. Shows the foundation of the home and walls being added to the frame of the home. *House & Garden.*

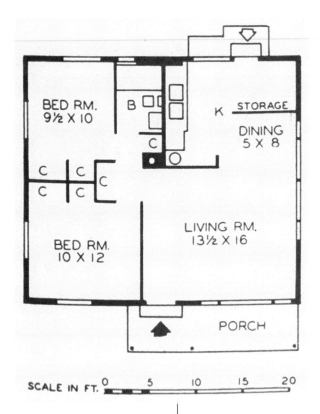

BED RM.
9½ X 10

B

K STORAGE

DINING
5 X 8

C C
C

C

C C

LIVING RM.
13½ X 16

BED RM.
10 X 12

PORCH

SCALE IN FT. 0   5   10   15   20

Floor plan of a typical prefabricated home built during the World War II era. *House & Garden.*

Air view: Photograph taken from an airplane or blimp.

Specifications: Detailed design requirements.

Demountability: Capability for easy disassembly.

On the site: At the factory.

Provision: A certain capability made beforehand.

houses and the **specifications** call for **demountability** as one of the major requirements.

Each unit has had to be erected **on the site**, then demounted, loaded into a truck, taken thirty or forty miles over rough roads, then re-erected at the residential site. By encouraging the design of prefabricated demountables, PBA hopes to be able to redistribute these houses as needed during and after the war.

PREFABRICATION ALONE could produce the demountable house. The object of prefabrication, generally, is to manufacture a house entirely within the walls of a factory, ship it out to the site in prebuilt sections. These sections are quickly joined together at the site and **provision** can be made so that they may be demounted with a minimum of waste. When a house of conventional construction is torn down the operation is necessarily accompanied by an unavoidable waste of valuable materials and equipment.

Homes for the men who make Martin bombers

STEPS IN THE ASSEMBLING OF THIS HOUSE

EACH HOUSE RESTS ON CONCRETE PIERS JOINED BY PRECAST CONCRETE RAILS

WALLBOARD PANELS ARE NAILED QUICKLY TO THE WOOD FRAME

5 men erect this house in less than 1 day's time

All-out production meant more than a new plant for the Glenn L. Martin Co. at Baltimore, Md. It meant providing comfortable, low-cost homes for some 30,000 new workers, their wives and families. A housing shortage already threatened; the need for the new houses was urgent.

Small homes designed by the U.S. government

This two-bedroom house is cheap and quickly built

Small homes designed by the U. S. government

This two-bedroom house is cheap and quickly built

The house illustrated here is one of 70 erected at the Army Medical Center in Forest Glen, Md., for the employees and their families. The Public Buildings Administration is erecting houses of similar plan in several areas throughout the country where this agency is given the job of providing new homes to accommodate an influx of workers on major defense projects

A pair of single-bedroom houses set back to back

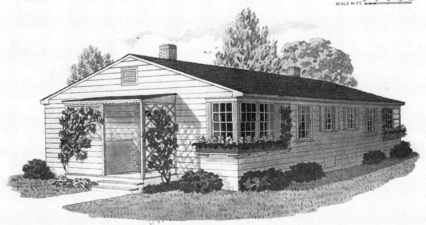

This type of house is intended for defense workers without children. Outstanding in all these PBA houses are the large windows and well-shaped living-dining rooms, also the compact kitchens, fully equipped except for refrigerators. Heating is by a coal-fired hot air furnace. After the war these houses are planned for possible use as low-rent homes for factory workers

Prefabricated two-bedroom home (top) and one-bedroom home (bottom) erected at the Army Medical Center in Forest Glen, Maryland. Both were built by the Public Building Administration for defense workers and their families. *House & Garden.*

The house illustrated here is one of 70 erected at the Army Medical Center in Forest Glen, Md., for the employees and their families. The Public Buildings Administration is erecting houses of similar plan in several areas throughout the country where this agency is given the job of providing new homes to accommodate an influx of workers on major defense projects.

A pair of single-bedroom houses set back to back

This type of house is intended for defense workers without children. Outstanding in all these PBA houses are the large windows and well-shaped living-dining rooms, also the compact kitchens, fully equipped except for refrigerators. Heating is by a coal-fired hot air furnace. After the war these houses are planned for possible use as low-rent homes for factory workers.

What happened next . . .

After the war most of the defense housing units were destroyed rather than moved. However, a significant number continued to provide housing for decades. Broad Creek Village in Norfolk, Virginia, was scheduled to be moved elsewhere within six months of the war's end. Nevertheless, most of its twenty-six hundred units remained in place and in use until 1957–58, when they were either demolished or demounted to make way for an industrial park. Linda Vista is part of the core of San Diego at the beginning of the twenty-first century. In 2002 the Atchison Village board of directors nominated the Richmond, California, subdivision for listing on the National Register of Historic Places. The register accepts districts, sites, and buildings of importance to American history and culture; the U.S. National Park Service administered it. Atchison Village is already part of the Rosie the Riveter/World War II Home Front National Historical Park.

Did you know . . .

- Public housing—that is, housing built or directly financed by government programs—first appeared in the United States in the 1930s. Public housing projects provided employment during the Great Depression (1929–41) and improved neighborhoods by replacing slums.

- During World War II (1939–45), public housing became known as "defense housing" because the government focused on constructing residential units for war industry workers and military personnel.

- President Bill Clinton (1946– ; served 1993–2001) signed the Rosie the Riveter/World War II Home Front National Historical Park Establishment Act in October 2000. The historic park is located in Richmond, California, site of one of the major shipbuilding yards during World War II. The park is a series of several parks and monuments linked by trails.

Consider the following . . .

- Working cooperatively with several other students, contact a local government housing authority and ask if a wartime housing project was built in your community. If there was such a project, what happened to it?

- Contact a large local housing construction company and ask how prefabrication is used in construction in the twenty-first century.

For More Information

Books

Polenberg, Richard. *America at War: The Home Front, 1941–1945*. Englewood Cliffs, NJ: Prentice-Hall, 1968.

Spinney, Robert G. *World War II in Nashville: Transformation of the Homefront*. Knoxville: University of Tennessee Press, 1998.

Periodicals

"Houses for Defense." *House and Garden* (February 1942): 25, 26, 31, 32.

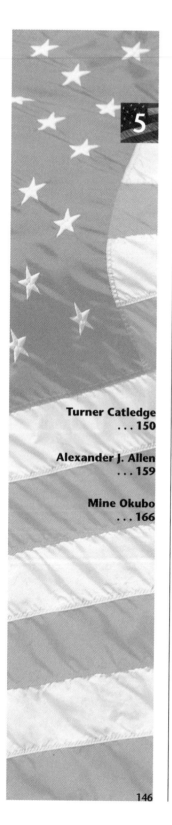

5 Black American and Japanese American Experiences on the Home Front

At the beginning of the twenty-first century, Americans who had lived through the experience of World War II (1939–45) still recalled the overwhelming unity and patriotism exhibited on the home front. After the Japanese attacked the U.S. military base at Pearl Harbor, almost all Americans fully supported the fight against the Axis powers of Germany, Italy, and Japan. Yet for some, this home front spirit was flawed with contradictions, even hypocrisy: The United States joined the war to protect freedom and democracy overseas, but freedoms on the home front were severely limited for people of color. Black Americans, who made up 10 percent of the U.S. population, faced strong racial prejudice and discrimination in almost every part of daily life. This discrimination had been present in the United States for eighty years, since the end of slavery. Japanese Americans lost nearly all their civil rights and freedoms after the Pearl Harbor attack. On February 19, 1942, President Franklin D. Roosevelt (1882–1945; served 1933–45) signed Executive Order 9066, which ordered all Japanese Americans to be removed from their homes and sent to ten internment camps for the duration of the war. Internment camps were a series of ten guarded camps, located mostly in the Western United States, where a total of 112,000 Japanese Americans and Japanese aliens were detained through the war for fear of sabotage or espionage.

Black Americans found no less discrimination in the U.S. military than in American society in general. When the United States entered the war in December 1941, tens of thousands of blacks were eager to join the military. Those who enlisted found themselves assigned only to home front units. They built barracks and other military base buildings, loaded and unloaded supplies, and maintained equipment. Blacks were denied officer status. At the beginning of the war, the Army Air Forces and the marines excluded blacks entirely, and in the navy, blacks served only as waiters. Nevertheless, black representation in the armed services grew from 98,000 in November 1941 to 468,000 in December 1942. Under political pressure on the home front, the army formed several all-black combat units and promoted blacks into officer roles. The navy broadened its recruitment of blacks and Marine Corps opened recruitment to blacks. Ultimately about one million blacks served in the military during the war. In spring 1943 there were 504,000 U.S. troops overseas, and 79,000 of them were black. Black American soldiers returned to the home front with a widened perspective of the world and with great expectations for a better future after developing their technical skills in the military.

On the home front, black American civilians fought for new opportunities and an end to racial discrimination, especially in the workplace. U.S. industry had begun mobilizing for the war effort in 1940. Industries that normally produced civilian goods started retooling to manufacture war materials such as guns, tanks, aircraft, ships, and countless small items that were used to build the larger items. At that time most black men held unskilled labor positions, and black women were domestic workers, predominantly maids. Family income among black Americans was very low compared to the family income of most whites. Although the war industries needed new workers for expanding production, they rarely hired blacks. When employers did hire blacks, they offered them only unskilled positions, such as janitors or garage attendants. In 1940 the U.S. aircraft industry employed over

100,000 workers, but only 240 were black. Many companies had an official "whites only" hiring policy. This open discrimination led President Roosevelt to issue Executive Order 8802 in June 1941. The order banned racial discrimination in war industries that received government contracts and in the federal government. Companies that failed to comply with this order risked the loss of very profitable government contracts for war materials.

In 1942, after the attack on Pearl Harbor pushed U.S. industries into full war mobilization, black employment slowly began to increase. However, blacks still faced discrimination in the workplace. When they applied for jobs, they would be told to go to the "door for blacks," and they were always hired into the lowest-paying jobs. To combat such discrimination and break down employment barriers, black Americans began the Double V campaign. "Double V" stood for military victory overseas and victory over racial discrimination on the home front.

By early 1943 employers faced an acute shortage of workers because so many men were leaving their jobs to join the military. War industries desperately needed replacement workers, and this situation gave black Americans employment opportunities they had never had before. Hundreds of thousands relocated to urban war industry centers, where housing was in short supply. Because of segregated housing policies in many cities, in which blacks and whites could not live in the same neighborhoods, blacks frequently ended up crowding together in the few areas open to them. Frustrated by the overcrowded housing in black neighborhoods and the more limited job opportunities for blacks than whites, racial tensions ran high by the summer of 1943.

The first excerpt is "Behind Our Menacing Race Problem," an article written by Turner Catledge and published in the August 8, 1943, issue of the *New York Times Magazine*. The article appeared a few days after race riots erupted in Harlem, a black ghetto (a densely populated slum inhabited by a minority group) in New York City, and two months after similar riots in Detroit, Michigan, a major war industry center. Catledge explores the complex issues involved in the "race problem." The second excerpt, "Alexander J. Allen," comes from *The Homefront: America during World War II* (1984), a book edited by Mark J. Harris, Franklin D. Mitchell, and Steven J. Schechter. Alexander Allen was the director of the Baltimore chapter of the National Urban League. In this excerpt he describes his struggles to persuade employers to hire black workers. Allen also recalls how blacks were keenly aware of the inconsistency of U.S. war goals. The United States fought to defend freedoms and democracy abroad but tolerated rampant racial discrimination on the home front.

The third excerpt comes from *Citizen 13660* (1946), a book written and illustrated by Mine Okubo. Okubo tells the fascinating story of a young Japanese woman's internment, first at Tanforan Assembly Center near San Francisco and then at Topaz in central Utah. Okubo describes daily life at the Topaz camp and shows how residents there managed to build a community and maintain some normalcy in their lives during their confinement.

Turner Catledge

Excerpt from "Behind Our Menacing Race Problem"
Written by Turner Catledge.
Published in the *New York Times Magazine*,
August 8, 1943.

"Whatever description may eventually be affixed to the riots that flared in Harlem . . . they did one thing for certain. They helped further to uncover one of the most embarrassing and most dangerous conditions in the United States today."

In 1942 and early 1943 U.S. industries moved into full war mobilization, and the unemployment rate dropped almost to zero. Anyone who wanted to work could find some sort of employment. Millions of men had left the labor force to join the military, so job opportunities opened up for black men and women that had not existed before the war. Approximately seven hundred thousand blacks relocated to large industrial centers during the war, hoping to find high-paying positions in the war industries. They journeyed to the large cities on the east coast and west coast and in the upper Midwest. These urban centers did not have enough housing for the newly arrived workers; they also lacked adequate outlets for recreation. Blacks generally had to live in severely overcrowded inner-city areas called ghettos. Owners of surrounding property blocked them from moving out of the ghettos to better housing by not selling to black buyers. On the job, many blacks still experienced prejudice and discrimination.

Racial tensions exploded in several U.S. cities during the hot, humid midsummer days of 1943. The worst racial incident occurred in Detroit, Michigan. On the evening of

June 20, during a heat wave, many blacks congregated at the only park open to them, Belle Isle. A rumor began to circulate that whites had mistreated a black woman and her baby. The rumor sparked a violent reaction and, after dark, groups of blacks moved through the city looting and fighting, retaliating for the rumored violence against the black woman. By the time order was restored, thirty-four people had died, including twenty-five blacks, and more than seven hundred people had been injured. Two months later a riot erupted in New York City's Harlem district. Looting and destruction of property left six people dead and three hundred injured.

The *New York Times Magazine* published Turner Catledge's article, "Behind Our Menacing Race Problem," a few days after the Harlem riot. In the article Catledge explores in depth the problem of race in America. He points out that those who look for simple explanations and answers will come up short. The causes, he explains, lie embedded in several centuries of history. Catledge says that the tensions that caused the rioting

125th Street in Harlem is full of mannequin parts and debris after stores were looted and display windows were smashed in a riot on August 2, 1943, which started after a clash between a white policeman and a black military policeman.
© Bettmann/Corbis.
Reproduced by permission.

stemmed from the civilian population shift, overcrowding, and job discrimination. Although jobs were available, promotions or advancements for blacks rarely occurred. At the end of his article Catledge acknowledges that both whites and blacks need to drop the prejudices and embrace a more cooperative relationship.

Things to remember while reading the excerpt from "Behind Our Menacing Race Problem" . . .

- Black American soldiers risked their lives to fight for freedom and democracy overseas, and they resented that their own country denied them basic freedoms and civil rights.

- During the war years, black Americans on the home front worked hard to achieve equal rights. Thanks to the wartime economy, they attained better jobs and better pay, but for the most part, white Americans resisted the push for racial equality.

Excerpt of "Behind Our Menacing Race Problem"

In the dissensions between whites and Negroes lie deep-rooted forces that grow in complexity.

*Whatever description may eventually be affixed to the riots that flared in Harlem last Sunday and Monday, they did one thing for certain. They helped further to uncover one of the most embarrassing and most dangerous conditions in the United States today. It is the situation, growing tenser by the week, between the Negro and white races. In spots throughout the country, particularly in the acutely crowded industrial centers in Northern and border States, we are witnessing new symptoms of an old sore which has been festering and breaking forth **intermittently** for **four-score years**. In all that time we have alternately tried to ignore the basic situation altogether or have treated it in a way that was bound to make it worse.*

*In the South we looked to the **strong arm**, to **Jim Crow** and to **physical fear**. In the North we turned to the politicians, to*

Dissensions: Strong disagreements.

Intermittently: Not continuously but from time to time.

Four-score years: Eighty years.

Strong arm: Law enforcement or private individuals using undue force.

Jim Crow: Jim Crow laws enforced racial segregation, the practice of keeping races separated in every aspect of life; such laws required, for example, separate schools, separate restrooms, and separate water fountains for whites and blacks.

Physical fear: Intimidation from American terrorist groups such as the Ku Klux Klan.

Hollow and unrealistic: Meaningless and not practical.

Oversimplification: Simplifying a complex matter so much that any real understanding is lost.

Ramified: Branched and intertwined.

Mores: Moral attitudes.

Blind alley: A mistaken direction.

Lay: Blame.

A mob of white men overturn a car belonging to an African American; the incident was part of race-related riots that took place in June 1943 in Detroit, Michigan.
© Bettmann/Corbis. Reproduced by permission.

Government action . . . In the one case the methods were cruel and inadequate. In the other they proved **hollow and unrealistic**.

This is no time, in the midst of a war, to make a turn around in these methods, even assuming it could be done. There is too much involved to make that possible within the twinkling of an eye. Public authority, therefore, is pushed up against the last resort in such cases, discipline.

The race problem in the United States tempts one ever to **oversimplification**, as this correspondent has learned during an investigation made recently in several cities with large Negro communities. Yet the problem is so **ramified** and runs so deep into the **mores** of the people as to lead one who attempts simplification into one **blind alley** after another. In the recent riots in Detroit, for instance, people were able to **lay** the whole tragedy to almost anything. Those who wanted to find **fifth column or Ku Klux Klan** activities—some observers went there with instructions to find such activities—had no great trouble in finding sufficient ground for so simple a conclusion.

Fifth column or Ku Klux Klan: Home front terrorist groups. Fifth Column was associated with foreign enemy support and the Ku Klux Klan promoted extreme racial prejudice.

*Those who wanted to blame the police did so largely with a lot to justify their conclusions. If you want to **charge it off to** bad housing and recreation, or to selfishness or industrialists, or the influx of new Negro and white workers from the South, or to criminals and hoodlums, as **Mayor La Guardia** charged off the disturbances in New York, you could take any of these simple **outs**. You could even blame it on the weather, for the spark that set off the explosion in Detroit was a fight that probably would never have happened had not the night of June 20 been hot and **sultry** and tens of thousands of people had gone to Belle Isle Park to get a breath of fresh air and got in each other's way.*

The truth is that each and every one of the factors suggested . . . was involved in some degree in the disturbance in Detroit. They are present in virtually every other industrial community of the North where the race problem has reared its menacing head.

In the South, where most of the Negro population still lives and where the division between the races is more evenly balanced numerically, the race problem has apparently not become as acute as a general rule as in the North. This is due to differences in social organization in the two sections as related to the races, and to the corollary fact that, even in this time of war, the South has retained its essentially rural characteristics. Many of the conditions which have bred new tensions or intensified old ones have not spread as yet throughout the South, with notable exceptions here and there.

*But there are **attributes** to the problem which are common North and South and virtually in every location in either section where there are large numbers of Negroes (the presence of the two races together makes the problem). . . .*

Behind all the immediate trouble . . . is an impatient, irresistible drive of the Negroes on the one hand for a fuller realization of the equality which has long been promised to them, but just as long denied. And on the other hand, a stubborn, deepening, and in some places broadening, resistance of the whites to that very aim.

"It's the old story of the irresistible force meeting the immovable object," was the way Wilbur LaRoe Jr., chairman of the new Inter-Racial Committee of the District of Columbia, put it. "Unless there is a relaxation somewhere along the line, there is bound to be trouble."

Nearly every other major factor connected with the question is a cause or an effect of this basic condition. First among more

Charge it off to: Blame it on.

Mayor La Guardia: New York City mayor Fiorello La Guardia.

Outs: Explanations or excuses.

Sultry: Humid.

Attributes: Various aspects.

American Home Front in World War II: Primary Sources

specific causes of tension is the matter of housing. It is indeed unfortunate that this simple word has been **bandied about** so much in the fight over social reforms that many people shy from it. But it becomes a stark reality in the race question when it is realized that in a city like Baltimore, for instance, Negroes are crowded into ghettos on an average of ten to the house, or 58,000 to the square mile; that in Baltimore and Chicago and Detroit they live almost altogether in the **white man's leavings**, in communities **rung so completely around by landlord covenants** that they are held virtual prisoners in these particular areas.

The crowding has been made more acute by the **influx** of new workers, both Negroes and whites, into the war factory areas. In Detroit the Negro population has increased more than 50 percent in five years. In Baltimore the Negro population, already around 200,000 out of roughly 1,000,000, is mounting at the rate of 2,000 per month.

Along with the new Negroes come new whites in many places. For the most part the whites have come from sections which **seethed** with anti-Negro prejudice. . . .

Negro soldiers are growing resentful, as they have shown in many places, when they are told that they are fighting for an empty world so long as "democracy" is being denied to their folks back home, and being denied even to him under the Army's and Navy's policy of segregation.

Just as housing has proved inadequate, so have the most ordinary recreational facilities. Detroit has only two major parks, only one near enough to the Negro ghetto to be of any use to its inhabitants and it is a constant **bone of contention** between Negroes and whites. In Baltimore there are said to be only four public tennis courts in which Negroes can play, only one pool in which they can swim.

Crime also has grown under such limitation. . . .

Police in Detroit, St. Louis, Indianapolis, Columbus, Pittsburgh and nearly every mid-Western industrial center are gloomy over the problem. Their gloom is increased by the belief, which is quite well grounded, that the Negroes are being **excited to antagonism** against the police. The Negroes in many places are being told by their leaders that police are their enemies to all intents and purposes.

The general civilian dislocations of the war; constant crowding of transportation facilities; line-ups at stores, banks and post offices; general relaxation of **civilities** and observances of minor

Bandied about: Casually used.

White man's leavings: Places white population moved away from.

Rung so completely around by landlord covenants: Restricted on all sides by agreements between property owners to prohibit blacks from moving into neighboring apartment buildings or houses.

Influx: Arrival.

Seethed: Was rampant; full of.

Bone of contention: The main point of a dispute.

Excited to antagonism: Encouraged to take hostile action.

Civilities: Courtesy among people.

laws and regulations—all those can and do easily take on an inter-racial character in times like these. People all too easily blame their irritations on others, and there is a certain added convenience to be able to blame them on persons of another race.

*The pressing necessity for using every available **unit of manpower** has **dissipated** one of the trouble sources so far as Negroes are concerned by breaking down the barrier to their employment in war industries. The problem of **upgrading** has come to take the place of the old barrier, however, and just last week a strike was staged by white riveters in a Baltimore shipyard when the management announced a program of training some Negroes for this type of job.*

*All these and many more specific elements which enter into the current Negro problem get back sooner or later to . . . the Negro taking this occasion to make a determined drive, come what might, for his "rights." One **faction** of the Negro leaders is insisting not merely on rights comparable or even equal to the whites; they want the "same" rights, which they translate to mean the privilege to use the same facilities as the whites—the same hotels, theaters, night clubs, etc. Segregation, the word and all it stands for, has become **anathema** to the Negro, so far as he is represented by his more vocal leaders of today.*

The whole picture is one in which one can see little hope of avoiding further trouble unless there is more of a spirit of give-and-take on both sides.

*There are leaders among both Negroes and whites who are realistic enough to work out a large part of this great human problem. One does not have to look very far to find them. But each group has first to cut through prejudices which have grown up on its own side through the years in which the question has been badly handled, prejudices which now have become active and **virulent**.*

Unit of manpower: Worker.

Dissipated: Lessened.

Upgrading: Job advancement; promotion to a better job.

Faction: A group within a larger group.

Anathema: Something intensely disliked.

Virulent: Intense and bitter.

What happened next . . .

The United States made very few gains toward racial equality during the war years. Black soldiers returning from overseas were often bitterly disappointed that prejudice and bigotry remained the norm despite the increased occurrences of whites and blacks working in the same industries and serving in the same military. Although President Roosevelt issued Executive Order 8802 banning racial discrimination in the war industries, he did not provide much other support for the cause of racial equality. He was consumed with the war effort and did not want controversial home front issues to detract from U.S. goals abroad. Discrimination continued to take place in nearly all aspects of American life and would eventually lead to the race riots of the 1950s and 1960s.

Black Americans did enjoy one notable success in the area of employment. In 1944 in Philadelphia eight blacks were hired as trolley car drivers, a position previously held by whites only. To protest, the white drivers walked out, halting the transportation system. The Fair Employment Practices Commission (FEPC), a group assigned to enforce compliance with Executive Order 8802, stepped in. President Roosevelt ordered eight thousand troops to go to Philadelphia to take control of the company, the strike ended, and the black trolley car drivers kept their jobs. The mere existence of FEPC made businesses think twice before pushing blacks out of jobs. However, the FEPC ceased to exist in 1946 since it was primarily established to resolve home front racial employment issues during the war though black leaders wanted to make it permanent.

Did you know . . .

- Franklin Roosevelt first entered office as U.S. president in 1933. However, he did not take any official action on civil rights until he issued Executive Order 8802 in 1941. This order was the first civil rights action taken by any president since the American Civil War (1861–65) era.

- Of the seven hundred thousand blacks who migrated to industrial centers during the war years, four hundred thousand came from the South.

Consider the following . . .

- Research the Jim Crow laws that were prevalent in the Southern states from the late nineteenth century through the World War II years. Report what you learn to the class.

- The author of this excerpt mentions many causes of the race problem. Make a list of them, including historical causes and the more immediate causes of the 1943 riots. Do you think the riots made Americans realize that racial problems needed to be addressed nationwide? Explain why you think they did or did not.

- Research the Civil Rights Act of 1964, which grew from the seeds planted by the Fair Employment Practices Commission (FEPC) during the war. Assess racial tolerance in your local community and discuss what race relations are like in the United States at the beginning of the twenty-first century.

For More Information

Books

Kelley, Robin D. G., and Earl Lewis. *To Make Our World Anew: A History of African Americans*. New York: Oxford University Press, 2000.

Periodicals

Catledge, Turner. "Behind Our Menacing Race Problem." *New York Times Magazine* (August 8, 1943): pp. 7, 16.

Web sites

The History of Jim Crow. http://www.jimcrowhistory.org/home.htm (accessed on July 31, 2004).

Alexander J. Allen

Excerpt from "Alexander J. Allen"
**Reprinted from *The Homefront: America during World War II*.
Published in 1984.**

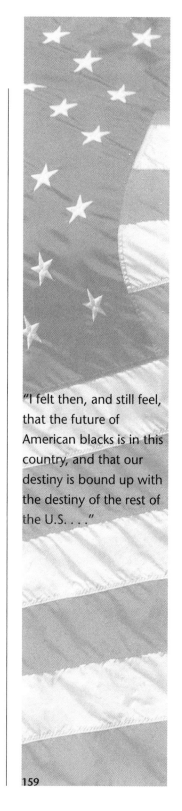

"I felt then, and still feel, that the future of American blacks is in this country, and that our destiny is bound up with the destiny of the rest of the U.S. . . ."

In this excerpt, Alexander J. Allen recalls that during the war years black Americans hoped for considerable progress in their fight to end racial discrimination on the home front. After all, part of the reason the United States joined the Allied war effort was to promote democratic ideals and stop the spread of fascism. (Fascism is a political movement led by a dictator. Support for a fascist dictator is commonly driven by a fanatical support of one's nation and race; in Germany, fascist politics led to severe discrimination against Jewish people and people of color.) Many people in the United States saw their country as a model of democracy. However, denying basic freedoms to black Americans, who made up 10 percent of the U.S. population, was hardly consistent with democratic ideals. Black American leaders were quick to point this out, and under their leadership the Double V campaign was born. "Double V" stood for victory abroad and victory at home over racial discrimination.

A resident of Baltimore, Maryland, Allen worked for the Baltimore chapter of the National Urban League. The National Urban League, a volunteer organization founded in 1911, was dedicated to ending racial segregation and discrimination.

The league sought to open new opportunities for blacks in U.S. society. Allen concentrated his efforts on placing black workers in war industry jobs. He viewed the war years as a period of opportunity for breaking down the employment barriers that blacks had faced for decades. If he and others like him were successful, he reasoned, employment prospects for blacks would be permanently improved.

Things to remember while reading the excerpt from "Alexander J. Allen" . . .

- Nationwide, black Americans were determined to break down employment barriers in the war industries.

- A majority of white Americans denied that employers practiced racial discrimination when hiring or promoting workers. They believed that blacks were unemployed or stuck in lower-level jobs because of personal shortcomings, not racial discrimination.

Excerpt from "Alexander J. Allen"

*When the war began, there were a number of blacks who were not enthusiastic about fighting it. They were sensitive to the **inconsistency** of a country that professed to be fighting for democracy and yet was not practicing it at home. But I felt then, and still feel, that the future of American blacks is in this country, and that our destiny is bound up with the destiny of the rest of the U.S. . . .*

*Certainly the blacks, as well as anybody else, and perhaps better than most, understood the negative side of **fascism** and **racism**. I was in Cleveland in school with **Jesse Owens**, and I remember when Hitler left the stadium at the 1936 Olympics because Jesse had defeated the best that **Aryan society** had been able to produce. So blacks were aware of what was wrong with **Hitler** and what was wrong with **Mussolini** and understood the reason for opposing the Nazi war machine as it began to take one country after another in Europe. But at the same time, blacks were extremely concerned over the fact that racism and bigotry and*

Inconsistency: Contradictory actions.

Fascism: A political movement led by a dictator, often built on a fanatical support of one's nation and race.

Racism: Prejudice against people of a particular race.

Jesse Owens: U.S. Olympic track and field athlete.

Aryan society: A supposed master race of non-Jewish white people, promoted by Hitler and his Nazi followers in Germany.

Hitler: Adolf Hitler, dictator of Germany from 1933 to 1945.

Mussolini: Benito Mussolini, dictator of Italy from 1922 to 1943.

American Home Front in World War II: Primary Sources

An African American draftsman employed at an arsenal during World War II. Skilled positions such as this one were hard for blacks to obtain due to racial prejudice on the part of many employers.
National Archives photo no. 208-NP-2HH-1.

*discrimination were a continuing practice in this country. Fascism was not a monopoly of Hitler, or of Mussolini, or the Japanese. It was something that we saw every day on the streets of Baltimore and in other places. We did not see much sense in the war unless it was tied to a commitment for change on the domestic scene. It made a **mockery** of wartime goals to fight overseas against fascism only to come back to the same kind of discrimination and racism here in this country.*

*So black leaders decided to fight a two-front war—one against the **Axis** and the other against bigotry at home. Both of them had to be defeated if this country was to live out its ideals. That was the philosophy of the Double V Campaign, which stood for victory at home and victory abroad. We felt it was an absolute necessity to take advantage of every opportunity to achieve change during this **period of ferment**, when people were perhaps more sensitive than they might otherwise be to the way the United States was viewed by its allies and by other people in the world.*

Mockery: An offensive imitation of.

Axis: The nations that fought against the Allies in World War II, including Germany, Italy, and Japan.

Period of ferment: A time full of great development and unrest.

In January of 1942 I went to work in Baltimore as the industrial-relations director of the Baltimore Urban League. It was an impressive title for a one-man operation. There was no department except myself and the secretary. But we worked trying to open up jobs for blacks in the building trades and the defense industries. In the beginning it was slow going. All the problems of racism and racial discrimination that were part of peacetime carried over to the war industries.

The Maryland State Employment Service, which became a branch of the U.S. Employment Service during the war, was part of the problem rather than a part of the solution. Even though President Roosevelt had signed an executive order that said all defense workers should be given equal consideration for job vacancies, that was just **so much verbiage**. **Actual practice** in Baltimore was that black workers were denied entrance to 39 Hopkins Place, where the best jobs were. Blacks were sent around the corner to the annex on Lombard Street, where they handled common labor and unskilled work. Even if you had a graduate degree in electronics, you would still be sent to the black entrance. And there were police to enforce it. If you resisted you might very well be arrested, as a number of people were. So many of the blacks would come to the Urban League offices to look for jobs, because they knew we were trying to place people in war industries. We'd go to work at the Urban League in the morning and the lines of people waiting to be interviewed would be two or three blocks long.

Trying to persuade the employers to hire black workers, you met with a lot of ignorance, and a lot of resistance. Many employers didn't have the courage to step out in a way that could conceivably subject them to criticism or abuse from their colleagues. To some degree there was a feeling that "I can't afford to be the first one. If somebody else would do it first, then I'll go along." That's not the kind of thing anybody likes to say about himself, though, so instead you'd get "Well, the time isn't right," or "Black workers don't perform," or "We're afraid that our white workers will walk out." Under Baltimore city law at that time, you not only had to have separate **toilet facilities** on the basis of sex, but you had to have separate toilet facilities on the basis of race. So they'd say, "Well, we'd like to do it, but we can't afford to set up a whole new set of toilet facilities." So one of the campaigns that the Baltimore Urban League undertook was to change the **municipal ordinance**. Eventually, we succeeded in doing that.

So much verbiage: Words, not action.

Actual practice: What actually happened.

Toilet facilities: Restrooms.

Municipal ordinance: Local city law.

For me the war period was a very compelling, very exhilarating era. There was a feeling that you had hold of something that was big and urgent and was not going to be here forever. There were opportunities for change which would not exist after the war was over.

*And we did begin to see changes. In some places employers **got a little religion**. They began to realize the inconsistency and **inequity** of discrimination. Sometimes it was pressure from the government. A lot of times it was pressure from local citizens, black and white, who felt a commitment, sometimes through the Urban League, sometimes through other organizations. But mainly what contributed to the change was the economics of the situation. Some companies just ran out of white workers to hire.*

The pressures of labor-market shortages simply forced many employers to change their attitudes toward what they might call marginal workers—blacks, other minorities, women—in nontraditional capacities. The denial of opportunity to people who were competent and desirous of work just didn't make sense economically.

Got a little religion: Changed their attitudes and became more accepting of minorities.

Inequity: Unfairness.

*War orders were **pressing**, they had jobs that needed to be done, so employers began to tap this long-neglected part of the labor market.*

*In 1942 the number of blacks in manufacturing industry in Baltimore was nine thousand. By 1944 they had increased to thirty-six thousand, which was a jump not only numerically but also percentagewise, from six percent of the work force to fifteen percent. After **VJ Day** the number dropped back to twenty thousand blacks, but they were twelve and a half percent of the work force. So the **retention rate** was far beyond the original expectation. Even though the peak had been passed, the employment picture for blacks was far better at the end of the war than it had been at the beginning of the war.*

What happened next . . .

Although progress was slow, racial discrimination among employers lessened. Many black leaders viewed the war years as a turning point on the road to improved economic status for black Americans. Blacks gained confidence in their ability to create change in American society, and they became even more determined to claim the same civil rights as white Americans enjoyed. Membership in black organizations such as the National Association for the Advancement of Colored People (NAACP) and the National Urban League increased dramatically. Organizations grew and became more effective in promoting black activism. Ultimately this activism led to the civil rights movement of the 1950s and 1960s.

Did you know . . .

- By 1945, 8 percent of war industry jobs were held by blacks, up from 3 percent in 1942, and only a tiny fraction of a percent in 1940.

- During the war years the number of black workers holding skilled positions significantly increased.

- In 1944 the National Labor Relations Board stopped certifying labor unions that excluded blacks from membership.

Pressing: Needing immediate attention; urgent.

VJ Day: Victory over Japan celebration day, September 2, 1945; the day Japan formally surrendered to Allied forces.

Retention rate: The percentage of workers who kept their jobs after the war.

- The National Urban League and the NAACP remain the two largest and most influential organizations promoting black American causes at the beginning of the twenty-first century.

Consider the following . . .
- Explain what Alexander Allen meant when he said, "For me the war period was . . . very compelling . . . You had hold of something that was big and urgent and was not going to be here forever."

- Allen states that the employment picture for blacks did improve. List at least five reasons why positive changes occurred. According to Allen, what was the most powerful reason for change?

- Read the "Sybil Lewis" excerpt in Chapter 3. Find examples of racial discrimination that Lewis, a black woman, experienced as a war industry worker.

For More Information

Books

Harris, Mark J., Franklin D. Mitchell, and Steven J. Schechter, eds. *The Homefront: America during World War II*. New York: G.P. Putnam's Sons, 1984.

Takaki, Ronald T. *Double Victory: A Multicultural History of America in World War II*. Boston: Little, Brown & Company, 2000.

Wynn, Neil A. *The Afro-American and the Second World War*. New York: Holmes & Meier Publishers, 1976.

Web sites

National Association for the Advancement of Colored People. http://www.naacp.org (accessed on July 31, 2004).

National Urban League. http://www.nul.org (accessed on July 31, 2004).

Mine Okubo

Excerpt from Citizen 13660

Reprinted from *Citizen 13660*.
Published in 1946.

"On April 24, 1942, Civilian Exclusion order No. 19 was issued and posted everywhere in Berkeley. Our turn had come."

On December 7, 1941, Japan carried out a surprise attack on a U.S. military base at Pearl Harbor, Hawaii. After this incident Americans feared the Japanese would attempt a similar attack on the U.S. mainland. They were also convinced that spies and saboteurs lurked within Japanese American communities. In 1941, 127,000 Japanese Americans—about 70 percent of them U.S. citizens—lived in the United States. California was home to 93,000, and another 19,000 lived in Oregon and Washington.

Within hours of the Pearl Harbor attack, FBI (Federal Bureau of Investigation) agents moved through Japanese American communities, arresting prominent individuals. Working without any evidence of wrongdoing, they arrested anyone who they thought might have feelings of loyalty toward Japan. The government closed banks run by Japanese Americans and froze the bank accounts of Japanese Americans. Agents searched Japanese American homes for items such as radio transmitters that might be used to signal Japanese ships close to the coastline.

Under heavy political, military, and public pressure, President Franklin Roosevelt signed Executive Order 9066 on

In 1942, Japanese-owned businesses on the West Coast were quickly closed as their owners were evacuated to relocation centers.
The Library of Congress.

February 19, 1942. The order required all persons of Japanese ancestry, whether U.S. citizens or not, to leave specific areas of California, Washington, Oregon, and Arizona. Japanese Americans in those areas were ordered to sell their possessions and check in at reporting stations for transportation to assembly centers. They could bring with them only what they could carry. Given only a few weeks to turn themselves in, they sold their houses, cars, and stores at very low prices. By obeying the president's executive order, Japanese Americans lost an estimated $400 million in property and income.

Gathering at the reporting stations, Japanese Americans registered as families, and each family received a number. Then they were taken to temporary quarters called assembly centers. These assembly centers were located at fairgrounds, racetracks, and stockyards not in use. On average, families would stay at assembly centers for a hundred days before leaving for permanent camps. In general, families were kept together when they moved to the permanent camps, but not always.

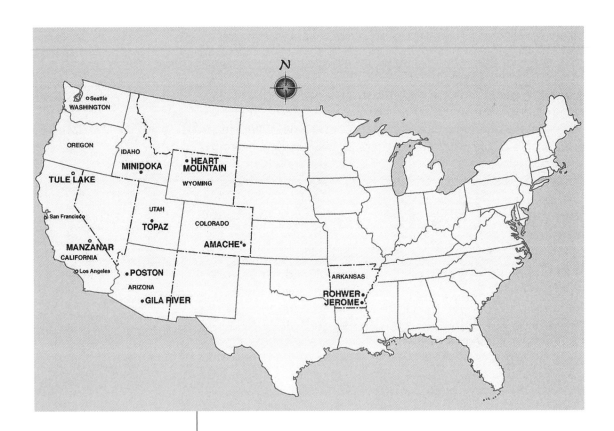

A map showing the locations of the Japanese internment camps constructed in the United States, where Japanese immigrants and Japanese Americans were held from 1942 to 1945.

© Maps.com/Corbis.

Reproduced by permission.

The U.S. government hastily constructed ten permanent internment camps in remote areas: two each in California and Arizona; one each in Utah, Wyoming, Colorado, and Idaho; and two in Arkansas swamplands. The guarded camps held a total of 112,000 Japanese Americans and Japanese aliens during the war for fear of sabotage or espionage. Japanese Americans who were forced to leave their homes were kept as prisoners at these heavily guarded camps for months—or in some cases, years.

Their living quarters were barracks; thin walls provided no sound barrier between rooms. Each room held one family, as well as cots, blankets, bare lightbulbs, and a potbelly stove for warmth. To make additional furniture, families scrounged for construction scrap materials at night. They ate their meals in large mess halls, and their school-age children attended classes that were held inside the confines of the camp. Despite the meager accommodations and lack of freedom, the resourceful

Japanese Americans managed to build a semblance of community life while they were held captive.

The last excerpt in this chapter comes from *Citizen 13660,* a book written and illustrated by Mine Okubo. Published in 1946, it was the first account of the Japanese internment experience. Born in 1912 in Riverside, California, Okubo held a bachelor's and master's degree in fine arts from the University of California at Berkeley. She traveled extensively in Europe, studying various art traditions and techniques. When her mother became gravely ill in 1939, she returned to the United States. After her mother's death, Okubo moved back to Berkeley, where her younger brother was enrolled at the university.

After the Pearl Harbor attack, Okubo and her brother were among the many Japanese Americans who were forced to leave their homes and check in at reporting stations. They became family unit number 13660, hence the title of Okubo's book. They were taken first to Tanforan racetrack, then Topaz internment camp in central Utah. At both locations Okubo wrote about her experiences daily and drew illustrations of what went on in the camps. She compiled her work and titled it *Citizen 13660.*

Things to remember while reading the excerpt from *Citizen 13660* . . .

- Japanese people who had immigrated to the United States but who were not U.S. citizens were known as Issei (pronounced EE-say). There were about forty-seven thousand Issei in the United States in the 1940s. Japanese Americans born in the United States (the children of Issei) were called Nisei (pronounced NEE-say). Nisei and their children, who were called Sansei (pronounced SAN-say), were U.S. citizens. Approximately eighty thousand Nisei lived in the United States during the war years.

- In the areas where internment took place, the policy affected all Japanese Americans, including those with only one parent of Japanese ancestry.

- After Japan attacked Pearl Harbor, Americans assumed the Japanese would attack the West Coast soon thereafter.

- The internment of Japanese Americans lasted more than three years. Internees were stripped of their rights, their dignity, and their property, though the government had no evidence that they were a security threat to the nation.

Excerpt from Citizen 13660

On April 24, 1942, Civilian Exclusion order No. 19 was issued and posted everywhere in Berkeley. Our turn had come.

*We had not believed at first that **evacuation** would affect the Nisei, American citizens of Japanese ancestry, but thought per-haps the Issei, Japanese-born mothers and fathers who were **denied naturalization** by American law, would be interned in case of war between Japan and the United States. It was a real blow when everyone, regardless of citizenship, was ordered to evacuate. . . .*

*My family . . . was scheduled to leave with the next to the last group at 11:30 a.m. on Friday, May 1, 1942. Our destination was Tanforan Assembly Center, which was at the Tanforan Race Track in San Bruno, a few miles south of San Francisco. We had three days and three nights to pack and get ready. My brother was excused from the University with a promise that he would receive his **B.A.** degree in June. . . .*

A guide was called to take us to our home, Barrack 16, Room 50. We went practically halfway around the race track and then diagonally across the center field through sticky mud and tall weeds. The ground was wet from the downpour of the day before. Those who had come on that day were drenched and their bag-gage was soaked. . . .

We followed the guide past the race track to the other side where the horse stables were. We passed many stables before Stable 16 was pointed out to us. It was an isolated building sur-rounded by tall weeds and standing high above the ground. . . .

We shook the mattresses and flattened them out and made our beds with the sheets and blankets we had brought along. We "hit the hay" around ten that night, but learned very quickly that

Evacuation: Force removal from an area.

Denied naturalization: Not allowed to change their citizenship.

B.A.: A Bachelor of Arts college degree.

Japanese Americans transferring from train to bus at Lone Pine, California, bound for the war relocation camp at Manzanar, April 1942.
The Library of Congress.

sleep was not to be easily won. Because the partitions were low and there were many holes in the boards they were made of, the crackling of the straw and the noises from the other stalls were incessant. Loud snores, the grinding of teeth, the wail of babies, the murmur of conversations—these could be heard the full length of the stable. Moreover, it was very cold and we were shivering. One blanket was not enough to keep us warm. We got up and opened the duffel bags and the suitcases and spread everything over our beds. Sleep finally overtook us around midnight. Thus ended our first day in the Tanforan Assembly Center.

The first month was the hardest because adjustments had to be made to the new mode of life. The naked barracks and white-washed stalls had to be fixed up into living quarters, and we had to get used to the lack of privacy of camp life. . . .

Although cooking was not permitted in the barracks and stalls, blown fuses often left us in the darkness, guiltily pondering whether it was our hot plate or our neighbor's that did the trick. . . .

Black American and Japanese American Experiences: Mine Okubo

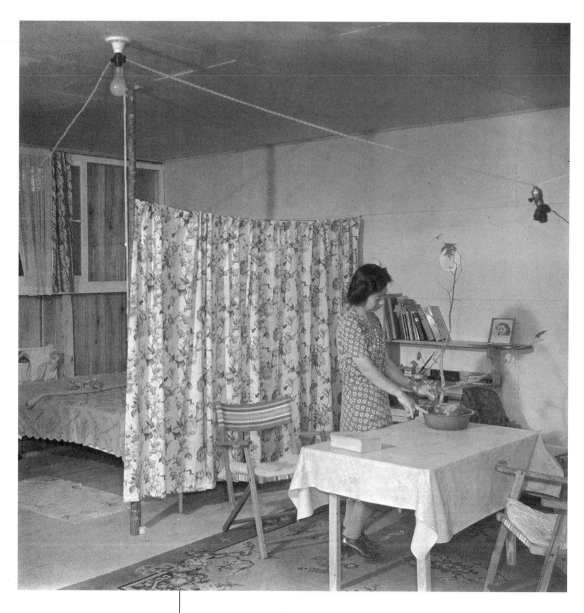

The typical interior of a barracks home at a Japanese relocation camp. Families had to hang sheets or blankets to create "rooms" within the bare, one-room living quarters.
National Archives photo no. 210-G-E291.

On September 9, 1942, the advance work group of 214 people left for the Central Utah Relocation Project to make preparations for induction.

On the 16th of September at five in the afternoon, my brother and I reported with our hand luggage to a newly constructed **bull pen**. We were assigned to Group 5, Section 8. Our train captain read off the names in the group. . . . We took our assignment (Block 7, Barrack II, Room F). . . . F was one of the end rooms.

American Home Front in World War II: Primary Sources

*It was a large rectangle (about 20 by 10 ft.) and completely bare, furnished only with a ceiling light and a closet space near the door. There were two windows to the north and one to the south. A three-inch layer of **alkali dust** covered the **masonite** floor. The room was unfinished, the bare wall beams and rafters giving it a skeleton-like appearance.*

When we went to Mess 7 for lunch we found a dining hall set for about three hundred people. It had a pleasanter atmosphere than the dining halls in Tanforan. Our first meal was served semi-family style, and it was good. . . .

Army cots were provided as in Tanforan Assembly Center. . . . Two Army blankets were distributed to each of us. The boys used two of the blankets to curtain off a room for me in one corner. . . .

*Topaz, the Central Utah Project, was a more or less permanent center. Therefore, the evacuees looked for work immediately upon **induction**. Everyone wanted a job for which he had been trained or had some skill. The **three of us** were accepted for work on the Topaz* Times, *at the professional rate of $19 a month, with an additional credit of $3.75 for clothing. The other rates of pay in the center were $12 and $16.*

*Our newspaper kept the residents informed about the center and the outside. Originally a **mimeographed** sheet issued three times a week, it later became a daily, with a Japanese section and a comic section. All news passed the censorship of the administration staff.*

After two months with the Topaz Times, *a small group of us decided to break away and start a fifty-page art and literary magazine. We called it* Trek. *Three issues appeared. . . .*

The entire Topaz project area occupied 17,500 acres. The center contained 42 city blocks, of which 36 comprised the residential area, one square mile in extent. At first we were not permitted beyond it, but later we could wander to the rest of the area.

All residential blocks looked alike; people were lost all the time.

Comfort was uppermost in the minds of the people. All were on the lookout for building material for partitions and furniture. Lumber and sheet-rock board were scarce and well guarded, but since building material was not furnished to the residents as promised, they became desperate. With the passing of time and the coming of cold weather, stealing no longer became a crime but an

Bull pen: Holding area.

Alkali dust: A very fine dust with a strong odor.

Masonite: A wooden sheet made from wood fibers pressed together.

Induction: Enrollment in the camp.

Three of us: Refers to Okubo, her brother, and young, male student who shared their barracks.

Mimeographed: Copied on a printing machine.

act of necessity. Everybody was out to get building material. There were guards everywhere, but the residents became skillful at dodging them; worried mothers were the most skillful of all. . . .

Each mess hall fed from two hundred and fifty to three hundred persons. Food was rationed, as it was for the civilian population on the outside. The allowance for food varied from 31 cents to 45 cents a day per person. Often a meal consisted of rice, bread, and macaroni, or beans, bread, and spaghetti. At one time we were served liver for several weeks, until we went on strike.

About five hundred arrivals from Tanforan were inducted every other day. . . .

The Boy Scout band welcomed each incoming bus, and there were welcome signs for the new residents.

Mass meetings of welcome were held at the different mess halls. The project director and other officials, including the drum and bugle corps, were on hand to give each new group an impressive showing.

The first snow fell in Topaz on October 13. The residents went wild with excitement; for most of them this was the first experience of snow.

Each family was given a pot-bellied stove. Ours was moved in with me. . . .

When the cold days came, the War Relocation Authority distributed **G.I. clothes** *to all those employed, both women and men. It was welcome if peculiar apparel—warm* **pea jackets** *and army uniforms, sizes 38 and 44, apparently left over from the first World War.*

In Tanforan we had ordered our clothing allotment from the Sears, Roebuck summer catalog. These clothes, with many substitutions, now began to arrive. Everyone was dressed alike, because of the catalog orders and the G.I. clothes.

An ice rink was constructed on the south side of the camp, and on cold days skating was a good sport. . . .

Each block had a laundry complete with washboards and clotheslines. Much time was spent in the laundry. There was plenty of hot water. . . .

There was a morning and evening rush to and from the washroom, of people in getas *(traditional [Japanese] wooden clogs), in underwear, in nightgowns, and in robes. Homemade* getas *took*

G.I. clothes: Military clothing.

Pea jackets: Double-breasted wool coats worn by navy sailors.

Community cooperative: Jointly owned and operated by camp inhabitants for a common purpose.

Canteen: Recreational facility.

the place of rationed shoes and boots. Because of the mud puddles, some people built their getas very high. . . .

A **community cooperative** was established. It provided a **canteen,** dry-goods store, beauty parlor, barber shop, cleaning establishment, shoe repair shop, and movies. . . .

School organization was an improvement over Tanforan. The curriculum followed the requirements of the State of Utah and the

Japanese American children attended school while in the relocation camps. Schools were the same barracks-type of building as the homes, and teachers were generally Caucasian.
© *Bettmann/Corbis.*
Reproduced by permission.

school was staffed by **Caucasian** teachers and by teachers selected from among the evacuees. . . .

Art and hobby shops were of great interest. The residents exhibited vases and desk sets of wood, toys, stuffed animals and dolls, garments and knitted ware, carvings of stone and wood, finger rings of cellophane or fashioned from toothbrush handles, peach seeds or beads, tools made of scrap iron, and beautiful hats made of **citrus-fruit wrappings** woven with potato-sack strings. Ingenious use was made of everything that could be found in the center.

Recreation halls had for equipment only what the evacuees were able to provide. Ping pong, badminton, and cards were the important indoor games. Basketball, tennis, golf, football, and baseball were the outdoor games—baseball was the favorite sport. . . .

Entertainments were given on makeshift stages in the mess halls and in the open. Talent shows and plays were presented. Later an auditorium was built.

There were **scrap-metal drives, bond sales, Red Cross drives**, and blood donations to help us keep up with the outside world. . . .

There were 150 in the first high-school graduation class. Rented blue caps and gowns added much color to the large out-door ceremony. The graduates were very serious. . . .

In the spring practically everyone set up a **victory garden**. Some of the gardens were organized, but most of them were set up anywhere and any way. Makeshift screens were fashioned out of precious cardboard boxes, cartons, and scraps of lumber to pro-tect the plants from the whipping dust storms.

In the evening there was the usual **bucket brigade** from the laundry buildings to the gardens. . . .

To provide enough meat and fresh vegetables, a variety of vegetables was produced on the project farms and the agricultural division raised cattle, chickens, and hogs.

The hogs ate everything we left, and ultimately we ate the hogs.

At harvest time everyone pitched in to help. . . .

The program of **segregation** was now instituted. One of its purposes was to protect loyal Japanese Americans from the

Caucasian: White Americans, predominately of European ancestry.

Citrus-fruit wrappings: Waxed paper that repels rain.

Scrap-metal drives, bond sales, Red Cross drives: Activities that contributed to the war effort. Here, Okubo describes that Japanese Americans imprisoned in the camps carried on the same home front activities that American citizens pursued in general across the nation.

Victory garden: Small fruit and vegetable gardens grown by individuals or families in their own yards and public places to add to the nation's production of food.

Bucket brigade: Water was in short supply in the relocation camps' desert settings, and it was not wasted. Water left from washing clothes was used to water the gardens.

Segregation: Keeping a particular group of people totally separated from others.

continuing threats of pro-Japanese agitators. Tule Lake, one of the ten original centers, was chosen as the segregation center for the disloyal. In the fall of 1943, thirteen hundred Topazians (about one tenth of the total) were sent there. . . .

The rules were becoming much less rigid. Block shopping was introduced, whereby a resident of each block was permitted to shop in the nearby town of Delta for the rest of the block. Special permits were arranged ahead of time by the administration. . . .

Many went fishing in the irrigation ditches, about three miles away on the outskirts of the project agricultural area.

Relocation programs were finally set up in the center to return residents to normal life. Students had led the way by going out to continue their education in the colleges and universities willing to accept them. Seasonal workers followed, to relieve the farm labor shortage.

Many volunteered for the army. Government jobs opened up, and the defense plants claimed others. The Intelligence Division of the army and navy demanded still others as instructors and students. My brother had left in June to work in a wax-paper factory in Chicago. Later he was inducted into the army. . . .

The day of my departure arrived. I dashed to the block manager's office to turn in the blankets and other articles loaned to me, and went to the Administration Office to secure signatures on the various forms given me the day before. I received a train ticket and $25, plus $3 a day for meals while traveling; these were given to each person relocating on an indefinite permit. I received **four typewritten cards to be filled out and returned after relocation**, and a booklet, "When You Leave the Relocation Center," which I was to read on the train.

I dashed to the mess hall for a bite to eat, then to the Administration Office, picked up my pass and **ration book** at the Internal Security Office and hurried to the gate. There I shook hands with the friends who had gathered to see me off. . . .

I was now free.

I looked at the crowd at the gate. Only the very old or very young were left. Here I was, alone, with no family responsibilities, and yet fear had chained me to the camp. I thought, "My God! How do they expect those poor people to leave the one place they

Four typewritten cards to be filled out and returned after relocation: A tracking system for checking-in through the mail periodically to show that Okubo was still employed, which was a condition of her leaving the camp in the first place.

Ration book: A series of four books the government issued during the war to regulate availability of certain items in short supply, such as sugar and coffee.

can call home." I swallowed a lump in my throat as I waved good-by to them.

What happened next . . .

In 1943 detainees who could show evidence of a job awaiting them outside the camp were permitted to leave. At first many of these jobs were in agriculture, because U.S. farms were suffering from a labor shortage. Before long, however, jobs in government departments, defense plants, and the military opened up, allowing roughly one-third of the camp detainees to leave between 1943 and 1944. The critical workforce shortages forced the government and employers to look at various sources for new workers, including the internment camps. Those not considered high risk were allowed to leave and join the workforce.

While still at the Topaz internment camp, Mine Okubo mailed her camp sketches to an art show in San Francisco. There her work received an award, and the award brought Okubo a job offer from *Fortune* magazine in New York City. Because she had a job, Okubo was allowed to leave Topaz and move to New York in January 1944. By December 1944, with an Allied victory looking likely, all the remaining detainees were freed. However, the last camp did not actually close until March 1946.

During their confinement, several thousand Japanese Americans angrily renounced their U.S. citizenship. In 1959 the U.S. government moved to restore their citizenship. In 1988, more than four decades after World War II, President Ronald Reagan (1911–2004; served 1981–89) signed legislation offering a formal apology to Japanese Americans and authorizing payment of $20,000 to each surviving detainee.

After regaining her freedom, Mine Okubo exhibited her artwork nationwide, and her work appeared in national magazines such as *Time* and *Life*. Her book *Citizen 13660* won the 1984 American Book Award, and it continues to be used in U.S. classrooms in the early twenty-first century. In 1991 the

Women's Caucus for Art presented Okubo with a Lifetime Achievement Award.

Did you know . . .

- Amache, in Colorado, was the smallest camp, housing seventy-three hundred detainees. Eleven thousand lived at the Heart Mountain camp in Wyoming, making it the third largest community in the state. Tule Lake, located on a dry lake bed in northern California, was the largest camp, holding about eighteen thousand detainees. Tule Lake detainees included those who were considered to be troublemakers or disloyal to the United States.

- The detention of Japanese Americans was legally challenged in the courts. In *Korematsu v. United States* (1944) the U.S. Supreme Court sided with the federal government, stating that the detention was a military necessity.

- In 1943 Nisei became eligible to join the U.S. military. Signing up in the camps, they formed the 442nd Regimental Combat Team. Composed entirely of Japanese Americans, this unit fought in Europe and became the most decorated army unit of World War II.

- Approximately 150,000 Japanese Americans lived in Hawaii in 1941; they made up one-third of Hawaii's population. U.S. officials decided not to detain Japanese Americans in Hawaii, because their businesses were an essential part of the Hawaiian economy.

Consider the following . . .

- On September 11, 2001, almost sixty years after the Japanese attack on Pearl Harbor, terrorists from the Middle East attacked the U.S. mainland, killing almost three thousand civilians. In response, the U.S. government investigated and deported many Middle Eastern people who were staying in the United States illegally. However, the government did not round up and detain American citizens of Middle Eastern descent or Middle Easterners who were legally in the country. Do you think the government's experience in detaining Japanese Americans and

Japanese aliens after Pearl Harbor affected its response to September 11?

- Why do you think historians believe it is crucial for Americans to remember the Japanese internment of World War II?

- Even though you have had the advantage of discussing and better understanding the dangers of racial prejudice, put yourself in the place of Americans on Sunday, December 7, 1941, as they listened to radio broadcasts about the Japanese attack on Pearl Harbor. Honestly assess what your feelings would have been toward those of Japanese descent.

For More Information

Books

Cooper, Michael L. *Remembering Manzanar: Life in a Japanese Relocation Camp*. New York: Clarion Books, 2002.

Inada, Lawson Fusao. *Only What We Could Carry: The Japanese American Internment Experience*. Berkeley, CA: Heyday Books, 2000.

Okubo, Mine. *Citizen 13660*. New York: Columbia University Press, 1946.

Stanley, Jerry. *I Am an American: The True Story of Japanese Internment*. New York: Crown, 1994.

Sun, Shirley. *Mine Okubo: An American Experience*. San Francisco: East Wind Printers, 1972.

Tunnell, Michael O. *The Children of Topaz: The Story of a Japanese-American Internment Camp*. New York: Holiday House, 1996.

Web sites

Japanese American National Museum. http://www.janm.org (accessed on July 31, 2004).

National Japanese American Historical Society. http://www.nikkeiheritage.org (accessed on July 31, 2004).

Through a Youngster's Eyes

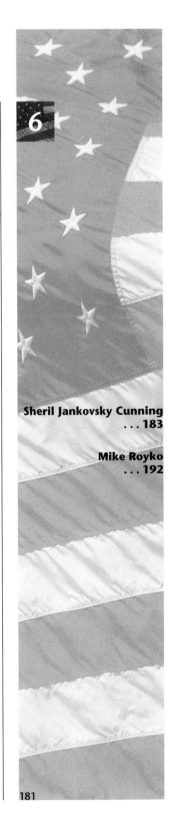

Like their parents, children were totally caught up in the news and activities of wartime America. When they played, they played war games; their heroes were fathers, uncles, and brothers serving in the military; their group and club activities involved collecting scrap metal, rubber, and paper, which were recycled for the war industries, and raising money to buy war stamps and bonds. They imitated their parents by planting their own victory garden row and putting together care packages to send to overseas soldiers and European children orphaned by the war. They were very quiet during air raids, obeying all their parents' instructions. They secretly feared that invaders might appear at their door. Many children thought of death for the first time when a family member or neighbor died in battle.

The two excerpts in this chapter describe wartime experiences of children. The first, "Sheril Jankovsky Cunning," comes from *The Homefront: America during World War II* (1984), a book edited by Mark J. Harris, Franklin D. Mitchell, and Steven J. Schechter. The second is "Mike Royko," taken from *"The Good War": An Oral History of World War II* (1984), a book by Studs Terkel. At the beginning of the war, Sheril Cunning was a seven-year-old living in sunny Southern California. Mike Royko was nine years of age and lived in an ethnically diverse Chicago, Illinois, neighborhood. Both were scared during air raid drills and blackouts. Both were familiar with air raid wardens. Sheril's father was the warden on her neighborhood block, and she worried about his safety during every air raid alert. Mike had an entirely different and amusing opinion of his air raid warden. Sheril was exposed to a variety of wartime activities, the same activities that took place nationwide in support of the war effort. Mike's experiences were limited to the happenings and talk in his immediate neighborhood. Both Sheril and Mike were left with lifelong vivid memories of the war years.

Sheril Jankovsky Cunning

Complete text of "Sheril Jankovsky Cunning"
Published in *The Homefront: America during World War II*.
Published in 1984.

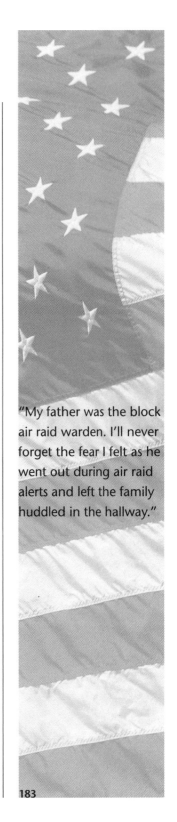

"My father was the block air raid warden. I'll never forget the fear I felt as he went out during air raid alerts and left the family huddled in the hallway."

Sheril Cunning lived in Long Beach, California, during World War II (1939–45). Long Beach was a prosperous, middle-class community. When the United States declared war on Japan on December 8, 1941, the town's casual, sunny disposition changed dramatically. Sheril, seven years old, saw the warm beaches where she played immediately blocked off; huge antiaircraft guns blocked her view of the water. Following civil defense recommendations, Sheril's mother put up heavy blackout curtains that prevented light from escaping from the house during air raid drills. The family had various plans to avoid harm in the event of an invasion.

Fears of Japanese attack or invasion were strong and real on the West Coast, especially during the first year of the war. In this excerpt Sheril remembers the fear and a variety of other experiences that reflect important aspects of home front life. She shares memories of air raid drills, food ration coupons, victory gardens, war bond rallies, and children's war games. She remembers rolling bandages at church with her grandmother and inviting soldiers who were strangers to Thanksgiving dinner. She also recalls her first experience with death in the family.

Things to remember while reading "Sheril Jankovsky Cunning" . . .

- After Japan's attack on Pearl Harbor, people living on the West Coast assumed the Japanese would also attack the U.S. mainland, along the western coastline.

- With vivid imaginations, children often pictured frightening wartime scenarios. To prevent or lessen children's anxieties, parents, teachers, and government leaders encouraged them to participate in the home front war effort. Gaining a sense of involvement helped keep children psychologically healthy during the war years.

"Sheril Jankovsky Cunning"

As a child growing up during the war in Long Beach, California, I lived constantly with the fear we might be invaded or bombed. We lived only three blocks from the beach, and before the war started we would walk down there with our mother and play in the waves and sand. But during the war the whole coast was blocked off from civilian use. All along the bluffs, they set up giant antiaircraft artillery and camouflage netting which to a small child appeared to be several stories high. You couldn't see the ocean anymore. All you could see was the guns and camouflage.

We also had air raid alerts which made the possibility of invasion seem very real. Because Pearl Harbor had been bombed and California was on the Pacific and close to the Japanese, we felt we could have a surprise air attack at any minute.

My father was the block air raid warden. I'll never forget the fear I felt as he went out during air raid alerts and left the family huddled in the hallway. The sirens would go off, the searchlights would sweep the sky, and Daddy would don his gas mask and his big hard hat and goggles and go out to protect the neighborhood.

Although we had blackout curtains, my parents didn't really trust them not to leak light. So we sat in a hall closet with all the doors closed in order to be able to have the lights on. We had a wind-up **Victrola** which we'd take in there with us. My mother

Victrola: A phonograph to play records.

would sing to us to keep up our spirits. But we couldn't help being afraid for our father. And afraid for ourselves. Our prime protector was out protecting someone else. It gave us the feeling of being abandoned. The searchlights and sirens struck great fear in our hearts and yet it was exciting.

Many of our games involved war themes. We made hideouts and plans (and alternate plans) in the event Long Beach would be invaded or bombed. My sister and I planned for situations in which we might be like the poor, starving children of Europe we saw in the **newsreels**, living without parents, in rags, in bombed-out buildings. We were convinced that if attacked only children would survive and all adults would be killed.

We had a back closet that we figured was the safest place in the house to hide in case of invasion. My mother stored all her old clothes in there in big rubber garment bags. We figured that nobody would find us behind those bags. But just in case they did, we kept a bottle of ketchup in the closet. We were going to douse ourselves with it and lie there as if we had already been bloodied and killed, so that they would walk away and not stick their bayonets into us.

What was funny is we always thought it would be the Germans who would invade. Although Japan was on the other side of that ocean out there in our front yard, we had very strong visions of **storm troopers** in big boots invading our shores. The Japanese were going to bomb us, but it was the Nazis who were going to open that closet door and see two little dead girls. I'm sure that came from the newsreels and Life magazine. Life came every week to **deliver the war to our doorstep** and **replenish** our fear.

The war also brought my first experience of death. I remember the day that we got the news that my cousin was killed when his troopship was torpedoed. Yet there were so many stories and movies around about someone coming back after being declared dead that I thought, Well, maybe they'll discover Jimmy alive someday. My mother tried to make me realize. "No, Jimmy is really dead. He was in the middle of the ocean. There isn't going to be any finding Jimmy." And I remember her crying, saying things like, "He was so young, he never hurt anybody, and he never had a chance to grow up and be a man." It was a long time after the war before I gave up my hope that he would return.

Newsreels: A short movie on current events often shown at movie theaters.

Storm troopers: A private German Nazi army known for their violence and brutality.

Deliver the war to our doorstep: At this time, most Americans did not own a TV; the photographs in Life, and other magazines, brought images of war to people's homes.

Replenish: Increase once again.

A popular World War II poster warning U.S. citizens not to put information into enemy (German, Japanese) hands. *National Archives photo no. 44-PA-82.*

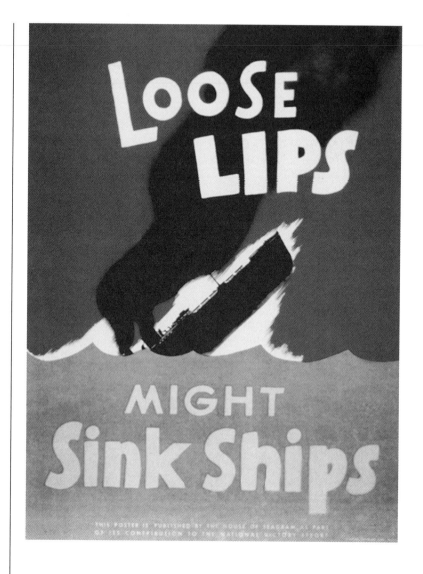

Besides the fear, the war also created a sense of distrust. I can remember posters everywhere with Uncle Sam holding a finger up to his lips. "SHHH." Don't give away secrets. "Loose lips sink ships." You weren't supposed to trust anyone. You heard it on the radio, saw it in the movies. They'd tell you even the nicest person could turn out to be a spy.

Yet, at the same time, there were also a lot of positive things about the war, a kind of game atmosphere and team spirit. I remember all the neighborhood women sitting around the kitchen table pooling and trading **ration coupons**. My grandmother

Ration coupons: Government-issued certificates that allowed a person to purchase fixed amounts of scarce consumer items.

... to Buy Canned, Bottled and Frozen Fruits and Vegetables; Dried Fruits, Juices and all Canned Soups

YOUR POINT ALLOWANCE MUST LAST FOR THE FULL

Plan How Many Points You Will Use Each Time Before

BUY EARLY IN THE WEEK

raised chickens so we often didn't need our meat coupons. And we made our own butter. So one month we might trade our meat or dairy coupons for sugar. The next month we might trade our sugar for steak or nylons. I know rationing was sometimes a hardship to my mother, but as a child seeing all these coupons trading back and forth, it was like watching a big Monopoly game.

Then everybody grew a victory garden. We had the most miserable, hard-as-cement, three-by-five foot plot of ground, and grew radishes and carrots as our contribution to the war. But radishes weren't anybody's **mainstay**, and our carrots never got bigger than an inch. Yet we all wanted to do our part for the war. You got caught up in the **mesmerizing** spirit of patriotism.

There was a huge neighborhood lot on our block where many people grew things. You could hardly walk in that plot. There were a dozen different kinds of squash, corn everywhere, beans growing on poles taller than my head. As a child it seemed like the **Garden of Eden**. Community spirit always ran high. Everybody grew something different and traded around.

War ration coupons were very familiar items to the children of World War II. Here, a teacher instructs her 6th grade class on how to use war ration coupons. *Courtesy of the FDR Library.*

Mainstay: Eaten regularly.

Mesmerizing: Engaging or fully consumed.

Garden of Eden: A biblical garden of plenty.

Young people wanted to contribute to the war effort just as much as adults did. One way for kids to help was by collecting their coins to help buy war bonds. *The Library of Congress.*

"**Even a little can help a lot - *NOW***"

Buy

U.S. WAR STAMPS BONDS

U.S. GOVERNMENT PRINTING OFFICE : 1942—O—455803 FORM DSS-405

ILLUSTRATION COURTESY OF LADIES' HOME JOURNAL

USO: United Service Organizations, a group made up of volunteers who provided support to servicemen.

My grandmother belonged to a sewing circle at the church, and she would take my sister and me with her. All the little girls were taken. We tore up sheets and we rolled bandages for the soldiers. And we made up little bags with shaving articles and cigarettes and chocolate bars which they sent to the hospitals.

*Then on Thanksgiving my grandmother would always call the **USO** and invite soldiers, total strangers, to come for dinner. We thought that was just great, having these handsome young men* *at our dinner table, people from areas of the country that we'd hardly ever heard of. We were very impressed.*

*The war **pervaded** every aspect of our lives. Even the Christmas parade. The tanks would go down Pine Avenue, great **hulking** machines, then Santa Claus would come. And we cheered for the tanks as much as we cheered for Santa Claus.*

*I remember the war bond rally at Bixby Park. It was one of the most memorable events of my life. The war made me special. I got to be on stage. My costume was American-beauty-rose satin and it had a big white lapel that went from my shoulders down to my abdomen and formed a V for Victory. I remember my mother sewing it, and I remember actually doing this tap dance on the stage in Bixby Park. Arm in arm, like the **Rockettes**, we formed a big V, and all the audience out in the park was cheering us on.*

*It was a time of many **dichotomies**. We were taught patriotism on the one hand, distrust on the other. Although there was great fear, there was also a good feeling, a believing in our country and our government, a sense of us all pulling together.*

The imprint of those times still remains. The sight of searchlights (now used as advertising spots) continues to produce terror in me, a run-and-hide, cover-the-head response. But I also long for the feeling of patriotism and the community spirit of those years.

What happened next . . .

On August 14, 1945, Japan announced it would surrender to the Allies. On August 15, a day that became known as V-J Day, for "Victory over Japan," wild jubilation broke out across the home front. In New York two million people gathered in Times Square to celebrate. Strangers danced and kissed. Some five tons of paper poured out of New York's windows and swirled down like snow. Japan formally surrendered on September 2. Sheril's family and citizens nationwide celebrated the end of the war.

Pervaded: Affected.

Hulking: Large and clumsy.

Rockettes: A famous New York female dance team that often hooked arms while in a line and performed high kicks in unison.

Dichotomies: Two opposing things such as thoughts, ideas, or situations.

Did you know . . .

- According to this excerpt, participating in a local war bond rally was one of the most memorable experiences Sheril had during the war. Children were often included in the rallies to remind adults that their children's future was a primary reason for fighting the war.

- In neighborhoods across the country, there were thousands of victory gardens like the one Sheril mentions; children were encouraged to plant and tend their own row in their family or neighborhood garden. Victory gardens produced one-third of all the vegetables eaten in the United States during the war years. This eased food shortages and made more food available for Allied forces fighting overseas.

- Because children enjoyed the competition of games, they were frequently called to participate in scrap metal or paper drives for the war effort. These drives were turned into competitions, such as who could collect the most.

Consider the following . . .

- List the various activities Sheril participated in during the war. Can you imagine American youngsters in the twenty-first century being equally involved in war-related activities on the home front?

- Care packages sent to soldiers or war orphans overseas could not weigh more than 5 pounds. Create a care package for an imaginary World War II soldier, and make another package that you think would have appealed to a European war orphan. (Items do not have to be new since the packages will not actually be mailed.) Check the weight of each package to make sure it does not exceed the 5-pound limit.

- Do some research to find out whether the Japanese actually launched attacks on the West Coast.

For More Information

Books

Harris, Mark J., Franklin D. Mitchell, and Steven J. Schechter, eds. *The Homefront: America during World War II.* New York: G.P. Putnam's Sons, 1984.

Panchyk, Richard. *World War II for Kids: A History with Twenty-One Activities.* Chicago: Chicago Review Press, 2002.

Schomp, Virginia. *World War II: Letters from the Homefront.* New York: Benchmark Books, 2002.

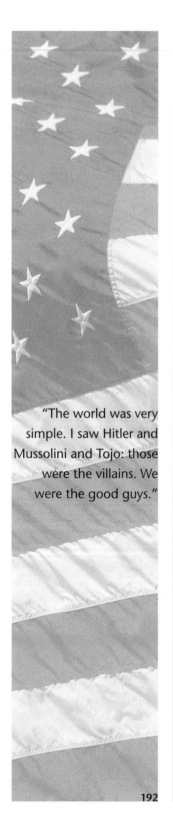

Mike Royko

Complete text of "Mike Royko"

Reprinted from *"The Good War": An Oral History of World War II*. Published in 1984.

"The world was very simple. I saw Hitler and Mussolini and Tojo: those were the villains. We were the good guys."

Mike Royko was nine years old in December 1941, when the United States entered World War II. He lived in a Chicago, Illinois, neighborhood made up of Polish, Irish, German, and Slavic immigrants. Mike's neighborhood was his entire world. The neighborhood included a tavern owned by his father, and the Royko family lived above the tavern. Mike's chief recollections of the war years revolve around his family and customers of the tavern.

In this excerpt Mike recalls that his sister, whose husband was stationed overseas, went to work in a war industry factory. He remembers her "sense of mission" about her work. He also describes the responsibilities he took on during air raid alerts.

Young Mike obviously had a knack for listening to adults talk, which served him well in the tavern; the "talk, talk, talk" did not escape him. He remembers lonely women, customer debates about Allied military strategy, and the atmosphere in the tavern after the United States dropped an atomic bomb on Japan. In the last paragraphs of the excerpt, Mike recalls how his neighborhood began to change at the end of the war.

Things to remember while reading "Mike Royko" . . .

- Although Chicago was far from either coast, the city's residents practiced air raid drills in earnest. Children believed there could be severe consequences if they did not perform well in the drills.

- Children viewed the war in simple black-and-white terms: The United States and the rest of the Allies were the "good guys," and Germany, Italy, and Japan were the "bad guys."

- Soldiers coming home from the war, especially those with medals, were the ultimate superheroes for many American children.

"Mike Royko"

I was nine years old when the war started. It was a typical Chicago working-class neighborhood. It was predominantly Slavic, Polish. There were some Irish, some Germans. When you're a kid, the borders of the world are the few blocks of **two-flats,** *bungalows, cottages, with a lot of little stores in between. My father had a tavern. In those days they put out* **extras.** *I remember the night the newsboys came through the neighborhood.* **Skid-row** *kind of guys,* **hawking** *the papers. Germany had invaded Poland: '39. It was the middle of the night, my mother and father waking. People were going out in the streets in their bathrobes to buy the papers. In our neighborhood with a lot of* **Poles,** *it was a tremendous story.*

Suddenly you had a flagpole. And a marker. Names went on the marker, guys from the neighborhood who were killed. . . .

Suddenly I saw something I hadn't seen before. My sister became **Rosie the Riveter.** *She put a bandanna on her head every day and went down to this organ company that had been converted to war work. There was my sister in slacks. It became more than work. There was the sense of mission about it. Her husband was* **Over There.** *She went bowling once a week. They had a league. I used to have to go with her, because the presence*

Two-flats: Two-story apartments.

Extras: Special editions of newspapers.

Skid-row: A district of saloons and cheap rooming houses frequented by vagrants and drunks.

Hawking: Selling.

Poles: Slang for emigrants from Poland in Eastern Europe.

Rosie the Riveter: A fictional female character who worked on assembly lines in the war industries. Rosie symbolized women factory workers during the war.

Over There: In combat zones overseas, fighting as a U.S. soldier.

A mother and her two sons take shelter in their basement during an air raid drill. Such drills were common in the United States during World War II, so that people would know what to do in the event of a real air raid emergency.
© Bettmann/Corbis.
Reproduced by permission.

Pariah: An outcast person.

of her little brother would discourage guys from making passes at her.

There was one sad case in the neighborhood. This woman's husband was overseas. I remember her as very attractive. She became pregnant: the neighborhood **pariah**. If they could have shaved her head and walked her through the streets, they'd have done it. She was an outcast and the talk—talk, talk, talk—of the neighborhood. She was very lonely.

If a guy came into the tavern with the wife or girlfriend of a guy who was overseas, somebody might have gone after him.

There was talk in the neighborhood about one guy who got a **Dear John letter**. The girl wasn't from our neighborhood, but it made for a lot of talk. He was one of ours. It was an "I am pregnant" letter. . . .

There was the constant idea that you had to be doing something to help. It did filter down to the neighborhood: home-front mobilization. We had a block captain. It was always some goof who wanted something like that, who could become a little official fellow. A sort of neighborhood guy who nobody would have ever noticed under normal circumstances. But he had his white helmet. He was the air-raid warden.

The siren would go off and everybody would turn off the lights. He would go around the neighborhood banging on doors and yelling, "Your lights are on." He'd write down people's names if they had a little light on in their apartments. I didn't like this.

Children in this Virginia neighborhood bring bacon grease and cooking fats to a collection spot. Fats and oils were used in the production of certain war materials during World War II.
Courtesy of the FDR Library.

Dear John letter: A letter written to end a close relationship.

Through a Youngster's Eyes: Mike Royko | 195

"Far-Away Father"

A steady stream of letters linked people on the home front with their loved ones who were fighting overseas. Many families made writing a group affair and sent letters at least once a week. Others wrote a letter or card every single day.

Children whose fathers were away from home on military duty were profoundly affected by the separation. Older children missed their fathers and longed to see them again. They lived in fear that their fathers might be killed in battle. Younger children and infants grew up without knowing what their fathers were like or what it was like to have a dad at home. Absent fathers anguished over missing milestones like a first step or a birthday.

Letters proved to be the best way to keep separated families close. The following excerpt comes from an article titled "Far-Away Father," written by Barbara S. Bosanquet and published in the June 1943 issue of *Woman's Home Companion*. The article advises mothers on the best ways to direct communication between a "far-away father" and his children. During the war years, advice articles such as this one, written with an overly simplistic tone, appeared frequently in popular women's magazines. It is interesting to ponder how a twenty-first-century woman would react to such advice.

'What color is Daddy's hair? How tall is he?' asks a four-year old English girl who has not seen her father since she was eighteen months old. She cannot remember him, yet she misses him. She bursts out with, 'Why can't my Daddy come to see me?'

Remarks such as these are now being heard in American homes. How shall we keep alive the feeling of the family as a unit?

Letters from the children to their father are one of the best links. Set aside a special time—say Sunday evening—and prepare pencils and paper for them.

My parents were downstairs running the tavern, so I'd have to turn out these damn lights. My younger brother and I would sit there in this absolutely pitch-black apartment. We were afraid that if we didn't, the air-raid warden would come by and the FBI would come and terrible things would happen. . . .

*We were all supposed to save fat—bacon grease and chicken fat. We believed that it would be used to make **nitroglycerine**. I don't think anybody ever turned it in. In our back yard, we had big coffee cans of fat and grease. . . .*

Nitroglycerine: An oily explosive liquid.

Father of course writes to the children. Short notes, funny stories and conundrums [puzzling riddles] are what they like.

One Englishman whose children are in America writes a monthly serial [stories that occur at regular intervals] for them about an imaginary family in England. He thus gets his everyday life across to seven- and nine-year-old daughters.

The knowing father always addresses letters separately to each child. He will ask questions about school and home. 'Dear Kathy, do you lisp without that tooth?'

Remind Father in advance about birthdays, so that he can send a special letter. You can also see to it that the most-wanted present bears a card from Daddy.

A father will feel cheated of his children as he realizes that he is losing months and perhaps years of their lives. He needs to have their daily life made real. Snapshots will help tremendously. Anecdotes [brief entertaining stories about some event] to show how often they talk of him will please him.

You will soon realize that children are upset in different ways by their father's absence. At a children's party the eight-year-old daughter of a naval officer on active duty was very jealous of her friends whose fathers were there. Her six-year-old sister that night dreamed of flying to her father's ship and bringing him home.

Children need men in the house. One grandfather was invited by his two grand-daughters whose father was in camp [at a military base] to come to Fathers' Day at their school. He was inspired to bring each of them a rose boutonniere [a flower worn in a buttonhole], which none of the fathers had thought of doing.

If your husband is on the battlefront you cannot always hide your anxiety. The older children are bound to feel the same way themselves. The sense of sharing this trouble, often unspoken, brings mother and children closer together. Anxiety is part of war. You can help the older ones to understand why their father must fight. The younger ones will accept the fact that Daddy is away "to help win the war," if you keep serene.

We'd listen to the radio every night. My father would turn it on to find out what was happening. The way a kid's mind could be shaped by those **dulcet** voices. The world was very simple. I saw Hitler and Mussolini and **Tojo**: those were the villains. We were the good guys. And the Russians were the good guys too. The war was always being talked about in the bar. Everybody was a military strategist.

The big event was my brother-in-law coming home, my sister's husband. He had been a combat soldier all the way

Dulcet: Pleasing or agreeable.

Tojo: Hideki Tojo, a Japanese military and political leader during World War II.

through. He had all his ribbons and medals on. He was the family hero. It was a constant thing in the neighborhood, guys comin' home from the war.

*Everybody was tacking **GI** on to everything. Do you know how many GI Lounges sprang up? Immediately after the **big bomb** was dropped on Japan, somebody opened the Atom Bomb Lounge on Milwaukee Avenue. Nobody really understood what happened. People couldn't grasp it. I don't remember any horror or regret. It was our weapon.*

*There were so many ex-GIs in the tavern. There wasn't a lot of sitting around talking about I did this, I did that. They just went about their business. The majority of guys from my neighborhood did not use the **GI Bill** for school. They used it for a loan for a home.*

That's when the younger couples started moving out. Guys got married and went lookin' to live somewhere else. The neighborhood got older and never really recovered. The guys went out to Park Forest, Rolling Meadows. They were the new suburban pioneers. Now that they fought, they came back and believed they were entitled to this type of life.

*Before the war, most of these people traveled by public transportation. Few people had cars. My father was considered a big help because he had a **La Salle**. It was a distinctive thing to own a car. Now, everybody had a car.*

*After the war my father put in a two-piece band that'd play on Friday night, a drummer and an accordion player. Pop songs, polkas, weddings. Every weekend there were weddings. These soldiers coming back were getting married. That's when the **baby boom** started. They were working, they had money. They were going out on Friday and Saturday nights. The vitality of the neighborhood was tremendous—until the move to the suburbs.*

What happened next . . .

By the end of the war, Mike was a budding teen. At the tavern he watched victory parties and weddings take place. However, the GI Bill made it possible for many new couples to

GI: Nickname for military servicemen derived from the term "government issue."

Big bomb: The atomic bomb; bombs were dropped on Nagasaki and Hiroshima, Japan, effectively ending the war with Japan.

GI Bill: A legislative act that provided extensive economic benefits to World War II veterans, including support for school expenses and low-interest loans for buying homes and starting businesses and farms.

La Salle: A make of car.

Baby boom: An unusually high birthrate after World War II between 1946 and 1964, leading to a population of 76 million children.

buy homes in the suburbs. As they moved away, Mike's neighborhood began to lose its energy.

Mike was seventeen when the Korean War (1950–53) started. In another excerpt from *"The Good War": An Oral History of World War II,* he described it as "our first embarrassing war." World War II soldiers from Mike's neighborhood were his heroes; assuming he would also come home a hero, Mike joined the military and went to Korea. By then, he was nineteen years old. When he got to Korea, however, he made a startling discovery. As he put it, "I didn't know anyone who was in Korea who understood what we were doing there." He also had trouble grasping who the good guys and the bad guys were in this conflict. Japan, once an enemy of the United States, was now an ally of the United States in the fight against communist North Korea and China. He recalls his confusion and embarrassment about the war:

> I was still mad at the Japs. The Japanese are now our friends, our pals. I'm going from Japan to Korea, where I'm supposed to fight the Chinese, who are now our enemies. A few years earlier I was mad at the Japanese and I was supposed to love the Chinese. Now I gotta love the Japanese and hate the Chinese. (Laughs.) That's when I decided something's wrong.

> I remember coming back from Korea, the hostility, the indifference. I was almost embarrassed being in Korea because we didn't win. We cut a deal. We got a draw. We had failed where our older brothers had won.

Always able to express his ideas in writing, Mike eventually became a well-known columnist for the *Chicago Tribune.*

Did you know . . .

- During World War II (1939–45) television was still new technology, and almost no one purchased a television between 1942 and 1945. Instead children gathered with their parents around the radio to hear entertainment programming and up-to-date news of the war.

- War games were the most popular games of the day. Children needed nothing more than a few blocks of wood and some street puddles to stage grand battleship fights.

- The GI Bill, passed in 1944, rewarded veterans of World War II by providing them with money for education. Through the bill veterans could also apply for low-interest loans to purchase homes, new businesses, and farms. The bill's benefits gave war veterans a boost toward a more prosperous life.

Consider the following . . .

- The radio was the main source of news in Mike's home. Research what types of programs radio stations offered for children in the early 1940s.

- Civil defense workers wore special patches on their sleeves to signify their designated roles in the home front war effort. A favorite pastime among children was learning to identify the various patches. Check sources in your local public library for images of civil defense insignia. Learn as many of the insignia as you can, and then make up a game that tests your knowledge.

For More Information

Books

Bailey, Ronald H. *The Home Front, U.S.A.* Alexandria, VA: Time-Life Books, 1977.

Harris, Mark J., Franklin D. Mitchell, and Steven J. Schechter, eds. *The Homefront: America during World War II.* New York: G. P. Putnam's Sons, 1984.

Schickel, Richard. *Good Morning, Mr. Zip Zip Zip: Movies, Memory, and World War II.* Chicago: Ivan R. Dee, 2003.

Terkel, Studs. *"The Good War": An Oral History of World War II.* New York: Ballantine Books, 1984.

Watters, Mary. *Illinois in the Second World War.* Springfield: Illinois State Historical Library, 1952.

Periodicals

Bosanquet, Barbara S. "Far-Away Father," *Woman's Home Companion,* (June 1943): p. 6.

Praise and Practical Advice

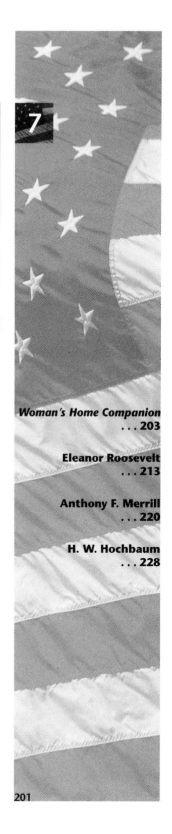

W ar spread across Europe and Asia in the late 1930s. As the fighting continued in 1940 and 1941, Americans hoped the United States could somehow stay out of the conflict. However, on December 7, 1941, Japanese bombers attacked a U.S. military base at Pearl Harbor, Hawaii, and in response the United States declared war on Japan. After this declaration, people on the home front had to make lifestyle changes and sacrifices so that all the nation's resources could be directed toward the war effort. Housewives were asked to plan nutritious meals despite the limitations of a strict food rationing system. They were also encouraged to plant victory gardens, volunteer for war-related community activities, and enter the wartime workforce. Millions of men also contributed to the home front war effort. Either too old for military service or disqualified from service for medical reasons, they kept the nation's economy running by working in war industries or taking jobs left by those who joined the military services. Men on the home front also took over traditionally male responsibilities, such as repair and maintenance of homes and cars, for neighbors whose husbands or sons were serving in the military.

The U.S. government printed and distributed pamphlets, articles, and posters that gave Americans practical advice on how to accomplish all they were asked to do. These materials also provided encouraging words for everyone involved in the home front effort. Articles full of encouragement and wartime advice dominated popular magazines too. Television had not yet arrived in homes, so magazines were the top visual entertainment medium. Most were published in a very large format, with many pictures and full-page advertisements. Magazines were a major source of news and lifestyle information during the war years, and most households subscribed to several.

Some magazines were geared especially to women's interests. These included *Woman's Home Companion, Ladies' Home Journal, House and Garden, McCall's,* and *Good Housekeeping.* All the excerpts in this chapter provide examples of the praise and practical advice such magazines offered. The first excerpt, "How You Are Helping," was originally published in the June 1943 issue of *Woman's Home Companion.* The article praises the sacrifices and courage of America's "wives and mothers, the sisters and daughters of our fighting men." The second excerpt is from a question-and-answer series called "If You Ask Me," which was written by Eleanor Roosevelt (1884–1962), the First Lady. The series appeared in *Ladies' Home Journal* from 1941 to 1949. Many American women looked upon Eleanor Roosevelt as a mother figure for the nation, and they took her words of advice to heart. The third excerpt is from "Washington and the Home Front," a piece written by Anthony F. Merrill and published in the March 1942 issue of *House and Garden.* Although it appeared in a women's magazine, this article was directed toward home front men, offering suggestions for keeping their homes in good repair. The fourth excerpt, "Still Keep 'Em Growing," was written by H. W. Hochbaum and published in the January 1944 issue of *House and Garden.* The article praises Americans for their successful victory gardens and urges them to plant even more in 1944. Notice how the articles excerpted in this chapter use patriotic language in their discussion of everyday home front activities and family relationships.

Woman's Home Companion

Excerpt from "How You Are Helping"
**Published in *Woman's Home Companion*,
June 1943.**

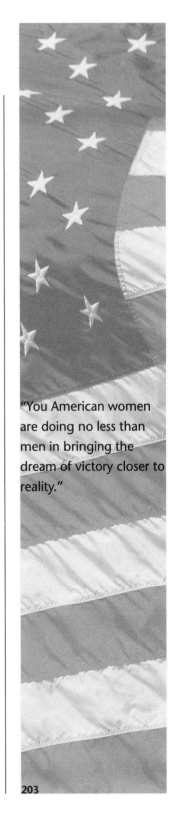

In preparation for an article praising the war contributions of America's women on the home front, the editors of *Woman's Home Companion* sent out a questionnaire to their Reader-Reporters in early 1943. Reader-Reporters were readers who volunteered to relay home front wartime activities that were occurring in their communities and share their own thoughts as the war progressed. Roughly one-third of them had immediate family members in the military. Likewise one-third had family members working in the war industries. Half of the Reader-Reporters volunteered for activities directly related to the war effort. These Reader-Reporters were representative of the female population nationwide.

As noted in "How You Are Helping," the questionnaire aimed to find out "just how deeply the war had penetrated women's everyday lives and their psyches." The final section asked Reader-Reporters to "Look into your hearts and write what you feel today." For their article, the editors of *Woman's Home Companion* used excerpts from the completed questionnaires. The portion of the article that is reprinted in this chapter features Reader-Reporter comments on a variety of subjects that

"You American women are doing no less than men in bringing the dream of victory closer to reality."

were topics of daily discussion for all Americans: rationing, volunteering, the need for patience, and a sense of community.

The article also pointed out that Americans always thought for themselves and approached topics from different angles. Some respondents opposed war and the horrors it created. Others grumbled about the wealthy few Americans who continued to spend on luxuries; others complained about supposed government inefficiency in spending their tax dollars. Most, however, wrote that they were eager to do whatever they could for the war effort. Some, sensitive to the ethnic diversity of the American population, called for the end of racial prejudice in America. Many yearned for peaceful times again.

Things to remember while reading the excerpt from "How You Are Helping" . . .

- By spring 1942 running a household was becoming more and more difficult: Shortages of basic consumer items became more common; men joined the military, leaving their wives in charge of all household duties; and many women began working outside the home as well, filling vacancies left by men who had entered the armed forces.

- Approximately 32.5 million American women worked at home running their households in 1943 and 1944. They were considered the backbone of the country during the war years.

- Whether a woman remained at home or entered the workforce, she was responsible for shopping, food preparation, cleaning the house, childcare, sewing, washing and ironing clothing, tending a victory garden, canning garden produce, and volunteering for war-related community activities.

Excerpt from "How You Are Helping"

Our Reader-Reporters are doing their glorious share in winning the war. Here they look into their hearts and reveal what lessons their sacrifices are teaching them.

Federal Security Agency
U. S. PUBLIC HEALTH SERVICE

H. PRICE

Foods that count keep him on the job

As the household members primarily in charge of food shopping and preparation, women were encouraged to buy wisely in order to keep their men in top condition for war efforts.
© K.J. Historical/Corbis. Reproduced by permission.

SOME DAY the world will thrill to the full story of how you women of America contributed to victory in World War II. Today we already can say, humbly and proudly, that we salute the wives and mothers, the sisters and daughters of our fighting men.

You American women are doing no less than men in bringing the dream of victory closer to reality. You are working in your homes, in volunteer centers, in war factories, in child-care centers. You are demonstrating **ingenuity** in changed circumstances. You are showing courage in **bereavement, stamina** in uncertainty. You are proving your ability to make cheerful homes for weary war

Ingenuity: Skillful cleverness.

Bereavement: Grieving over the death of a loved one.

Stamina: Endurance.

workers, to feed children nutritious meals despite shortages and rationing, to economize and sacrifice to win the war.

This picture is no optimistic dream or wishful thinking. Through our panel of Reader-Reporters across the nation, the WOMAN'S HOME COMPANION *is enabled to look into the lives,* **aspirations** *and deeds of a representative* **cross section** *of our millions of readers. And what we see today thrills us—and should send a chill through the hearts of the* **Axis leaders***.*

Today more than 35 percent of our Reader-Reporters have one or more members of their immediate families in the armed forces.

Today more than 36 percent of our Reader-Reporters have one or more members of their immediate families working in war plants or making supplies for our armed forces. . . .

In addition almost 50 percent of our Reader-Reporters are doing volunteer war work outside their homes—and they average seven and one-half hours of work every week.

Recently we sent to our Reader-Reporters a questionnaire designed to indicate just how deeply the war had penetrated their lives. The last question was this: "Look into your hearts and write what you feel today."

The answers reveal not only that the women of America are working overtime to **lick** the Axis, but that the sacrifices and hardships of war are bringing a heartening new significance to our American democracy.

"The people," writes a housewife on the Atlantic seaboard, "are willing and anxious to make every sacrifice. Imagine **griping** about rationing when so much is at stake. Better to ration unnecessarily than to have wished we had been rationed."

Scarcely a single Reader-Reporter protests against the hardships of rationing. Of course they don't pretend that it makes housekeeping any easier, but they accept it quietly as an **inevitable prelude** to victory. And they have learned new values. For example listen to this woman in the middle west:

"As I find myself with fewer and fewer material things, I remember my childhood, barren in money, rich in memories. My father made our Christmas presents and my mother was an artist in **makeshifts**. There is no real poverty except poverty of the spirit."

Aspirations: Desired goals or ambitions.

Cross section: A representative sample.

Axis leaders: Leaders of Germany, Italy, and Japan.

Lick: Defeat.

Griping: Complaining.

Inevitable prelude: A necessary condition leading up to.

Makeshifts: Making do with what is available for gifts and wrappings.

RATINING SAFEGUARDS YOUR SHARE

U. S. GOVERNMENT PRINTING OFFICE. 1943 — O—493734

Office of Price Administration

A New Englander writes: "God sent us a sweet baby girl and my husband happened to be transferred from one post to another and was home when the baby was born. This brought me great comfort."

*Another: "My husband and I preferred a movie or visiting old friends to **cultivating** our neighbors. War has knit our family closer and we share the new-found feeling with our neighbors."*

*Here's a woman who is working as a bookkeeper while her husband works in a war plant. Does she feel that they are doing enough? No! "The biggest problem among us civilians today is patience and understanding, especially among women," she writes. "We must remember that war workers working long hours are **keyed up to the breaking point**. Store clerks are rushed to death and rationing and shortages aren't their fault. We must learn to take these things **in our stride**."*

Nobody pretends that the adjustment to an empty place at the table is easy. "My only son is a gunner on an army bomber,"

Food rationing was generally accepted by Americans who wanted to do whatever they could to help win World War II. This poster aims to explain the benefit of rationing during the war years.
The Library of Congress.

Cultivating: Improving relations with.

Keyed up to the breaking point: Worn out and stressed to a high degree.

In our stride: Keep a steady pace to meet goals.

writes one mother. *"At first I am ashamed to say I cried a good deal. Then I realized that I was making my husband and daughter unhappy. I busied myself with Red Cross and volunteer aid work and put my faith in God. I realized that my behavior was a denial of all the faith I had tried to instill in my children. Now I have found myself again and am carrying on with thousands of other mothers."*

These are honest sentiments from the hearts of the women of America. They are working in Red Cross centers, civic defense, salvage committees, child-care centers, hospitals, war factories, to say nothing of the armed forces themselves.

*"I'm a **Wave**,"* writes one girl. *"Naturally we miss our men but if we buckle down and do our job well, they'll be coming back soon. . . ."*

Americans are individualists. They do not conform to rigid patterns, as do the women of **totalitarian states**. They have and express their own opinions. A woman on the Atlantic seaboard writes: *"The war oppresses me with a feeling of living in a nightmare. I find that I cannot rejoice in the news that so many thousands have been killed, even if they are the enemy. I see **gallant** youngsters eagerly setting out to drop bombs on civilians of other nations. Every decent human value seems twisted."*

There is a bit of grumbling. Some who are putting all their spare cash into war bonds cannot understand why others are indulging in luxuries. Some complain of **Washington inefficiency**. Some protest against high wages to war workers.

But most of our Reader-Reporters prove that they are Americans in spirit as well as name. Their sentiments are symbolized by those of a woman in New England.

*"Today women no longer ask what they can do. They do it. By thousands in our **arsenal city**, they pack the bus lines, **throng** the entrances to the **armory building** and other war factories. They wear slacks, tie bandannas around their curls and carry lunch boxes. Their faces are weary and their steps drag when they end their shifts. What drives these tired girls and young **matrons**? Big money or patriotism? Or both? Never mind. They are making **munitions** in our common cause.*

*"In restaurants waitresses are in their sixties and even seventies. It hurts you to see them carrying heavy trays—until you see the pride in their bright eyes. **Grandsons, maybe, in Africa?**

Wave: Reference to the WAVES, Women's Auxilliary Volunteer Emergency Service, a U.S. Navy volunteer service for women.

Totalitarian states: Countries where every aspect of life is tightly controlled by a dictator and all citizens must conform.

Gallant: Heroic.

Washington inefficiency: The U.S. government's perceived misuse of money.

Arsenal city: A community where military equipment and weapons are manufactured or stored.

Throng: Crowd.

Armory building: A place where military equipment and weapons are manufactured or stored.

Matrons: Married women, often with children.

Munitions: Various types of ammunition, such as grenades and bombs.

Grandsons, maybe, in Africa?: Refers to Allied forces fighting against German forces in North Africa from 1942 to 1943.

I'm Proud... my husband
wants me to do my part

SEE YOUR U. S. EMPLOYMENT SERVICE
WAR MANPOWER COMMISSION

Women during World War II wanted to contribute to the war effort in whatever way they could. For some, this meant tending a victory garden in the backyard while continuing to take care of their families, for others it meant taking a war industry job outside the house.
The Library of Congress.

"*Heavy planes roar steadily over your tiny apartment. Your caller says, 'Don't they make you frightfully nervous?' 'No,' you say, 'they reassure me. They're ours, thank god.'*

"*You go to the church of your own preference. On the way you pass your Greek newsstand, your Italian grocer, your Jewish tailor, your French hairdresser, your Irish **druggist**. Tolerance is no longer a mere word.*"

Women are doing wartime duties but yearn eventually to live in peace. . . .

Druggist: Pharmacist; a person who prepares medical prescriptions for customers.

*These women are giving serious thought to all the victories, large and small, that must be won. Writes a New England housewife: "There's a day coming when the Negro race will have a **place in the sun**. And the anti-Jewish sentiment **cropping out** is tragic."*

*"Both my sister and I work," says another. "The war has taught me that we must have **more Christianity** toward all people, both here and abroad. Social and racial prejudices must stop."*

*"I believe," writes a New England teacher, "that the world of the future can be educated for peace rather than for war. Didn't Hitler prove that you can teach children to grow up as you wish when he educated them for **Nazism**? I feel that a woman should be **at the peace table**, a woman interested in humanity rather than economics or finance."*

From the Pacific Coast, "Some day this will be over. I believe that a better world is in the making—better living conditions for more people, a greater understanding between races."

What happened next . . .

On May 7, 1945, Germany surrendered. On August 14, 1945, Japan surrendered. The war was over, and Americans flooded the streets in jubilation. The food and material shortages ended within months, the men came home, working women became housewives again—though in some cases reluctantly, and the U.S. economy began a peacetime march to prosperity. However, lasting peace proved elusive. The United States had forced Japan's surrender by dropping atomic bombs on the cities of Hiroshima and Nagasaki; more than 120,000 Japanese citizens were killed. With this act, the world entered the nuclear age, and all nations had to live with the knowledge that potential enemies could annihilate them with nuclear weapons. By the late 1940s the United States and the Soviet Union, the two nations that possessed nuclear weapons, had become opponents in the so-called Cold War (1945–91). The Cold War was an intense political and economic rivalry that fell just short of military conflict but inspired a massive buildup of weapons on both sides. This Cold War rivalry

Place in the sun: An equal social and economic status with white Americans.

Cropping out: Appearing on the scene.

More Christianity: Adopt principles of the Christian faith; love one another, treat each other with respect.

Nazism: Allegiance to a political party that controlled Germany, more formally known as the National Socialist German Worker's Party, led by Adolf Hitler from 1920 to 1945.

At the peace table: Directly involved in peace negotiations.

between the United States and communist countries would sometimes flare up in armed conflict. In 1950 the United States entered the Korean War (1950–53) fighting against communist North Korea and Chinese forces.

Contrary to the hopes of many people on the home front, the grim experience of World War II did not lead to immediate improvements in social and racial attitudes. After the war's end, it took almost twenty years to achieve major civil rights legislation in the United States. Congress passed the Civil Rights Act in 1964.

Did you know . . .

- In 1940 only 15 percent of all married women in the United States worked outside the home. By war's end one in four, or 25 percent, were in the workforce. Mothers with children younger than six years of age were urged to stay home, so very few young mothers sought employment.

- The first food rationed was sugar. On May 5, 1942, War Ration Book One, popularly known as the "Sugar Book," appeared. It gave each individual the same number of stamps for sugar purchase; the stamps were the only legal way to obtain refined sugar. On November 29, 1942, coffee rationing began. In early 1943 rationing for meat—including beef, veal, pork, lamb, butter and oils, and cheese—went into effect.

- Women served as volunteers in various organizations, including the American Red Cross, the Office of Civilian Defense, and the United Service Organizations (USO). They also volunteered to work on war bond drives, which were concentrated campaigns to sell bonds that would help finance the war effort.

Consider the following . . .

- After delving into the various topics presented in this book, imagine yourself as a home front woman—a housewife or a workforce woman—in the middle of the war years. Write your own response to "Look into your hearts and write what you feel today."

- At your public library, ask a librarian to help you find the November and December 1942 issues of *Good Housekeeping*. Look up two articles: "Thanksgiving, Don't Skip It This Year" in the November issue and "Plan Your Holiday Meals This Way and You'll Meet Uncle Sam's Recommendations for Nutritious Meals" in the December issue. Prepare several of the ration-conscious recipes offered in these articles.

- Identify and discuss the personal Attributes that women needed to make it through the war years.

For More Information

Books

Sinnott, Susan. *Doing Our Part: American Women on the Home Front during World War II.* New York: F. Watts, 1995.

Whitman, Sylvia. *V Is for Victory: The American Home Front during World War II.* Minneapolis, MN: Lerner, 1993.

Winkler, Allan M. *Home Front U.S.A.: America during World War II.* Arlington Heights, IL: H. Davidson, 1986.

Periodicals

"How You Are Helping." *Woman's Home Companion* (June 1943): pp. 20, 82.

Eleanor Roosevelt

Excerpt from "If You Ask Me"

**Written by Eleanor Roosevelt.
Published in *Ladies' Home Journal*,
August 1943.**

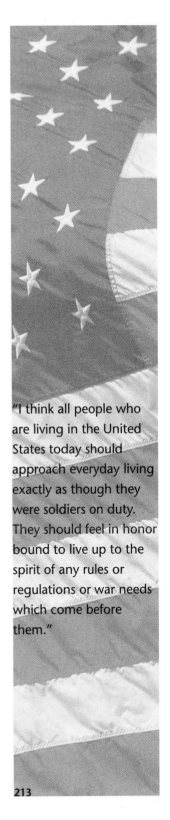

E leanor Roosevelt (1884–1962), wife of President Franklin D. Roosevelt, wrote a monthly question-and-answer column titled "If You Ask Me" for *Ladies' Home Journal* from June 1941 until the spring of 1949. The First Lady tackled all sorts of questions, addressing national and international issues and dispensing practical advice on family matters. In this excerpt her responses cover a wide range of topics, including freedom of the press and the division of household chores between husbands and wives. During the war years her answers always reflected consideration of the country's united war effort. The following questions and answers come from *Ladies' Home Journal* issues that were published between August and November 1943.

"I think all people who are living in the United States today should approach everyday living exactly as though they were soldiers on duty. They should feel in honor bound to live up to the spirit of any rules or regulations or war needs which come before them."

Things to remember while reading the excerpt from "If You Ask Me" . . .

- When the United States entered World War II, Eleanor Roosevelt had been the nation's First Lady for almost nine years.

- Unlike any First Lady before her, Eleanor Roosevelt took a leading role in national affairs. With tireless efforts and compassion she had shepherded Americans through the dark years of the Great Depression (1929–41), the worst economic crisis in U.S. history, when record numbers of people were unemployed.

- Throughout the 1930s Americans had become accustomed to writing personal letters to the First Lady, asking for her help.

Excerpt from "If You Ask Me"

[Question, August 1943 issue] *Considering the fact that radio stations are licensed by the **existing Administration** and therefore exist only by grant of power from whichever party is **in the ascendant**, combined with the fact that radio is so heavily under war censorship, don't you think it would be best to inform people that radio will always be a thoroughly censored medium?*

[Answer] *Radio licenses are granted by the Federal Communications Commission. This commission is an independent bureau, established by an act of Congress, June 19, 1934. It is not controlled politically. It is composed of seven members and functions as a unit.*

It seems to me that though, of course, the radio has to be censored on war information, just as newspapers are, it is as free a medium of information as there is in the country, though, like the newspapers, it is naturally affected and colored somewhat by its sponsors. Advertising naturally has considerable effect both on the radio and on newspapers and magazines. . . .

[Question, August 1943 issue] *Don't you think doctors, farmers, war workers, and so on, with **T gas cards**, and others with **C gas rations** who use their gas for personal driving, and other ration cheaters, should be **classed with strikers** in wartime?*

[Answer] *I think all people who are living in the United States today should approach everyday living exactly as though they*

Existing Administration: U.S. president, his staff, and cabinet members.

In the ascendant: In political power.

T gas cards: Gasoline ration cards that allowed truckers to purchase all the gas they needed.

C gas rations: Cards issued to people who performed essential work that required the use of additional gasoline.

Classed with strikers: Equating ration cheaters with striking laborers. Most Americans considered the laborers who went on strike during the war as unpatriotic.

In uniform: In military service.

were soldiers on duty. They should feel in honor bound to live up to the spirit of any rules or regulations or war needs which come before them.

There will arise border-line cases in which it is hard to decide whether they should follow one course or another. In such cases I think they must do what common sense dictates and what will help them to meet their personal obligations in the best possible way. By doing so they will, of course, help the community situation as a whole. . . .

[Question, September 1943 issue] *How can I have the baby my husband and I want—and should have as our contribution to the future of our country—as my husband is **in uniform** and I have to work to support myself? What is a **white-collar** wife to do now that the baby nurses are all in the defense industry?*

[Answer] *There are nearly always people who would rather take care of babies or who, for one reason or another, have to work at something different than defense work. You will have to try hard to find one of these people if you want to keep on with your job. Otherwise you may have to find ways of **getting on** for a while on whatever your husband can send you and stay at home yourself to take care of the baby. If your husband is a private and you have no one else in the family who can help you out, you may find it impossible to support yourself and a baby; but if you have someone who can help you and you can manage to get along for a while on what your husband sends, you may later be able to find someone whom you can pay, or perhaps a nursery where you can leave the baby for the time when you are at work. . . .*

[Question, September 1943 issue] *I've heard that every soldier is entitled to a **furlough** before he goes overseas, and yet my husband and many of the men in his outfit are being **shipped** without having been granted a single furlough since their **induction** four or five months ago. Is this fair?*

Many Americans turned to Eleanor Roosevelt for advice and encouragement during her time as first lady.
AP/Wide World Photos.
Reproduced by permission.

White-collar: Professional worker who does not perform manual labor.

Getting on: Making do.

Furlough: A brief leave of absence from duty.

Shipped: Shipped overseas for military duty.

Induction: Enrollment into the military.

[Answer] *It is very unfortunate when that happens to a man, but I have known it to happen in a number of instances. It only happens, however, when the needs of war require it; and you have to realize that from the time a man goes into the Army, while he will be given every consideration that is possible, there is one greater consideration, and that is the good of the country and the good of the service, and everything else must be* **subordinated** *to it. We just have to be grateful when the furloughs come through, but try to be resigned when they do not. . . .*

[Question, October 1943 issue] *What is your opinion of the wives of servicemen who follow their husbands around from camp to camp? Do you think it keeps up the morale of these men to have their wives near, regardless of the conditions of the camp towns and the general high cost of living in them?*

[Answer] *I am quite sure that it is good for the morale of the men to have their wives near, if it is possible for them to put up with whatever conditions they may meet without grumbling, which would make it harder for the men. If a wife realizes that she must take second place as against the war job which her husband must do, and that she is there primarily to help him do that job, she will endure difficulties and discomforts cheerfully and be happy that they have a chance to be with each other for a little longer.*

If a woman has this attitude, I am sure she will find endless ways in which to help her husband and other men in the camp, and her presence will always be welcome.

[Question, October 1943 issue] *When a woman puts in an eight-hour day at a war job and has a family to look after, too, don't you think it is only fair that her husband should do half the housework?*

[Answer] *I should think it would be a little difficult to divide the housework equally, but any husband who really cares for his wife will naturally help her in any way he can. . . .*

[Question, November 1943 issue] *Do you believe that our soldiers and workers in defense plants should work on Sunday?*

[Answer] *When there is need to do so, I think all of us should work on Sunday. There is a* **parable** *in the Bible which I think very clearly suggests the fact that work which is needed should always be done.*

[Question, November 1943 issue] *It has always been my belief that everyone has a right to live. Now I am asked to send my*

Subordinated: Considered less important.

Parable: A story that provides a moral lesson.

husband off with my blessing to destroy the lives of other men. Do you think this is right?

[Answer] *I am afraid that when it is a question of either destroying someone else or being destroyed, there is very little choice for most of us, and those of us who believe that people have a right to live until they die from natural causes must work for peace between wars, because, once war starts, our natural instinct for self-preservation is going to make all of us fight.*

Eleanor Roosevelt was a big proponent of women entering the workforce.
Courtesy of the FDR Library.

What happened next . . .

Mrs. Roosevelt continued writing this column throughout the war. Publication of the column stopped in spring 1949. However, Americans continued to seek the First Lady's wise advice and commentary, which she provided in various forms until her death in 1962.

Did you know . . .

- Eleanor Roosevelt understood firsthand the loneliness of military families on the home front and the sacrifices they made. Her sons James, Elliott, Franklin Jr., and John served in the military. Her daughter Anna's husband, Captain John Boettiger, served in Europe. The First Lady was a constant source of support for both her own family and her nation.

- A prolific writer, Eleanor Roosevelt produced another column, "My Day," which was regularly published in newspapers across the country. She wrote the column from January 1936 until her death in 1962. Mrs. Roosevelt also authored numerous books about her life and national and international issues.

Consider the following . . .

- The war effort posed great challenges for Americans on the home front and raised questions about employment practices, family life, the ethics of war, and many other issues. Choose a wartime issue that interests you, and devise a question to Mrs. Roosevelt concerning that topic.

- Have a classmate write a response to the question you asked Mrs. Roosevelt. The response should include both facts and compassion, just as Mrs. Roosevelt's responses always did.

- At your public library ask a librarian to help you find issues of *Ladies' Home Journal* from 1941 through 1945. Locate Mrs. Roosevelt's column in these issues, and read more of her responses to readers' questions.

For More Information

Books

Chadakoff, Rochelle, ed. *Eleanor Roosevelt's "My Day."* New York: Pharos Books, 1989.

Hareven, Tamara R. *Eleanor Roosevelt: An American Conscience.* Chicago: Quadrangle Books, 1968.

Roosevelt, David B. *Grandmere: A Personal History of Eleanor Roosevelt.* New York: Warnerbooks, 2002.

Roosevelt, Eleanor. *The Autobiography of Eleanor Roosevelt.* New York: Harper & Brothers Publishers, 1961.

Periodicals

Roosevelt, Eleanor. "If You Ask Me." *Ladies' Home Journal* (August–November 1943).

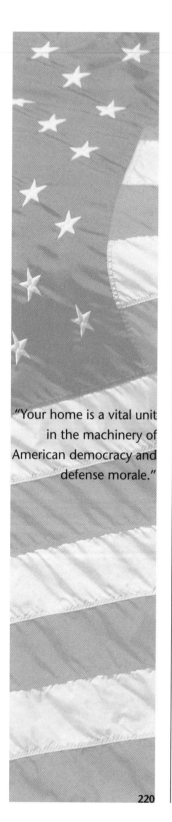

Anthony F. Merrill

Excerpt from "Washington and the Home Front"
**Written by Anthony F. Merrill.
Published in *House and Garden*,
March 1942.**

"Your home is a vital unit in the machinery of American democracy and defense morale."

Women on the home front were expected to sew most of their own clothes, grow their own vegetables in backyard victory gardens, and plan nutritious meals despite food shortages and a strict rationing system. Advice on how to accomplish these goals appeared regularly in women's magazines, and historical accounts of wartime sacrifices and ingenuity on the home front generally focus on women's activities. However, between thirty million and forty million American men also contributed on the home front, working in all capacities as part of the U.S. labor force. Those men were also responsible for household duties such as home and car maintenance. Fulfilling such duties required creativity and extra planning, because many parts and materials were in short supply during the war. The following article, "Washington and the Home Front," is a pep talk filled with humor and practical advice designed to rally men to their duties of home maintenance and repair.

Things to remember while reading the excerpt from "Washington and the Home Front" . . .

- The government estimated that single-family homes in the United States in the early 1940s were worth $80 billion.

- During the war government propaganda suggested that maintaining a home in good repair was a patriotic duty. However, the military had first access to all the raw materials that normally went into manufacturing supplies for home construction and maintenance. Therefore, civilians had an extra challenge in finding the supplies they needed to complete their home maintenance chores.

- Easily hired during peacetime, professional repairmen became scarce during the war years: Many joined the military or took war industry jobs. With repairmen in short supply, a do-it-yourself approach was a necessity rather than a hobby.

Excerpt from "Washington and the Home Front"

A report on the priority and housing agencies' attitude toward the war-time problems of home maintenance and repair.

Your home is a vital unit in the machinery of American democracy and defense morale. **Uncle Sam** *does not intend that it shall break down because of a leaky roof, a worn-out furnace grate, or a broken washing-machine part. On the contrary, America's homes, and America's investment in homes are the serious concern of several important branches of government.*

True, the Army and Navy need, and are taking, many of the raw materials and fabricated pieces which ordinarily go into home construction, but this won't prevent the essential repairs which your house occasionally requires—not for an unpredictably long time, at any rate.

Uncle Sam: A fictional character, dressed all in red, white, and blue, used to represent the United States. Beyond the character, the term itself, "Uncle Sam," represented the United States.

War Bond Campaigns

The War Finance Committee, a special wartime government agency charged with financing the war effort, directed war bond campaigns. By the end of 1945 the committee had raised and deposited into the U.S. Treasury $185.7 billion from war bond sales. Buying war bonds allowed individual Americans to express their patriotism and contribute to the war effort. By the end of the war more than eighty-five million Americans had invested in bonds. Not only did Americans aid in financing the war, they also derived a great moral boost by helping in the march to victory. The government and private industry continuously praised Americans for buying bonds.

Bonds could be purchased in two ways, through a Payroll Savings Plan or during a War Bond Loan campaign. Employees participating in the Payroll Savings Plan had a certain amount of money deducted from each paycheck and put toward the purchase of bonds. The War Finance Committee directed eight War Bond Loan Campaigns, the first running from November 30, 1942, to December 23, 1942, and the eighth starting on October 29, 1945, and ending December 8, 1945. Total sales in each drive exceeded the set goal. To promote the drives, corporations and organizations donated advertising space in newspapers and magazines. Companies contributed approximately $180 million in advertising space—in print, on billboards, and on radio—during the war years.

Through special radio productions and on cross country tours numerous Hollywood celebrities participated in the campaigns. Singer Kate Smith (1909–1986) and actress Dorothy Lamour (1914–1996) were key contributors to the success of war bond campaigns.

Campaign	Dates	Sales
First War Loan	11/30/42–12/23/42	$13 billion

Donald Nelson's: President Roosevelt's appointee in January 1942 as head of the War Production Board (WPB) that would make important decisions about directing raw materials to war industries.

Delude: Mislead.

That's the optimistic word from **Donald Nelson's** War Production Board. . . . Washington [D.C.] has not forgotten, either, that the American home is what we are fighting for, and it wants the American people to know that it hasn't forgotten.

Attitudes of supply bureaus

But—every official in the supply control bureaus urges the home-owner not to **delude** himself on the importance of civilian needs. If it's a scarce article and the military wants all of it, or an item that's off the store shelves because of war-order demands

Second War Loan	4/12/43–5/1/43	$18.5 billion
Third War Loan	9/9/43–10/2/43	$19 billion
Fourth War Loan	1/18/44–2/15/44	$16.7 billion
Fifth War Loan	6/12/44–7/8/44	$20.6 billion
Sixth War Loan	11/20/44–12/31/44	$21.6 billion
Seventh War Loan	5/4/45–6/25/45	$26 billion
Eighth War Loan	10/29/45–12/8/45	$21 billion

How bond investment worked

War bonds were bought for one half their face value, a $50 bond cost $25, a $25 bond cost $12.50. The government paid interest on the purchase price. Investors held onto their bonds for a predetermined period of years. At the end of that period the buyer could cash his bond for the full face value, doubling his original investment.

A less expensive way to buy a bond was through purchase of war stamps. War stamps were pasted into a war stamp book. When the book was filled it was turned in for a bond. Schoolchildren often filled war stamp books as a class project.

Each purchased bond was a loan to the government. The government had to repay the purchase price with interest but over a period of years. This allowed the government to receive up-front money for the war effort, then allowed it to pay back the money over a period of years. This is how, for decades, individual Americans have purchased large items such as homes and cars: a loan from a bank for up-front money that is repaid with interest over time by the individual.

Derived from the John W. Hartman Center for Sales, Advertising, and Marketing History, Duke University Web site: http://scriptorium.lib.duke.edu/adaccess/warbonds.html (accessed on August 2, 2004).

upon the manufacturing plants, it won't be available for the home-owner, no matter how badly he needs it.

That's the whole story in a nutshell. . . . At the moment the prospects of keeping your home in good shape are excellent, but if unexpected war demands alter the picture, you may have to let your home go to pot. The gloomy extreme is this—we are in a "total war" so all-inclusive of everyday civilian life that even our homes, through their enforced neglect, may serve as weapons. In other words, if your home has to go to rack and ruin in order that the Army may have everything it needs, then in so serving the

Go to pot: Go without needed repairs.

All-inclusive: Affecting everything.

Enforced neglect: Lack of maintenance and repair, brought about by wartime shortages of building materials.

Go to rack and ruin: Fall into disrepair.

nation your home will become a weapon against our enemies. That's very long-range **speculation**, indeed, yet defense officials are determined to present the public with the grim **potentialities** of the situation so that a complete sacrifice, should it ever be demanded, will not come as a horrid shock.

Home repair possibilities

However, today and for the immediate future, you may safely assume that you will be able to preserve your home in its present condition without hindering the war effort. Of course new private construction or non-defense remodeling receives no sympathy in Washington [D.C.], and if you haven't all the materials on hand for this work, you'd better not bother anyone by asking for them. If you can afford a new sunporch, you can afford **defense bonds** and the government agencies prefer **priority allocations in the latter**. But if it's a repair you're interested in, you may expect courtesy and assistance from one end of town to the other, within reasonable bounds.

What are primary repairs

Repair and maintenance, when translated into things, mean new paint and roofing, and replacement of worn-out heating, plumbing and electrical equipment. Check these principal repair factors against the war demands and you **have the picture**.

First; paint. While government agencies like to **needle** the **necessity-howlers** by remarking that a house won't collapse just because it needs a coat of paint, in reality there seems to be promise of a continuing supply of paint on the shelves of your local hardware store. . . . You'll have paint brushes, too, in spite of the fact that the Navy recently took over every bristle in the country. After that move the Navy found itself with a five-year supply of bristles, more than it needs, and now they are being gradually fed back into the market. . . .

Available roofing materials

There is a **sufficiency** of roofing materials—asphalt, slate and wood—and no shortage seems to be coming up. You may have difficulty finding supplies at your regular dealers, but there will be enough if you shop around. To illustrate—at this writing some areas are experiencing nail shortages, Philadelphia in particular. An **OPM** survey **ascertained** that there are enough nails and

Speculation: Prediction.

Potentialities: Possibilities.

Defense bonds: Reference to war bonds, government certificates sold to the public to raise money to finance war.

Priority allocations in the latter: Investment in defense bonds rather than consumer spending on unnecessary home improvements.

Have the picture: A figure of speech for understanding something.

Needle: To prod someone into action with pointed comments.

Necessity-howlers: Those who claim that a repair is absolutely necessary when it is not.

Sufficiency: Enough of a supply.

OPM: Office of Production Management; a federal agency that allocated materials to war industries after prioritizing the most critical production needs.

Ascertained: Determined.

producing facilities throughout the nation to meet the normal demand, and after a time the individual areas may experience relief. Meanwhile they will have to wait for their nails, for the government is serving nothing up on silver platters which can just as well come on a paper plate.

In the matter of things mechanical, OPM long ago took steps to insure the manufacture of replacement parts for all household machinery, heating, plumbing and electrical equipment. The manufacturer of a household replacement part has little difficulty in getting a priority whereas . . . the manufacturer of the machine itself may be turned down entirely. This means that you can fix the old furnace, washing machine, or gas stove, but you won't be able to buy any new ones when the dealer's present floor stock is exhausted. An exception on the new item ban are bathtubs, washbowls and toilets. Since those are iron and ceramics they are still being supplied distributors, the **pinch** being on steel, not iron.

Constant change in available materials

Priorities work on a day-to-day basis, since the War Production Board is highly sensitive to the daily fluctuations in supply and demand. Discovery of new stockpiles may **ease up** a **commodity**. The completion of a government contract may have the same effect on a factory for a brief time. On the other hand, a new war gadget may add one or more major materials to the critical list. That's Uncle Sam's system; know exactly what's available for civilian distribution and get it to the citizens through the manufacturers. The government is not going to grant you a personal priority on your individual household problem. Washington is a busy town, and it expects Mr. Citizen to **hump** around a bit and locate his own supplies. They may not have been routed right to your corner store, but look around and have patience with the distribution slow-up. You'll get what you want most of the time. And supposing you don't get what you want. Let the man they call **"the Boss"** in the defense agencies have a word.

Boss Nelson looked the shortages in the eye recently, and had this to say about them, "I don't like them and you don't like them, but they are a part of the war; until Hitler is licked we are going to have them whether we like them or not, and because we don't like them, I would like to post a question to you and all the rest of America.

Pinch: Shortage of supply.

Ease up: Relieve some restrictions on production of consumer goods that use that particular material.

Commodity: A product of industry.

Hump: Hustle.

"The Boss": Reference to Donald Nelson, head of the War Production Board.

*"Which would you prefer: to put up with shortages such as we have had so far, for year after year—ten years, fifteen years, perhaps longer—or to put up with some really **terrific** shortages for one or two years and get the job over quickly?*

"I don't think there is much doubt about the answer."

What happened next . . .

Homes generally did not "go to pot" during the war years. Most homes were kept in good repair, and most shortages of maintenance supplies were temporary. During the shortages, men became masters at "making do"—that is, getting by with limited resources—a skill all Americans had learned during the Great Depression (1929–41).

At the end of the war, millions of soldiers returned from overseas, got married, and started families. These new families needed somewhere to live, and consequently the demand for homes reached an all-time high. Construction of new homes dramatically increased, creating a boom in the rest of the economy as manufacturers scrambled to produce enough construction materials to meet demand.

Did you know . . .

- Housing experts urged homeowners to make roofing, plumbing, and heating their first priorities.

- Soon after the United States entered the war, men checked their toolboxes and purchased any needed items while retailers could still get them. Tools were made of steel, and by early 1942, when this magazine article was written, all steel was being diverted to the war industries.

- During the war the government rationed many of the materials normally used for home construction, including copper (used for screening, flashing, and plumbing), chrome (used for fixtures), zinc (used in brass and galvanized hardware), and cork (used in the most common type of flooring, linoleum).

Terrific: Large.

- Articles for the home, such as light fixtures, changed in style to save on materials needed for war production. Formerly fancy and decorative with a lot of metal trim, they became designed purely for providing light with a simple glass bowl around the light bulb.

Consider the following . . .

- If you had owned a home in the United States during World War II, do you think government agencies and local hardware or lumber businesses would have helped you with a plan to build a new family room? Would they have been more or less likely to approve of a bathroom remodeling project?

- If you were a young person on the home front in the 1940s, what skills might you have asked your father or grandfather to teach you?

- Find at least four phrases that directly state or subtly suggest that homeowners had a patriotic duty to keep their homes in good repair.

For More Information

Books

Lingeman, Richard R. *Don't You Know There's a War On? The American Home Front, 1941–1945.* New York: G. P. Putnam's Sons, 1970.

Periodicals

Merrill, Anthony F. "Washington and the Home Front." *House and Garden* (March 1942): pp. 10, 42.

H. W. Hochbaum

Excerpt from "Still Keep 'Em Growing"

**Written by H. W. Hochbaum, Chairman, Victory Garden Committee, U.S. Department of Agriculture.
Published in *House and Garden*,
January 1944.**

"As long as the war lasts and for years after we're going to need all the home-grown and home-preserved food we can possibly raise. Without it, we'll be sunk."

"Still Keep 'Em Growing" is a good example of the frequent magazine and newspaper articles that encouraged Americans on the home front to pull together to help achieve victory overseas. Originally published in the January 1944 issue of *House and Garden,* the article is a call to arms. The author, H. W. Hochbaum, chairman of the federal government's Victory Garden Committee, praises victory gardeners (those who planted small private gardens to add to the nation's commercial food production) for their highly successful efforts in 1942 and 1943. He also urges them to plant even more gardens in 1944.

During spring 1942 Americans planted six million gardens. In 1943 the War Food Administration called for eighteen million garden plots. Approximately twenty million were actually planted. The gardens were planted not only in backyards but in public parks, vacant lots, school yards, and even prison yards. Victory gardens produced millions of tons of fruits and vegetables, easing the burden on commercial farmers, who were struggling to feed Allied forces and civilian populations overseas. Victory gardens were a major avenue that allowed civilians on the home front to contribute meaningfully to the war effort.

Things to remember while reading the excerpt from "Still Keep 'Em Growing" . . .

- Victory gardens were a key symbol of the will of Americans to pitch in for victory. The gardens gave people of all ages a sense of contributing to the war effort.

- During World War I (1914–18), food was in short supply in the United States, so Americans planted vegetable gardens in their backyards; they called them victory gardens. When the United States entered World War II in December 1941, Americans did not need any prodding from the government to begin their victory gardens. They began planting as soon as the ground thawed, in spring 1942.

Excerpt from "Still Keep 'Em Growing"

Official to Victory gardeners—keep 'em growing. Even if peace should be declared tomorrow—still keep 'em growing. Don't let up even for a moment. As long as the war lasts and for years after we're going to need all the home-grown and home-preserved food we can possibly raise. Without it, we'll be sunk. With it we can meet the ever-growing demands with which we are and shall be faced. . . .

This means that every farmer, every Victory gardener in town, suburb and city will want to re-enlist in our garden army and that 25 percent more Victory gardeners must enroll this year. It means that many new community gardens must be developed for and by urban people. It means we must work to obtain the greatest possible amount of vegetables from every garden for home consumption. . . .

*So, you Victory gardeners, let's go! You did well last year— superlatively well. **Green** as you were (many of you), often forced to work with soil so raw and poor that it looked hopeless to experienced gardeners, despite cold Spring weather, floods,*

Green: Inexperienced.

Supplies to help homeowners plant their own victory gardens were easily found at the local hardware or grocery store. Here, a man purchases seeds and top soil to start his victory garden.
The Library of Congress.

droughts, bugs and diseases you produced nearly 8 million tons of vegetables. That was more than the total commercial production for fresh sale for civilian and non-civilian use. *Moreover, some 4 or 5 billion jars and cans of home-produced and purchased vegetables and fruit were put up by our homemakers. . . .*

One of the finest things that has come out of the Victory garden program is the neighborliness and community spirit

*evident wherever people garden together. And in countless back-yards and community gardens people also found space and time for flowers. This is as it should be. Ours is a roomy country. We have ample space most everywhere, except in the crowded city areas, to grow the vegetables we need. . . . We owe it to **Johnny and Joan** as they come marching home that the old home and the old home town welcome them with more flowers and greenery.*

*In war time, above all times, our health must be safeguarded. This challenge to the Victory gardener is more than that of pro-ducing food, as such. As a nation, we need to have more of the protective vegetables and fruits in our daily diet. A recent study of the workers in a huge aeroplane manufacturing plant brought out that nearly one-third of the workers had less than a safe amount of vitamin C in their blood. And yet the home garden, **judiciously** planted, can produce much of the daily supply of this vitamin, as well as supplies of vitamin A, and the minerals, lime and iron. Perhaps many of our industrial workers may not be able to have a Victory garden. But then a lack of appreciation of the need for*

Johnny and Joan: Slang reference to men and women who served overseas in the military.

Judiciously: Wisely.

vegetables, particularly the green and leafy kinds, tomatoes and yellow vegetables also seems common, on the part not only of our war workers but of our population generally. Our food habits are not up to standard, and many people still frankly don't care for vegetables. But our gardeners are learning. . . .

*The challenges to everyone who can get a hold of a suitable piece of ground this year are great. We as a nation will need all the food that we can produce on our farms and in our Victory gardens. Patriotism, prudence, thrift, health and spiritual well being dictate that we must earnestly garden as never before, produce and preserve as much as possible of the family's food supply. Then we shall all live better in these **strenuous** times. Then we shall know that our army and navy forces will get the kinds and qualities of food they must have. Then we shall know that we are helping our allies and also that we are aiding in restoring some of the ravaged and starved nations to health and happier living.*

What happened next . . .

After harvesting their crops, victory gardeners consumed some of the produce and preserved the rest by canning. Canning took place in many U.S. kitchens. Although the process is called "canning," the produce is actually put in glass jars. After being carefully heated, cooled, and sealed, the jars could be kept on a pantry shelf for years. Housewives often proudly displayed rows and rows of jars full of their garden produce.

Did you know . . .

- Estimates indicate that victory gardens produced more than one-third of all the vegetables grown in the United States during the war years.

- Approximately 70 percent of the vegetables consumed by Americans on the home front came from victory gardens.

- The Department of Agriculture recommended that 100 to 125 quarts of fruits and vegetables a year be canned for each member of a household.

Strenuous: Highly active, stressful.

Consider the following . . .

- Go to the Library of Congress Web site (http://www. loc.gov) and pull up photographs of victory garden posters printed and distributed by the U.S. government. Create your own poster encouraging Americans to plant a victory garden.

- Research, plan, and plant a small victory garden on school property or at home.

- Choose a fruit or vegetable to can. Locate a book that explains the canning process; then buy canning supplies at a grocery store. With adult supervision, use the home economics classroom or your home kitchen to can your chosen fruit or vegetable.

For More Information

Books

Bentley, Amy. *Eating for Victory: Food Rationing and the Politics of Domesticity.* Urbana: University of Illinois Press, 1998.

Hayes, Joanne L. *Grandma's Wartime Kitchen: World War II and the Way We Cooked.* New York: St. Martin's Press, 2000.

Periodicals

Hochbaum, H. W. "Still Keep 'Em Growing." *House and Garden* (January 1944): pp. 13, 60.

Newlyweds and Families

Job opportunities in the war industry spurred approximately twenty million Americans—about 15 percent of the total population—to leave their homes and move to war industry centers, usually large urban areas, for work. Also moving about the country were some fifteen million men who had joined the armed services. Servicemen moved continuously around the nation to take on shifting assignments. In an attempt to stay close, the wives and children of servicemen often followed them to each base. Like war industry boomtowns, communities where military bases were located experienced serious overcrowding. Many local residents rented out space in their homes to the military families. If a soldier was sent overseas, his wife and children generally returned to their hometown, often moving in with other family members. If a serviceman shipped out while his wife was pregnant, he knew he probably would not see the baby until he or she was a toddler. Babies conceived just before the husband left were called "good-bye" babies.

Separation, loneliness, and homesickness became part of the military experience. However, most Americans who endured such feelings felt that they were suffering for a worthy cause. The dramatic circumstances that drew the United States into the war—namely, Japan's surprise attack on Pearl Harbor, which killed thousands of U.S. servicemen—created an overwhelming sense of patriotic duty, a resolve to pull together to defend the nation and help the Allies achieve victory. Therefore, the families of servicemen kept grumbling and complaints at a minimum. They waited, hoped, and prayed for safe return of their soldiers.

The first excerpt, a personal interview with Hazel M. Hanes, is a firsthand account of a woman's experience following her husband from base to base during the war years. In the excerpt, Hanes describes how she kept up with her new husband, O.C., as he took on different military assignments. O.C. trained in Texas to be an Army Air Forces pilot, and during 1944 he flew fifty-three missions in Italy. He returned to Hazel uninjured, strong, and confident.

The second excerpt is "A Busload of Strangers," published in the 1999 collection of memoirs *I'll Be Home for Christmas: The Library of Congress Revisits the Spirit of Christmas during World War II*. In this piece, Olive Nowak recalls a snowy December night in Minnesota when she boarded a crowded bus that was taking servicemen and other travelers home for Christmas. Olive fondly recalls the "spell of fellowship" during the bus ride. Just as in all other years, Christmas during the war years was a season of peace and goodwill in the hearts of Americans.

Hazel M. Hanes

Excerpt from a personal interview with Hazel M. Hanes
As told to Sharon M. Hanes on November 20, 2003.

The storyline of lovers separated by the war was a popular one in Hollywood movies of the 1940s. However, in reality, not a lot of couples experienced a wartime separation. Only 8 percent of the fifty million wives in the United States had husbands in the military, and these men were not always sent overseas. However, the percentage was higher among younger wives: Of all the wives between the ages of twenty and forty-four, 11 percent had husbands in the military; among wives younger than twenty, 40 percent had husbands who were military men. During World War II (1939–45) approximately 70 percent of American servicemen served overseas. In this excerpt Hazel Hanes speaks about what it was like to have her newlywed husband, O.C., prepare to go to war as a pilot with the Army Air Forces.

Things to remember while reading the interview with Hazel M. Hanes . . .

- Because the military needed gasoline for tanks, jeeps, and other machinery, gas was rationed for civilians. Most civilian drivers were allowed 4 gallons of gas per week; at the

time, the average car could travel only about 60 miles on 4 gallons. Therefore, buses and trains had to be used for travel and they were always very crowded.

- Before the war most young Americans had never traveled far from their hometowns.

- In towns where military bases were located, housing was in short supply, so residents frequently rented rooms in their homes to military personnel and their families. Sometimes rents were very high. But in most cases, out of respect for the difficulties young military families faced, residents asked a reasonable rate, and lasting friendships often developed.

Excerpt from the interview with Hazel M. Hanes

On **December 7, 1941**, life changed for all of us. I was a nineteen-year-old bride of five months. The next four years were the best of times and the worst of times. The best included the patriotism, **camaraderie**, and togetherness in a common purpose that everyone seemed to feel. We made many new friends, and traveled back and forth across the country. The worst was saying goodbyes and not knowing what the future might hold.

My new husband, O.C., wanted to fly. Thankfully the Air Force lifted the restriction for married men to enter pilot training. He loved airplanes and the idea of becoming a pilot so much I am convinced he would have divorced me to enter pilot training. In late 1942 O.C. went to Brooks Air Field in San Antonio, Texas, for exams and to be **classified** (or rejected, "perish the thought"). He remained at Brooks for pre-flight training. I lived with my parents in Dallas, Texas, worked for the Federal Security Agency (FSA), and saved my money. I was able to visit O.C. when he had a day off. This meant riding the bus or train all night, visiting him on base or, if he could get away, going into town for dinner, then back to Dallas. O.C. next went to Coleman, Texas, for 6 weeks of primary training. At last he was flying. Next he went to Sherman, Texas, and finally back to San Antonio for advanced training. I continued keeping up with him as best I could, riding buses or the train for visits.

All traveling was very trying and tiring. The buses and trains were packed and many times there was standing room only. On one long train ride I was fortunate to have a seat. My seatmate was on his way home after serving in the Pacific and was very weary. As night descended and the lights were lower we all tried to sleep. His head kept falling on my shoulder. After several times of pushing him away, I decided "What the heck," that could be part of my war effort. He had several hours of sleep and when he awakened he was embarrassed, but looked rested.

By the time O.C. got back to Brooks in San Antonio I had saved enough money to join him. Somehow through word of mouth at the base, O.C. found a nice suite of rooms in a house which we were able to rent. In September 1943 he received his wings and was commissioned as a second lieutenant. How very proud I was of him. That evening we went to dinner at the Officer's Club. Next it was home to Dallas for a two-week leave.

December 7, 1941: The day Japan attacked Pearl Harbor, Hawaii, forcing the United States to join World War II.

Camaraderie: Good fellowship.

Classified: Assigned to a prospective role in the military based on mental and physical characteristics.

Family and friends had **pooled** ration stamps for food and gas to celebrate his accomplishment.

After O.C.'s leave and our visit with family, we left for the west Texas town of Pecos for training in a **B-17** and for crew assignments. I remember how nice the ranchers were to us. I lived in a hotel and sometimes when I was eating lunch in a cafe a rancher would leave money with the cashier to pay for the lunch.

Pooled: Combined.

B-17: Four-engine bomber.

O.C. Hanes (front row, third from left) with his B-17 bomber crew in 1944.
Sharon M. and Richard C. Hanes. Reproduced by permission.

After Pecos we started our cross-county travel, first to Dyersburg, Tennessee. We spent Christmas of 1943 in Dyersburg where we rented a room from a nice family. I remember eating at a restaurant called the "Hut" many times. We would give our meat ration coupons to the owner so he could use them for more meat. Soon O.C. was moved to Langley Field in Virginia. It was from Langley he left for overseas duty based in Foggia, Italy. He completed 53 missions. Back at home, we all said a lot of prayers! It was difficult to hear of so many **casualties**—friends we had made along the way plus boys we had grown up with.

O.C. was one of the fortunate ones who returned. That was in Fall, 1944. He was reassigned to Bryan, Texas, for instrument flight training. Then we went to Williams Air Base in Chandler, Arizona, where O.C. instructed new pilots in B-17 operation. We were learning so much about our country and its people. Traveling coast to coast and observing how others lived and coped with the war and shortages of everything. After Arizona, orders came to report to Roswell, New Mexico. O.C. was to instruct pilots in flying

Casualties: Those who are killed or wounded.

The Sullivans

Mr. and Mrs. Thomas Sullivan of Waterloo, Iowa, hung a white banner with five blue stars in their window. Each blue star represented one family member serving in the military. Banners were in windows of homes across the country, but most held only one or, at most, two blue stars.

All five of the Sullivans' sons had enlisted together in the navy shortly after the United States entered World War II in December 1941. They insisted on serving together on the same vessel. In November 1942, the five Sullivan brothers died together when their ship was sunk by the enemy near Guadalcanal in the western Pacific Ocean. Their parents removed the banner with five blue stars and replaced it with a banner bearing five gold stars. A gold star symbolized a military man or woman who had died in service to the United States. No single family since the American Civil War (1861–65) had lost so many members in wartime military service.

B-29s. After several months word was received his squadron would soon have orders to the Pacific, but the war ended in mid-1945 before those orders came. There was a big sigh of relief and lots of celebrating.

After his discharge from the Air Force, it was back to "Big D"—and home and family. There was a problem—no housing. Like most others we moved in with family.

We were looking forward to "living." Finally in December 1946 we celebrated Christmas with our beautiful baby boy and our first very own Christmas tree. Life was good.

What happened next . . .

For the majority of couples separated by military service, the end of the war brought joyous reunions. Many couples chose to start a family and set up their own household. Americans had saved a good amount of their earnings during

B-29s: Long-range bombers.

Big D: A popular abbreviation for Dallas, Texas.

the war years, because there were few consumer goods available for them to buy. Once the war was over, they were eager to spend; they wanted all the comforts they had done without during wartime. Companies that had mobilized to manufacture war materials quickly went back to production of cars, appliances, televisions, and the many other consumer goods that had not been available during the war. Americans were happy to buy such items, and their postwar spending stimulated the booming U.S. economy. The United States had entered World War II after a decade of economic woes due to the Great Depression (1929–41), but the nation emerged from the war with a thriving economy, excellent employment opportunities, and a population that was generally optimistic about the future.

Soon after the war, a second boom got underway. The so-called baby boom began in late 1945: At that time, many couples started families, confident that peacetime and the strong economy would last. Hazel and O.C. Hanes settled in Dallas, Texas, and like many other young couples, bought a home and began their family. Their first child was born in 1946.

Did you know . . .

- The Servicemen's Readjustment Act of 1944, better known as the GI Bill, provided money to military veterans for college expenses or vocational training. Veterans who furthered their education under the GI Bill also received a monthly monetary payment while they were in school. The GI Bill also provided low-interest loans for veterans who wanted to buy or build a home.

- Many Americans joined the middle class for the first time, a new growing segment of U.S. society consisting of business and professional people and skilled workers. Those in the middle class had sufficient income to cover basic expenses with money leftover to purchase consumer items considered non-essential.

- Life was so good for so many Americans that few people recognized or acknowledged that most black Americans (roughly 10 percent of the population) and other minorities still faced racial discrimination on the home front. Despite the booming economy, most minority groups in the United States lived in poverty.

Consider the following . . .

In a way, World War II was easy for Americans to understand: The Allies (Britain, France, the United States, and other countries) were the "good guys," and the Axis powers (Germany, Italy, and Japan) were the "bad guys." With its persecution of the Jews and aggressive land grabs, Nazi Germany represented a great evil. Fighting against Germany and the other Axis powers during the war, Americans had no doubt that they were on the side of justice. This feeling of national unity would greatly diminish in the 1950s and 1960s as the nation became involved in controversial foreign wars for which the purpose of U.S. involvement was less well understood. Meanwhile inner city areas in the United States declined into poverty, and race riots would result.

- Discuss important occurrences that contributed to this loss of unity.

- Did those challenges and the resulting diversity of opinion strengthen or weaken the United States?

- What occurrence at the beginning of the twenty-first century returned Americans, at least for a short period of time, to a united spirit?

For More Information

Books

Harris, Mark J., Franklin D. Mitchell, and Steven J. Schechter, eds. *The Homefront: America during World War II*. New York: Putnam, 1984.

King, Larry, ed. *Love Stories of World War II*. New York: Three Rivers Press, 2001.

Litoff, Judy B., and David C. Smith, eds. *Since You Went Away: World War II Letters from American Women on the Home Front*. New York: Oxford University Press, 1991.

Schomp, Virginia. *World War II: Letters from the Homefront*. New York: Benchmark Books, 2002.

Other

Hanes, Hazel M. Interview by author. Dallas, Texas, November 20, 2003.

Olive Nowak

Excerpt from "A Busload of Strangers"

Reprinted from *I'll Be Home for Christmas: The Library of Congress Revisits the Spirit of Christmas during World War II*. Published in 1999.

"It didn't promise to be the best of Christmas Eves—America was in the midst of World War II."

By Christmastime 1943 the United States had officially been at war for two years. Millions of American men were stationed away from home and family. Many of them were overseas in very dangerous situations, about as far from the warmth, security, and joy of Christmastime as one could be. On the home front, wreaths appeared on doors as always; stockings were hung, trees decorated, and presents wrapped. Young children tried to be very, very good. However, despite outward appearances and the usual happy activities of the Christmas season, Americans were feeling great uncertainty and fear. Stories of wartime horrors were trickling out of Europe, and people on the home front experienced high anxiety as they waited to find out whether their loved ones would be sent overseas or whether soldiers already in combat would ever return.

As Christmas Eve approached, people on the home front began traveling home for the holiday. Buses and trains were hopelessly overcrowded with servicemen, war industry workers, government employees, and military wives and their children. Olive Nowak managed to get on board one such bus.

As the bus worked its way through snowy Minnesota late at night, she had a memorable experience. She tells about her journey in the excerpt that follows.

Things to remember while reading "A Busload of Strangers" . . .

- By late 1943 Americans were longing for an end to the war.

- Christmastime is usually considered a time of hope, and the war years were no exception. It was the one national holiday that continued to be enjoyed as closely as possible following the usual peacetime traditions. It would be the one day some war industries would briefly pause their production.

- The war effort and the unity that existed after Pearl Harbor led to a special sense of community and helpfulness. People reached out to one another more than in more normal times.

"A Busload of Strangers"

It didn't promise to be the best of Christmas Eves—America was in the midst of World War II.

By the time I arrived at the little bus depot in Albert Lea, Minnesota, a crowd of impatient travelers, many of them servicemen, were waiting for the bus. I was eager to get home to my family. My younger brother was already talking about enlisting in the Marines. This might be the last Christmas we would be together for a long time. My thoughts were also on a certain soldier overseas who was very special to me.

There was a collective sigh of relief as the bus rounded the corner, then dismay when after a few passengers departed, we saw it was still full. The bus driver shook his head sadly as he told us there wasn't any more room.

Suddenly a young sailor called out, "Hey, if there's a cute blonde out there, I'll be glad to hold her on my lap!" Amid the

Christmastime at a Washington, D.C., bus terminal in December 1941. Everyone wants to rush home for the holidays to share time with their families in this time of war. *The Library of Congress.*

laughter of the crowd, other bus passengers then began calling to the driver, "Put them all on—we'll share our seats so no one has to be left behind." Within minutes, there were three and four people snuggled into seats for two, some people sitting in others' laps.

As our busload of strangers sped through the night, someone began softly singing Silent Night. One by one we all joined in, until every passenger was singing—Joy to the World; Away in a

American Home Front in World War II: Primary Sources

A Christmas Wedding

In a brief piece titled "Christmas, Wartime, and a Wedding," published in *I'll Be Home for Christmas* (Delacorte Press, 1999), Esther Carlson describes her special wartime Christmas wedding. More marriages occurred in 1942 than ever before in U.S. history. In the face of wartime uncertainties, relationships were intense. Young dating couples dreaded the possibility—or certainty—of overseas military assignments and long-term separation; they feared they might never see each other again. Some couples married after only a few dates. Young women who followed this path were called "war brides." Surprisingly, many of these "rushed" wartime marriages—including Esther Carlson's—lasted over fifty years.

December 25, 1942, was, and always will be, the most memorable Christmas to me because it was also my wedding day.

My fiance, Harold, was in the military service; he was stationed in Long Beach, California, and I had come out from Denver to visit him in November. We decided to marry as soon as possible.

I got a job with Western Union, rented a small apartment in Los Angeles—and waited for the only dates Harold could get leave: late Christmas Eve and Christmas Day. My mother sent me a pretty bridesmaid dress I had once worn—that was my makeshift wedding gown, bought a gardenia from a street vendor to carry as my bouquet.

When Western Union finally closed at midnight on Christmas Eve, I rushed home to pick up my dress, then dashed for the streetcar to take me to the church—where Harold was pacing nervously back and forth, waiting. Within a few minutes of arrival, I'd changed into my dress and was walking down the aisle on the arm of an old friend of my parents. Harold and I spoke our vows at 1:30 A.M. in front of ready-made but unknown guests—a full congregation who had just heard the benediction to a traditional Christmas Eve ceremony. How startled they must have been to hear the wedding march follow a Christmas carol! Afterward, a kind young couple—again, strangers—used their precious rationed gas to drive us back to the apartment. Our wedding may have been "rushed," but our marriage hasn't been—it's lasted 51 years!

Manger; White Christmas; I'll Be Home for Christmas. We laughed, we sang, we shared candy and cookies. And we watched, misty-eyed, as departing servicemen, who only a few minutes before had been so cool, cried unashamedly as they were embraced by waiting wives, mothers, and fathers. When the bus reached my destination, the remaining passengers shouted out, "Merry Christmas, Happy New Year!"

When the war ended, my "special" soldier returned home, and we were married. Since then, we have spent many happy

*Christmas Eves together with our children, and, more recently, our grandchildren. Yet I doubt if I'll ever again experience the same feeling of peace and contentment that came over me that night during the war. As I stood there, watching the bus disappear into the night, I was eager to be home but reluctant to break the **spell of fellowship**. The snow had stopped falling, and the sky was studded with stars. I thought of the awe that must have gripped the hearts of those long-ago shepherds who had once gazed at a star over Bethlehem. And I understood that even in the midst of war there could still be "Peace on earth, good will to men". . . .*

What happened next . . .

There would be only one more wartime Christmas Eve, in December 1944. By Christmas 1945 the war had ended, and soldiers were back home reunited with loved ones.

Did you know . . .

- During the war years Christmas Day became the only holiday on which all work in the United States stopped and everyone rested. On December 24, 1942, President Franklin Roosevelt delivered a Christmas Eve message to the nation. In that speech, published in *The Public Papers and Addresses of Franklin D. Roosevelt, 1942 Volume,* the president said, "It is significant that tomorrow—Christmas Day—our plants and factories will be stilled. That is not true of the other holidays we have long been accustomed to celebrate. On all other holidays work goes on—gladly—for the winning of the war. So Christmas becomes the only holiday in all the year."

- Songwriter Irving Berlin (1888–1989) wrote the music and words for "White Christmas." Singer Bing Crosby (1903–1977) first sang the song for the nation on Christmas Day, 1941, on the popular radio variety show "The Kraft Music Hall." The song was an instant megahit on the home front and with U.S. servicemen overseas, and it remained popular

Spell of fellowship: The increased closeness developed with fellow citizens.

throughout the war. The words to the song made people separated by war long to be together again at home for Christmastime.

Consider the following . . .

- Find sheet music or a recording for "White Christmas" and "I'll Be Home for Christmas" and experience for yourself the effect of these songs.

- Search for information about famous entertainers who traveled across the country and to foreign outposts with the United Services Organization (USO) at Christmastime to bring joy and a bit of home to the troops.

For More Information

Books

Hayes, Joanne L. *Grandma's Wartime Kitchen: World War II and the Way We Cooked*. New York: St. Martin's Press, 2000.

Heide, Robert. *Home Front America: Popular Culture of the World War II Era*. San Francisco: Chronicle Books, 1995.

Hoopes, Roy. *Americans Remember the Home Front: An Oral Narrative*. New York: Hawthorne Books, 1977.

Library of Congress, comp. "A Busload of Strangers." In *I'll Be Home for Christmas: The Library of Congress Revisits the Spirit of Christmas during World War II*. New York: Delacorte Press, 1999, pp. 44, 82.

Where to Learn More

Books

Bailey, Ronald H. *The Home Front, U.S.A.* Alexandria, VA: Time-Life Books, 1977.

Bernstein, Mark, and Alex Lubertozzi. *World War II on the Air: Edward R. Murrow and the Voices That Carried the War Home.* Naperville, IL: Sourcebooks, 2003.

Carl, Ann B. *A Wasp Among Eagles.* Washington, DC: Smithsonian Institution Press, 1999.

Cooper, Michael L. *Remembering Manzanar: Life in a Japanese Relocation Camp.* New York: Clarion Books, 2002.

Cooper, Michael L. *Fighting For Honor: Japanese Americans and World War II.* New York: Clarion Books, 2000.

Daniels, Roger. *Prisoners Without Trial: Japanese Americans in World War II.* New York: Hill and Wang, 1993.

Freidel, Frank. *Franklin D. Roosevelt: A Rendezvous with Destiny.* New York: Little, Brown & Co., 1990.

Fremon, David K. *Japanese-American Internment in American History.* Springfield, NJ: Enslow Publishers, 1996.

Gilbert, Bill. *They Also Served: Baseball and the Home Front, 1941-1945.* New York: Crown Publishers, 1992.

Gluck, Sherna Berger. *Rosie the Riveter Revisited: Women, the War, and Social Change.* Boston: Twayne Publishers, 1987.

Goodwin, Doris Kearns. *No Ordinary Time: Franklin and Eleanor Roosevelt, the Home Front in World War II.* New York: Simon & Schuster, 1994.

Greene, Bob. *Once Upon a Town: The Miracle of the North Platte Canteen*. New York: William Morrow, 1992.

Hartmann, Susan M. *The Home Front and Beyond: American Women in the 1940s*. Boston: Twayne Publishers, 1982.

Heide, Robert. *Home Front America: Popular Culture of the World War II Era*. San Francisco: Chronicle Books, 1995.

Hoopes, Roy. *When The Stars Went To War: Hollywood and World War II*. New York: Random House, 1994.

Lingeman, Richard R. *Don't You Know There's a War On? The American Home Front, 1941-1945*. New York: G. P. Putnam's Sons, 1970.

Nathan, Amy. *Yankee Doodle Gals: Women Pilots of World War II*. Washington, DC: National Geographic Society, 2001.

New York Times. *Page One: The Front Page History of World War II as Presented in the New York Times*. New York: Galahad Books, 1996.

Panchyk, Richard. *World War II For Kids: A History With 21 Activities*. Chicago: Chicago Review Press, 2002.

Schickel, Richard. *Good Morning, Mr. Zip Zip Zip: Movies, Memory, and World War II*. Chicago: Ivan R. Dee, 2003.

Schomp, Virginia. *World War II: Letters From the Homefront*. New York: Benchmark Books, 2002.

Stanley, Jerry. *I Am An American: The True Story of Japanese Interment*. New York: Crown, 1994.

Takaki, Ronald T. *Double Victory: A Multicultural History of America in World War II*. Boston: Little, Brown and Company, 2000.

Terkel, Studs. *The Good War: An Oral History of World War Two*. New York: Pantheon Books, 1984.

Tunnell, Michael O. *The Children of Topaz: The Story of a Japanese-American Internment Camp*. New York: Holiday House, 1996.

Warren, James R. *The War Years: A Chronicle of Washington State in World War II*. Seattle: University of Washington Press, 2000.

Winkler, Allan M. *Home Front U.S.A.: America During World War II*. Arlington Heights, IL: H. Davidson, 1986.

Zeinert, Karen. *Those Incredible Women of World War II*. Brookfield, CT: The Millbrook Press, 1994.

Web Sites

The Army Nurse Corps. http://www.army.mil/cmh-pg/books/wwii/72-14/72-14.htm.

Army Women's Museum, Fort Lee, Virginia. http://www.awm.lee.army.mil.

Civil Air Patrol. http://www.cap.gov/about/history.html.

Coast Guard Auxiliary History. http://www.uscg.mil/hq/g-cp/history/Auxiliary%20History.html.

"Dorothea Lange and the Relocation of the Japanese." *Museum of the City of San Francisco*. http://www.sfmuseum.org/hist/lange.html.

Fly Girls. PBS Online. American Experience. http://www.pbs.org/wgbh/amex/flygirls.htm.

Japanese American National Museum. http://www.janm.org.

Rosie the Riveter Trust. http://www.rosietheriveter.org.

United Services Organization. http://www.uso.org.

The WASP WWII Museum. Avenger Field, Sweetwater, Texas. http://www.waspwwii.org/museum/home.htm.

The Women's Army Corps: A Commemoration of World War II Service. http://www.army.mil/cmh-pg/brochures/wac/wac.htm.

World War II Era WAVES. http://www.history.navy.mil/photos/prs-tpic/females/wave-ww2.htm.

Index

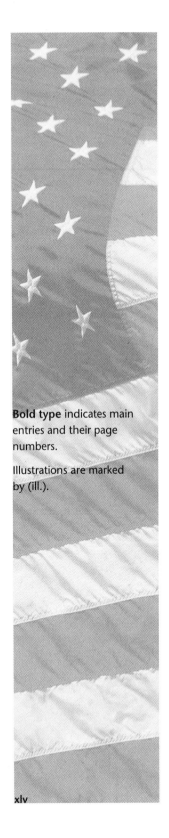

Victory gardens, 187, 190, 228–232, 230 (ill.), 231 (ill.)

V-J Day (Victory over Japan), 189

Volunteer farm laborers, 100–101, 101–105, 102 (ill.), 106

Volunteer Port Security Force, 47, 48, 50–51

Volunteers in civil defense, 35, 42–43, 44, 46–55
air raid wardens, 47 (ill.), 49 (ill.), 182, 184–185, 195–196
aircraft spotters, 51 (ill.)
Red Cross canteen workers, 60 (ill.)
women, 41 (ill.), 52, 54 (ill.), 58, 60–61
young people, 50 (ill.)

W

Wages
dissatisfaction with, 17
for black Americans, 147
for factory workers, 92, 132
for farmwork, 106
for women, 86–87, 92, 104, 106

War bonds, 47, 188 (ill.), 211, 222–223

War brides, 247

War Finance Committee, 47, 52–53, 222

War Food Administration, 228

War industry. *See* Factories and factory workers; Industrial mobiliztion; World War II: job opportunities created by

War stamps, 188 (ill.), 223

"Washington and the Home Front"

(Anthony F. Merrill), 202, **220–226**

"We Are Going to Win the War" (Franklin D. Roosevelt), 3, **22–31**

"We Choose Human Freedom" (Franklin D. Roosevelt), 18–20

"What to Do in an Air Raid" (U.S. Office of Civilian Defense), **36–43**

"While Their Parents Build Planes" (Frances Duncan), 96–97

Wickard, Claude R., 101

Willow Run manufacturing plant, 12, 124–125, 130 (ill.), 131

Wilson, Meredith L., 101

WLA. *See* Women's Land Army

Woman's Home Companion, 202, **203–210**

Women
as civil defense volunteers, 41 (ill.), 52, 54 (ill.), 58, 60–61, 211
as factory workers, 73–74, 82, 87 (ill.), 88 (ill.), 93 (ill.), 217 (ill.)
as farm laborers, 70–71, 100–101, 101–105, 102 (ill.), 105–106
as homemakers, 204, 211, 216
as Reader-Reporters, 203, 206
as working mothers, 96–97, 96 (ill.), 211
in aircraft industry, 75 (ill.), 77 (ill.), 81 (ill.), 82, 85–89, 86 (ill.)
attitudes toward, 73, 74, 88, 101, 103–104, 134
employment opportunities for, 32, 68–71, 69

(ill.), 73–74, 79 (ill.), 84, 100, 125, 209 (ill.)
general responsibilities of, 204, 216
magazines for, 202
population and demographics, 68

Women's Land Army (WLA), 70–71, 100–101, 102–105, 102 (ill.), 103 (ill.), 106

Work. *See* Employment

Workers. *See* Farm laborers and farming; Labor and labor unions

Working conditions, 17, 24, 86–88, 89, 91, 93–94, 98–99

World War II
American attitudes toward, 6, 20, 95, 204, 208
casualties during, 20, 35, 210, 235, 241
censorship during, 23, 26, 43, 214
economic advantages of, 111, 135
end of, 189, 210
financial cost of, 24, 47, 66, 222–223
job opportunities created by, 13, 20, 68–71, 74, 84, 100, 122, 125, 148
major events in, 4, 12, 15, 20, 22, 25–26, 31
U.S. involvement in, 2–3, 5, 108, 159
veterans of (soldiers/GIs), 193, 197–198, 199–200, 242

Wyoming, civil defense in, 57, 58–62, 66

Y

Youth. *See* Children and young people